FRED & ROSE

The Full Story of

Fred and Rose West

and the Gloucester

House of Horrors

HOWARD SOUNES

sphere

SPHERE

First published in Great Britain in 1995
by Warner Books
Reprinted 1995, 1996 (three times), 1997, 1998 (twice),
1999 (twice), 2000, 2001
Reprinted by Time Warner Paperbacks in 2002
Reprinted 2003 (twice), 2004 (twice), 2005
Reprinted by Time Warner Books in 2005
Reprinted 2006 (three times)
Reprinted by Sphere in 2007

11 13 15 14 12 10

A CIP catalogue record for this book
is available from the British Library.

ISBN 978-0-7515-1322-6

Maps by Will Unwin
Graphic of 25 Cromwell Street by Paul Weston

Typeset in Bembo by M Rules
Printed and bound in Great Britain by Clays Ltd, St Ives plc

Papers used by Sphere are from well-managed forests
and other responsible sources.

MIX
Paper from
responsible sources
FSC
www.fsc.org   FSC® C104740

Sphere
An imprint of
Little, Brown Book Group
Carmelite House
50 Victoria Embankment
London EC4Y 0DZ

An Hachette UK Company
www.hachette.co.uk

www.littlebrown.co.uk

'[Sounes] tells a clear, straightforward tale ... It is a story of obsessive love as well as obsessive murder'
Paul Baker, *The Times*

'a comprehensive account'
Duncan Campbell, *The Guardian*

'The great strength of [Sounes'] book lies in its in-depth and detailed background information going back several generations'
David Hardy, *Gloucester Citizen*

Howard Sounes, who was born in Welling, a suburb of South East London, in 1965, was working as a news reporter for the *Sunday Mirror* in 1994 when he broke the first major stories in the case of Frederick and Rosemary West. Sounes went on to cover the West story extensively for the *Sunday Mirror*, then the *Daily Mirror*, up to and including Rose West's trial in the autumn of 1995. This book, *Fred & Rose*, was first published in December 1995, shortly after Mrs West's conviction on ten counts of murder; it was a bestseller at the time and has remained in print ever since, becoming one of the most widely-read true crime books.

Shortly after *Fred & Rose* was published, Howard Sounes resigned from the *Daily Mirror* to pursue a career as a full-time author. His subsequent books have included a biography of the American writer Charles Bukowski (*Locked in the Arms of a Crazy Life*); biographies of the musicians Bob Dylan (*Down the Highway*), Paul McCartney (*Fab*) and Lou Reed (*Notes from the Velvet Underground*); a book about Amy Winehouse and other musicians who died at the age of twenty-seven (*Amy, 27*); a history of the arts in the 1970s (*Seventies*); and *Heist: The True Story of the World's Biggest Cash Robbery*.

For more information visit, www.howardsounes.com

In memory of
Betty and Ray Sounes
and Reginald Davis

CONTENTS

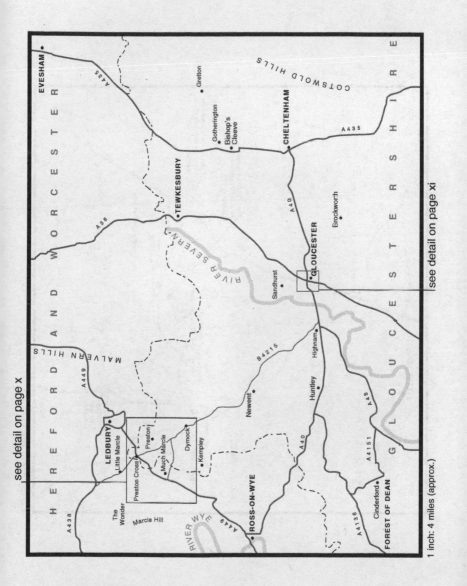

The Gloucestershire–Hereford and Worcester border. See overleaf for detailed maps of the boxed areas.

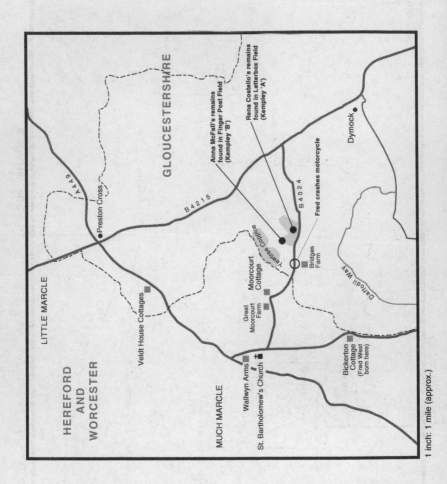

GLOUCESTERSHIRE

Anna McFall's remains
found in Finger Post Field
(Kempley 'B')

Rena Costello's remains
found in Letterbox Field
(Kempley 'A')

Fred crashes motorcycle

Dymock

B 4024

Preston Cross

B 4215

A 449

Yewtree Coppice

Bridges
Farm

Daffodil Way

LITTLE MARCLE

Veldt House Cottages

Moorcourt
Cottage

Great
Moorcourt
Farm

Bickerton
Cottage
(Fred West
born here)

HEREFORD
AND
WORCESTER

MUCH MARCLE

Wallwyn Arms

St. Bartholomew's Church

1 inch: 1 mile (approx.)

*The area around Much Marcle, where Fred West grew up, and where he
buried the remains of Rena Costello and Anna McFall.*

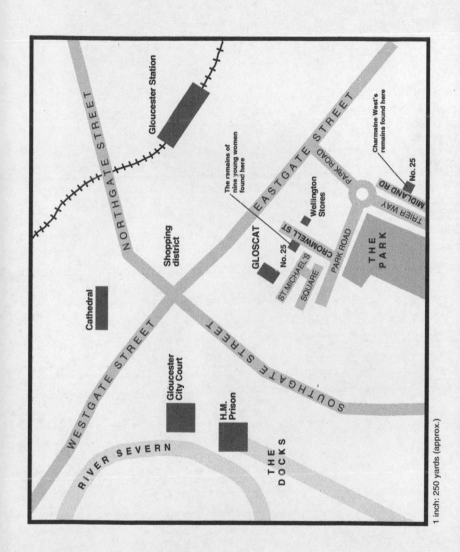

The following labels appear on the map:

Gloucester Station

NORTHGATE STREET

EASTGATE STREET

PARK ROAD

Charmaine West's remains found here

No. 25

MIDLAND RD

TRIER WAY

The remains of nine young women found here

Wellington Stores

GLOSCAT

No. 25

CROMWELL ST

Shopping district

ST. MICHAEL'S SQUARE

PARK ROAD

THE PARK

Cathedral

WESTGATE STREET

SOUTHGATE STREET

Gloucester City Court

H.M. Prison

RIVER SEVERN

THE DOCKS

1 inch: 250 yards (approx.)

Simplified street map of Gloucester, showing Midland Road and Cromwell Street, where the Wests spent their twenty-four years in the city.

PREFACE

IN THE LAST days of February 1994, articles began appearing in Gloucester's evening newspaper about human remains being uncovered under the garden of a house in the city. The address of the house was 25 Cromwell Street. The bones – for that is all the remains were after several years in the ground – had been tentatively identified by police as those of one of the daughters of the household, a girl named Heather West. She had not been seen alive since 1987, when she was aged sixteen. Her father, Fred West, a 52-year-old jobbing builder, and her mother, Rose, a 40-year-old prostitute, were arrested and questioned about the discovery. Rose was released after a few hours, but Fred was charged with Heather's murder.

It was an interesting case – a man who had apparently killed his teenage daughter and hidden her under the patio – but it was by no means unique. Murders within families, generically known to the police as 'domestic' killings, are relatively commonplace. For this reason, and the fundamental fact that Fred West had been charged – severely limiting what could properly be reported – the investigation at first received little coverage in the national media. The *Daily Mirror*, for example, printed just two short paragraphs on the morning of 1 March, under the headline DAD FACES DEATH CASE.

This situation changed slightly a few days later when it

emerged that the police had discovered the remains of two more young women at Cromwell Street. The story was given more space and prominence in the press, even reaching the front pages under the headline GARDEN OF EVIL, but was still overshadowed by other news.

I was employed at the time as a staff reporter for the *Sunday Mirror* newspaper in London. Just after lunch on Saturday 5 March I took an unexpected telephone call from a source in Gloucestershire, a person whom I am bound by a confidence not to identify. I was told that, over the last few hours, there had been sensational developments in the 'Garden of Evil' case – developments of which the press were unaware, partly because the police officers attached to the inquiry team had been sworn to secrecy.

Fred West had committed an astonishing number of murders, far more than had previously been suspected. The remains of young women were buried not only in the garden of 25 Cromwell Street, as had been supposed, but also in the cellar of the house; under the bathroom floor; under the extension of a second property nearby; and in fields on the outskirts of the village where Fred West was born. The police calculated there were at least nine more victims to be found, making – with the remains of the three already discovered – a possible total of twelve. An experimental radar device used over the previous twenty-four hours had indicated at least five graves in the cellar alone. While I listened to this incredible information on the telephone, trying to note every detail of what had happened, police officers were using pneumatic drills to break up the concrete floor.

I was told that the dead were probably all young women. The likely victims included lodgers, hitch-hikers, and girls snatched from bus stops. Fred West was talking freely about these girls, and from the casual way in which he discussed their fates, detectives believed he had almost certainly killed many more.

Even in those first few moments it was clear this was to number among the most extraordinary murder cases in British criminal history.

I worked on the story with the *Sunday Mirror*'s crime reporter, Chris House, who was able to corroborate what I had been told. Pondering the introduction to our article, which would appear on the front page, we cast about for a new name for the investigation, a phrase more appropriate than 'Garden of Evil'. We came up with HOUSE OF HORRORS. In retrospect it may not have been the most original idea, but it is the name that has stuck and has been widely used since. It first appeared in connection with the Wests on page one of the *Sunday Mirror* that weekend; following on from the headline was a lengthy article breaking the story of the macabre contents of 25 Cromwell Street, and the existence of the other graves, thereby revealing the true scale of the case.

The remains of several more young women were indeed recovered from inside 25 Cromwell Street over the following days, and enormous media interest came to focus on that plain semi-detached house. Journalists arrived in Gloucester from all over the country, and the world, eager to discover everything about the West family. There had not been such a newsworthy British murder story since 1983, when civil servant Dennis Nilsen was found to have killed fifteen young men. In many ways, the West case was more comparable to that of Myra Hindley and Ian Brady, who had murdered a number of children in the late 1960s.

The following weekend I wrote a second article, this time reporting that the human remains found at the house had been cut into pieces and that there was evidence of sexual torture. A week later I identified the exact location in the fields near Fred West's childhood home where the police were soon to dig for more victims. The front page of the 27 March issue of the *Sunday Mirror* reported that the remains already recovered were not complete: many bones were missing, especially from the feet and hands. This would later prove to be a most unsettling mystery.

It became apparent that such mayhem could not be the work of Fred West alone, although he was the only person to be charged at this stage. It seemed likely that Rose had been as much involved in the murders as her husband, and that it was her appetite for sadistic lesbian sex which had been the motivation for most of the killings.

On 10 April 1994 I reported that arrests would be made regarding sex abuse at Cromwell Street, and on 21 April Rose West was brought before magistrates, charged with raping a young girl. It was this that first put her behind bars. On 24 April, I reported that she was being closely questioned about the murders of her daughter Heather and another young girl. The next day, Rose was charged with murder for the first time. On 1 May I wrote that she would now be charged with murdering all nine women found at Cromwell Street, and as the weeks went by, this also happened.

A great number of newspaper articles have subsequently been devoted to this story, but they do not sufficiently explain the murders or the nature of the people involved. To attempt to understand why so many young women died in and around 25 Cromwell Street, it is necessary to learn about the personalities of, and relationship between, Fred and Rose West. Newspapers, and indeed policemen, are never very interested in this. It is enough for them to describe the murderers as 'evil' and 'psychopathic', leaving us none the wiser as to what motivated such violence. But there *is* relevant information to discover.

In the chapters that follow I have tried to set out the story of the lives of this extraordinary couple as factually and dispassionately as possible. My purpose is not to excuse their crimes, but to help explain *how* Fred and Rose developed into people capable of such behaviour. The reader will notice that there is little personal comment in the main part of the book. I do hold strong opinions regarding all aspects of the story, but have reserved these views for the Epilogue.

NUMEROUS people helped me in my work on *Fred & Rose*, which took more than eighteen months to research and write. I am grateful to them all, but want to thank the following individuals, and organisations, in particular: Fred West's brother and sister-in-law, Doug and Christine West; Rose West's mother, Mrs Daisy Letts; the Editors and staff at Mirror Group, especially Chris House; Alan Samson and Andrew Gordon at Little, Brown/Warner; Karen Tas; and Gloucester Police, including, most notably, Detective Superintendent John Bennett, who has been as helpful as the restrictions of his difficult job permitted.

THE victims of this case are very many, and are not limited to those dozen young women who are now known to have been killed by Fred and Rose West. The dead all leave relatives and friends who will never be able to forget what has happened. How many other victims the Wests claimed, and the sorrows of their loved ones, will probably never be known. There are also those who have been abused by the Wests as children, or have witnessed the sexual and physical abuse of others. I would like to end by offering my sympathy to all the people who continue to suffer the consequences of these tragic events.

PROLOGUE

THE GULLS FROM Gloucester docks perch on top of 25 Cromwell Street, crying and flapping their wings noisily as Fred West comes home. The birds have nested in the space between the roof and the gutter of his house, and are a constant nuisance. Fred glares up at them as he opens and then closes behind him the black and gold front gate.

He pauses to cast an eye over his property. Fred is extremely proud of this modest semi-detached house, and has made a great many improvements since he and his wife, Rose, moved here twenty years ago. An unusually ornate house sign, fashioned in wrought iron, represents the care he has lavished on the building. *25 Cromwell Street* is picked out in curly white letters set in a black frame. The address is also painted on the black plastic rubbish bins in the tiny front yard.

Some years ago Fred rendered the outside walls with sand-coloured concrete, and this is still in fair condition, although there are dark streaks at the top where rainwater runs down through faults in the Victorian guttering. The three sash windows, spaced one above the other at the front, are hung with net curtains. Their frames are pea-green. Facing Fred is a second pair of iron gates, about six feet tall, painted grey and fastened with a lock in the middle. The key is under a stone.

As Fred reaches down to pick up the key, he sees one of the young student girls from the bedsitters making her way to the local shop, the Wellington Stores. There is a college at the back of Fred's house, and many of the students rent accommodation in Cromwell Street because it is cheap and convenient. Fred earns extra money by carrying out odd jobs for the landlords of these bedsitters, and recently mended a handle on the window of this particular girl's room, so he calls out a cheery hello. His rural Herefordshire accent seems out of place here in the inner city.

The student likes Fred and his wife, as most of the neighbours do. When she was unwell recently, and staying home from college, Mrs West offered to visit the chemist for her, saying, 'I'm only a couple of doors away if you need me.' So the girl stops to speak with Fred, and asks after the health of the couple's large brood of children.

Fred says he hopes she has a boyfriend to take her out tonight. If not, she is very welcome to come over to Number 25 and have a drink with him and Rose; they could watch a video together. There is a lewd tone to the way he speaks, and the student can see why some of her friends warned her not to be in when he called to mend the window lock. He had made an odd comment then, about having slept with hundreds of women and fathering over forty children. It seemed such an absurd boast that she laughed out loud.

He is not even a handsome man. He has a wide face and distinctive, simian features, a protruding jaw and small crooked nose. His hair is such a dark brown that it appears black, and grows in an unruly clump. Long, old-fashioned sideburns spread down the sides of his jaw. His teeth are badly decayed and one of the two front incisors is chipped, accentuating a gap. Fred is of medium height and limps when he walks. He is slightly over-weight around the middle, but despite this appears fit and strong.

The student assumes Fred is in his late forties, maybe older. He invariably wears the same navy-blue donkey jacket that he has on today, a dark patterned sweater and blue jeans; his hands are grimy and he has not shaved. But it is his brilliant blue eyes that are most striking.

They say goodbye. Fred unlocks the double gates and carefully locks them behind him again. He opens the front door, which has been stained dark brown in an attempt to make it look like oak. There is a square glass panel at eye level and a small electric coaching lamp on the wall. A lucky horseshoe is nailed above the door, reminding Fred of the country village where he grew up.

Inside Number 25 there is an odd, fusty smell. The small hallway is painted lime green. On the left is a locked door, and there is another door directly ahead. Fred calls out: 'Rose! Rose!' in his gruff way. There is no answer so he walks through the second door, which leads into his 'tool room'. Apart from Fred's building equipment, there is also a washing machine and spin-dryer in here. He passes through another door and down a step into an open living area, featuring an arched breakfast bar with a Formica surface and stools set before it. There is also a sofa upholstered in green velour, a television, and a cream dial telephone on a shelf. The walls are covered with artificial pine boarding speckled with dozens of knots, and there is a wooden pillar in the middle of the room supporting the roof. This extension, and all of the fittings inside, are the result of Fred's passion for DIY.

Several children sit around. Some are white-skinned; others black. They range in age from toddlers to teenagers. They had been chattering amongst themselves, but fall silent as 'Dad' walks into the room, dropping his heavy bag of tools on the floor. 'Where's your mum?' asks Fred. One of the teenagers quietly replies that their mother is upstairs, adding that she is with one of 'her friends'.

Fred takes off his jacket and walks back through the tool

room, unlocking the door on the right in the hallway. He locks it behind him again and walks up a flight of approximately seven steps. At the top, Fred turns and climbs a further short flight, taking him up to a landing which leads into another lounge.

There is a large walk-in bar by the window, stocked with a variety of drinks. A mural of a tropical island covers one wall. On the carpet by the sofa are two glasses, still with a little alcohol in the bottom, and an ashtray. A cloud of cigarette smoke lingers.

Fred notices that a video has been left on. The picture is of poor quality – the colours are too bright and there is little definition – but it is clear what type of film it is. A young woman is wearing a bizarre costume made of pieces of shiny black material and straps. Only her eyes and mouth can be seen through holes in the mask she is wearing. A man is touching her from behind, and she appears to be in pain. Fred turns the volume down, but the sound of a woman moaning still emanates from somewhere in the room. It is amplified in a tinny way, as if from the speaker of a cheap radio.

Fred settles himself on the sofa, moving a cushion embroidered with the word MUM, and reaches down to an intercom which is plugged into the skirting board. The intercom has a speaker attachment, and he holds this to his ear: Fred can now hear two people having sex in another part of the house. Most of the noise is made by a woman. She is breathing hard and shouting as if she is being hurt. Fred can hear flesh being slapped.

He listens to his wife having sex as the afternoon light fades and everything except the glowing television picture diminishes into gloom. Sometimes Rose makes so much noise that she can be clearly heard even without the intercom. The sound comes from the room directly above the bar. When it eventually stops, Fred puts down the intercom. Momentarily at a loss as to what to do, he decides to move his van round to the front of the house.

Outside, the orange street lights have come on. It is a dowdy, unattractive area, and most of the properties are neglected, with rubbish piled up by the doors. Police sirens wail through the city, and a loud argument can be heard from the upstairs window of one of the bedsitters.

Because Cromwell Street is so central, shoppers and office workers park their cars here. Fred often finds that he has to leave his van around the corner in Cromwell Terrace, and then move it again after six o'clock so it is safely in front of his property before he goes to bed. When he has moved the van, Fred sits in the cab for a moment, watching as the door of his house opens and a small West Indian man comes out. The man looks left and right, quickly, furtively. Behind him in the doorway, a plump woman with dark hair clutches together a dressing gown of faded pink towelling. The man hurries away in the direction of Eastgate Street, and the woman closes the door.

The fluorescent light is on in the breakfast bar area, making the pine walls appear a queasy yellow colour. Rose is in the kitchen preparing Fred's supper. She is in her late thirties, of medium height and quite fat. Her hair is glossy – almost black – and cut short, but it falls down at the front over her eyes. Rose wears large spectacles with coloured plastic frames, and gold-coloured hoop earrings. Her skin is olive, and a fuzz of fine black hair grows on her upper lip. Apart from the dressing gown, she wears slippers and long white nylon socks. When she turns to get the salt from the unit behind her, she sees that one of the children is sitting on the work-surface. 'Fucking get off!' she yells, striking out with her hand.

'You made a right old row, Rosie,' says Fred – not as a rebuke, but as if he is complimenting her. Rose is at the sink now, opening a bag of frozen peas with scissors. 'He enjoyed it, evidently,' she agrees, nodding to some five-pound notes by her purse. 'Says he is coming again next week.' Fred rolls himself a cigarette contentedly.

Dinner is a simple affair: defrosted food with slices of white bread and a glass of tap water. Fred eats quickly, talking to Rose

as he does so about all he has done in the day. He has been at
Stroud Court, a home for autistic people near the village of
Nailsworth. His employers are paid to carry out maintenance
work for the institution. Fred says that, when he was driving
back to the depot near Stroud, he saw a woman by the side of
the road holding her skirt up for him. He could see 'everything'. Neither Rose nor the children react to this, considering
Fred to be 'off in a world of his own'.

He then asks the family if they can guess who he saw as he
was driving along Barton Street that evening. Without a pause
he answers his own question: 'I seen Heather!' The mention of
this name transforms the atmosphere in the room; suddenly,
everybody is listening to Fred.

Heather is Fred and Rose's first-born daughter. None of the
children have seen her since she apparently left home several
years earlier. It is difficult for the younger ones even to remember what their sister looked like, because all her photographs
have disappeared from the house. 'I come down Barton Street
and there she was. She is a working girl now, mind. She is,
what's'name, selling drugs and that. I called out "Hi, Heather!"
but I couldn't stop,' says Fred.

The children ask, 'How did she look, Dad?' making no comment about Fred's claim that their sister is a prostitute and a
drug dealer. He used to say she was a lesbian, because she never
had a boyfriend. The children think Fred is 'sex mad'.

'She looked rough. But she must be making a good bit of
money, mind,' Fred replies.

Rose's face becomes flushed, and she glares at Fred angrily.
She jumps up from the sofa, snatches his plate and pushes past
him into the kitchen, scraping the left-overs into the red pedal-
bin by the door. Fred falls silent. He knows how fierce Rose's
temper can be, and that she does not like him talking about
Heather.

He sits and watches the back of Rose's head. She is standing at the glass doors that lead out into the back garden. Rain is falling, making the coloured patio slabs shiny. It was wet like this when Heather died. Fred's gaze drifts across to the edge of the patio by the fir trees, and then his blue eyes glaze over thoughtfully.

The telephone rings abruptly – it is for Fred. He is called out by one of the local landlords to visit a bedsitter down the street. A bath has overflowed and the ceiling of the room below is ruined; the landlord wants Fred to patch up the damage and then arrange a time to repair the plaster. He will be paid in cash, and Fred is never known to turn down extra work – even on a Friday night – so he goes out.

WHEN he returns home, most of the lights are off and the house is quiet. He turns on the television just in time to watch a late news bulletin. Fred has no patience with most programmes, but always tries to catch the headlines.

Rose is in bed in their room on the top floor of the house. Fred undresses and climbs in beside her, turning off the light. He regrets having mentioned Heather's name today, upsetting Rose, but he thinks they should try and maintain the fiction that their daughter is still alive.

Thinking of Heather reminds him of all the other girls who have died. Fred puts his arms around Rose and closes his eyes.

Faces flicker in his mind like ghosts, and then there is blackness.

I

THE BLUE-EYED BOY

THE VILLAGE OF Much Marcle lies just off the A449 road, halfway between the market towns of Ledbury and Ross-on-Wye, in rich Herefordshire countryside one hundred and twenty miles west of London. The Malvern Hills are to the north, the Wye Valley is to the west and the Forest of Dean to the south. Gloucester, the nearest major city, is fourteen miles away across the River Severn.

At the beginning of the Second World War, Much Marcle was a village of approximately seven hundred people, most of whom were employed on the land. An ancient settlement dating back to the Iron Age, the unusual name of the village derives from Old English, meaning 'boundary wood'; the prefix 'Much' sets it apart from the neighbouring hamlet of Little Marcle. The local accent is distinctive: Gloucester is pronounced 'Glaaster' and sentences are often concluded with the word 'mind', pronounced 'minde'.

There are several grand residences in the village, including a Queen Anne rectory and Homme House, the setting for a wedding scene in the Victorian book *Kilvert's Diary*. Much Marcle's other notable buildings are the half-timbered cottages, the red-brick school house, the Memorial Hall and cider factory.

Standing on opposite sides of the main road are Weston's Garage and the Wallwyn Arms public house, and along the lane from the Wallwyn Arms is the thirteenth-century sandstone parish church, St Bartholomew's, distinguished by its higgledy-piggledy graveyard and imposing, gargoyled tower.

The surrounding countryside is a pleasing sweep of green pasture and golden corn, with orchards of heavy cider apples and venerable perry pear trees left over from the last century, geometric hop fields and ploughed acres of plain red soil.

In fact it is such an uneventful place that a landslide during the reign of Elizabeth I long remained the most fantastical event in Much Marcle's history. For three days in 1575 there was much fear and excitement in the parish when 'Marclay Hill . . . roused itself out of a dead sleep and with a roaring noise removed from the place where it stood', destroying all in its path, including hedgerows, two highways and a chapel. A wall of earth and stone fifteen feet high was the result of the mysterious upheaval, and it is marked to this day on Ordnance Survey maps as 'The Wonder'.

The Marcle and Yatton Flower Show and Sports Fair has been held in a field on the edge of the village on the last Saturday in August since the 1890s. It is the main summer event in the area, a descendant of the more ancient Marcle Fayres. Stallholders sell food, fancy goods and clothing; there are also fairground rides, exhibitions and sports, including a five-and-a-half-mile road race between Ledbury and the village.

IT was during the August of 1939 when the man who would become Fred West's father sauntered down the lane from the nearby hamlet of Preston, heading for the Marcle Fair. Walter West, a powerfully built young farm hand, was born in 1914 and had been raised near the town of Ross-on-Wye. He was intimidated as a child by his army sergeant father, a forbidding character who was decorated for his service in the Great War of 1914–18. Walter complained that even when the old man came out of the army, he did not leave its disciplinarian ways behind.

With little education, barely able to read or write, Walter had left school at the age of eleven to work on the land. His maternal grandfather was a wagoner, employed to tend farm horses and their tackle; Walter became the wagoner's boy.

He had married for the first time when he was twenty-three, to a nurse almost exactly twice his age. One of twin sisters, Gertrude Maddocks was a 45-year-old spinster with a long, kindly face. She married Walter in 1937, and they set up home together in Preston. Walter went to work at Thomas' Farm nearby.

Gertrude was unable to have children, so the couple decided to foster a one-year-old boy named Bruce from an orphanage. Two years into the marriage, Gertrude met a bizarre death when, on a hot June day, she was stung by a bee, collapsed and died as young Bruce stood helplessly by. Walter found her body sprawled on the garden path when he returned home. After the funeral, he realised that he was unable to care for his adopted son on his own and handed the boy back to the orphanage.

Walter always spoke fondly of his first wife, despite the considerable age gap between them and the brevity of their marriage. He kept her photograph and the brass-bound Maddocks family bible among his most valued possessions for the rest of his life.

It was two and a half months after Gertrude's funeral when Walter attended the 1939 Marcle Fair. He was loafing along between the attractions when he came to a needlework stall, where a wavy-haired girl was displaying her work. The girl was shy and unforthcoming, but Walter eventually discovered that her name was Daisy Hill and that she was in service in Ledbury. Her parents lived in a tied cottage called Cowleas, on a sloping track known as Cow Lane near Weston's cider factory in the village. Her father, William Hill, was a familiar figure in the area: a tall, skinny man with a large black moustache who tended a milking herd of Hereford cattle. His family had been in Much Marcle, mostly working the land, for as long as anyone could remember, and were sometimes mocked in the village as being simple-minded. Because they were named Hill, and their home was built on a slight rise, the family were known as 'The Hillbillies'.

One of four children, Daisy Hannah Hill was only sixteen years old when she met Walter. She was an unworldly young girl, short and squat of figure with a plain face and a gap between her two front teeth. Daisy was flattered and surprised by the attentions of this mature man, and accepted Walter's invitation to take a turn with him on the swing-boats. They whooped excitedly as they rode through the air above the green countryside, marvelling at how far they could see.

They courted for a while as Walter continued to live at Preston, a half-hour walk from the home of Daisy's parents. He then took a job as a cow-man, like Daisy's father.

Walter married Daisy at St Bartholomew's on 27 January 1940. Before the service, friends and family gathered under the ancient yew tree outside the church porch, making sure their ties were straight and their shoes clean. Where Walter's first wife had been so much older than himself, there was comment among the guests that the second Mrs Walter West was a girl of only seventeen. Daisy wore a white dress with a veil, gloves, and little silver slippers; she carried tulips and a lucky horseshoe. The groom was a burly man who looked older than his twenty-six years. He was dressed in his good dark suit, draping his pocket-watch and chain across his waistcoat, and wore a carnation in his buttonhole. When it came to signing the parish register, Walter betrayed his lack of education by printing his name in large childish letters.

He had found living in Preston upsetting after Gertrude's

death, so the newly-married couple set up home at Veldt House Cottages, just off the A449 main road. Daisy fell pregnant with their first child almost immediately.

She was eight months into her term, and alone in the house, when there was a knock at the door one evening. Daisy did not like opening up when Walter was out milking, but the visitor would not go away, so she had little choice. Confronting her was a stern-looking policeman in full uniform. Daisy was such a nervous and unsophisticated young girl that she found the sight of the policeman deeply unsettling, even though there was nothing for her to worry about. He explained that there had been a road accident outside the cottage: a man had been knocked off his bicycle and the policeman wanted to know whether she had witnessed anything. Daisy gabbled that she had not, and quickly said goodbye. But the visit had so excited her that, by the time Walter returned home, his wife had gone into labour. A tiny baby daughter was born prematurely later that night and given the name Violet. She died in the cradle a few days later.

Walter and Daisy then moved into a red-brick tied cottage at a lonely but pretty junction in the village known as Saycells' Corner. The surrounding fields were covered with wild flowers, and a footpath known as the 'Daffodil Way' cut across a nearby meadow.

Bickerton Cottage was almost one hundred years old, and very primitive. It had neither electricity nor gas, and its water was drawn from a well in the garden by hand pump. To the left of the front door was a living room with an antiquated iron cooking range; both this room and the scullery had stone floors and low ceilings. A small flight of narrow stairs led up to two box-like bedrooms. The windows of the little house were four tiny squares that looked out over an orchard of apple trees and, on the other side of the lane, a large willow. The Wests kept chickens and a pig in an outhouse behind the cottage; this was also where they emptied the bucket that was their only toilet.

Once settled in, Daisy became pregnant again. She took to her bed in late 1941 to give birth for the second time, groaning with pain throughout a bleak autumn night. A fire was built in her bedroom and water was set to boil on the range downstairs. Daisy could hear the barking of foxes and the hoot of owls as the clock ticked away the hours of darkness. At last, as the sky lightened with the dawn, a healthy baby boy was born, gulping his first breath at 8:30 A.M. on 29 September 1941.

Four weeks later the proud parents carried their son down the lane, through the gate of St Bartholomew's and into the chill of the nave. The Reverend Alexander Spittall bent to his work over the Norman tub font. He murmured the baptism, as the water trickled through his hands, naming the screaming infant Frederick Walter Stephen West. It would soon be abbreviated to Freddie West and, later on, to Fred West.

THE joy and pride that Daisy felt were obvious for all to see. She took little Freddie to her bed each night, where she cuddled and petted the boy, often to the exclusion of her own husband. Hers was a beautiful baby: the curly hair that would later grow so dark was straw-yellow at first, and everybody marvelled at his astonishing blue eyes, shining like two huge sapphires. Daisy displayed Freddie's christening card in a prominent position in the cottage. Illuminated in gold, red and blue like a page from a sacred book, the card read: 'He that Believeth and is Baptised shall be Saved.'

DAISY gave birth to six more children over the following decade, in conditions of considerable poverty. For several years it seemed as if she had hardly given birth to one child before falling pregnant with the next.

The Second World War brought the additional hardship of rationing to the village. Walter earned only £6 per week, and the family quite literally had to live off the land. Windfall cooking apples and other fruit could be collected free from the orchard behind the cottage; chickens were kept for eggs and to provide a bird at Christmas. Walter brought pails of unpasteurised milk home from the farm each day, and in the evening and at weekends, tended his vegetable garden. Daisy baked her own bread and worked at her laundry in an iron tub behind the cottage. As she washed, Daisy cooed and fussed over Freddie, who stared back at her from his cradle with his big blue eyes.

The next baby, John Charles Edward, arrived in November 1942, just thirteen months after Fred. The relationship between the two boys would be the closest and most complex of any of the children. Walter and Daisy seldom left their sons alone, and seemed to care for them very much. John Cox, who has lived next door to Bickerton Cottage since 1927, remembers: 'They thought a lot of the children. If ever they went off, they took the kiddies with them on their bicycles.'

Daisy gave birth to her third son within eleven months of having John. David Henry George was born on 24 October 1943, when Fred was two, but suffered from a heart defect and died a month later. It was partly because of his death that Daisy wanted to move on from Bickerton Cottage.

They went to live at a house named Hill's Barn in the village. Daisy again fell pregnant. Her first daughter, Daisy Elizabeth Mary, was born in September 1944, and came to look most like her mother: they would be known to the family as 'Little Daisy' and 'Big Daisy'.

In July 1946 the family moved for the last time, to the house where Fred grew up. Moorcourt Cottage was tied to Moorcourt Farm, owned by Frank Brookes, where Walter found work tending to the milking herd and helping with the harvest. Despite being called a 'cottage', it is actually quite a large building, semi-detached with two chimney stacks and a dormer window set in the tiled roof. It stands on the outskirts of Much Marcle at a bend in the Dymock road, surrounded by open country. Looking out of the front windows there are uninterrupted views of the fields stretching away to May Hill in the distance. Cows low in the meadows, and the spire of St Bartholomew's, within an embrace of yew trees, is just visible over to the right of the panorama.

In the autumn after they moved into Moorcourt Cottage, Daisy gave birth to her final son, Douglas. At first he shared his mother's bed, as the other babies had, but was then put in with Fred and John. Kathleen – known as Kitty, and the prettiest of the girls – was born fourteen months later; Gwen's birth in 1951 completed the family. Daisy, having borne eight children in ten years, was now a heavy-set 28-year-old woman, hardened by life and quite different in looks and character to the timid teenager Walter had married.

Conditions at Moorcourt Cottage were basic. Eight slept in three cramped bedrooms: one for Mr and Mrs West, one for the three girls, and one for the boys, where Doug took the single bed and Fred and John shared the double. A tin bath was set in front of the parlour fire on wash nights, the children bathing under the watch of a pair of crude ornamental Alsatian dogs Walter had won at the Hereford Fair. Toilet facilities consisted of a simple bucket which had to be emptied each morning into a sewage pit, and rats were a constant pest. When Daisy saw one crossing the yard, she would blast at it with Walter's shotgun – one of Fred's abiding memories of his mother was of her shooting at 'varmints'.

Of the six surviving children, Fred was his mother's favourite. Coming after the tragedy of Violet's death he was particularly precious; the son that Walter had wanted and the answer to Daisy's prayers. As the baby grew up he could do no wrong; younger brother Doug described Fred as 'mammy's blue-eyed boy'. Daisy believed whatever Fred told her and took his side in squabbles between the children. For his part, Fred adored his mother and did exactly as she said.

The bond between them was perhaps unnaturally close. 'Fred came first with Daisy, even in front of Walter. She thought the world of Fred,' says her sister-in-law, Edna Hill. Partly as a result of this mollycoddling, Fred was a spoilt, dull and introverted child.

He was also scruffy. Daisy did her best to dress him nicely, in baggy shorts held up with braces, cotton shirts and sleeveless Fair Isle sweaters, but Fred always managed to look unkempt. Thick, curly brown hair grew up in a little bush on top of his head – just like his mother, whose looks he had inherited. Doug and John looked more like their father, and also got along with him, which Fred never did. There had been an awkwardness between father and son from the day Daisy brought Freddie into her bed.

Walter was well-liked in the village. He was a regular at the Wallwyn Arms on Saturday nights, and was sociable enough to organise the once- or twice-yearly village outings to the seaside, usually to Barry Island in South Wales. The day trips were the only holiday most of the villagers ever had, and they would pose for group photographs upon arrival to mark the occasion. Fred tends to look happy when he is photographed with his family, as long as his father is not in the frame. One snapshot shows Fred laughing uproariously with brother Doug as his mother clowns about with a neighbour. But when Walter's stern face was in the picture, as it is in the surviving photograph of the Barry Island trips, Fred looks distinctly uncomfortable.

AT the age of five, Fred was enrolled in the village school – the only one he ever attended, serving for both his junior and senior education. The backwaters of Herefordshire were slow in improving education standards after the war, and there was no secondary school in the area until 1961. The West brothers walked the two miles there and back every day, joining up with groups of other local children along the way.

Discipline was strict. Classmates remember Fred as being dim, dirty and 'always in trouble' because of his slovenly performance. He was regularly given the slipper. After the age of eight, he was old enough to be caned along with the rest of the children. Daisy was outraged by the regular punishments which Fred tearfully reported back to her. His class squealed in delight at the sight of Mrs West, dressed in one of her big floral frocks with her hands on her hips, haranguing their teacher after Fred had been hit. Fred became known as a mummy's boy partly because of these scenes, and was repeatedly mocked and bullied.

After school, and at weekends, the children were expected to work. If Fred or his brothers and sisters wanted to buy an ice cream or a bar of chocolate, they had to earn the money to pay for it. There were also regular household chores, like chopping wood for the fire, that they had to carry out for no reward.

The jobs they worked at outside the house followed the seasons of the year. Spring found Fred leading his younger brothers and sisters on an expedition up the Dymock road to Letterbox Field, where they would gather bunches of wild daffodils to sell at the roadside: the countryside around Much Marcle is famous for daffodils and a blaze of colour in the spring. Years later, Fred stole back across the same fields to bury the corpse of his first wife.

In the long dog-days of summer the local women and children rose early to meet the hop truck. This rumbled out of the village along dusty lanes to the pungent hop fields, where they worked until the light faded. They also picked strawberries and other soft fruit. The children, with their own little baskets, toiled alongside the adults, their fingers becoming sticky as they worked.

Harvest promised the exciting summer sport of 'rabbiting', which in turn would lead to delicious pies and roasts for the undernourished families. Beaters walked through the wheat just before the harvesting machines began to work; then boys, armed with sticks, followed along the edges of the field and clubbed any rabbits that sprang out. The cull was a necessary part of feeding the poor of the village, and the rabbits were shared out at the end of the day with an extra one or two going to large, needy families like the Wests. 'They were for eating, oh aye,' says Doug West, licking his lips. 'We would take them home, skin them and eat them. My mum was a good cook – rabbit stew, roast rabbit, anything.'

Autumn evenings were spent at home, listening to the *Dan Dare* adventure series on the radio and playing darts. The Wests owned a wind-up gramophone complete with a collection of scratchy 78s. At one stage, Fred took up the Spanish guitar, but he had little patience and the instrument soon became an ornament hung up on the wall in the front room. During the severe West Country winters, the children pulled on their moth-eaten cardigans and went sledging on Marcle Hill.

Fred was a quiet boy, with few friends of his own, relying on his family, particularly John, for companionship. Although John was a year younger, he was physically stronger than Fred and, probably out of jealousy of his favoured brother, bullied him. The third boy, Doug, who was small enough to be left out of their fights, remembers that 'John used to beat the hell out of Fred'.

Walter milked the herd morning and evening. On Sunday Daisy would sometimes keep him company, leaving the children on their own, and this is when the trouble often started. Fred developed the habit of going outside the cottage and pulling faces at John through the window, until his younger brother became so enraged that he punched at Fred. The windows were made of small panes and John's little fists were enough to knock the glass out. Naturally Walter was furious when he returned, warning them not to do it again and threatening a beating if they disobeyed him. Sometimes he would be provoked into taking the thick leather belt from his work trousers to hit the boys.

*

THE Wests were cut off from the world in their lonely cottage, and it is possible they became closer than is natural. There have always been rumours in the village that Daisy West harboured something more than motherly love for Fred – it is said she took her eldest son back into her bed when he was aged about twelve, and that she seduced him. This would not have been such an unusual act for a community like Much Marcle: deviant sex was not uncommon in the Herefordshire countryside. In *Cider with Rosie*, for example, his account of an idyllic childhood between the wars, Laurie Lee wrote about a community very similar to Much Marcle, pointing out that sexual transgressions 'flourished where the roads were bad'.

Even if it is true that Daisy seduced Fred – and her family cannot confirm the story – it was probably Walter who was the dominant influence upon Fred's emerging sexuality. In later life Fred often spoke about his father's sexual appetites, claiming Walter indulged in one of the greatest taboos of all: having sex with children. Fred claimed that Walter abused young girls, and spoke openly about it, saying that what he did was natural and that he had a right to do so. Fred grew up with exactly the same mentality, never thinking that having intercourse with a child might be wrong. He maintained that 'everybody did it'.

Away from home, Fred's first sexual experiences took place in the golden fields around Moorcourt Cottage. Shortly after he entered puberty, Fred was taking part in fumbling sex games here. 'We used to dive in the hay, take pot luck and go for it,' he later bragged, saying that he had cared little about the age or identity of the girls involved.

Fred's formal education was soon over. He had learned little at school, and left at the age of fifteen without taking any exams, being barely numerate and unable to read or write beyond the level of a seven-year-old. He had displayed some talents, though: Fred was artistic and drew with instinctive accuracy; in his final years at school he had taken woodwork classes and showed an aptitude for practical work, constructing a three-legged milking stool and a bench. Both of these were presented to his mother.

He went to work with Walter on Moorcourt Farm and the neighbouring Bridges Farm. The land was a mixture of arable and livestock; corn and potatoes were grown, and cows and sheep reared. As the youngest labourer, Fred had to muck in, doing whatever jobs the older farm hands passed on to him.

IT was an unkempt, dull-looking youth who stood in mud up to his Wellington boot tops each day. His brown hair was uncombed and his old checked shirt torn. Tufts of adolescent beard stuck out from his chin, and his teeth were yellow because he rarely bothered to clean them. When asked a question, Fred would look away and either mumble or gabble his answer, making it hard to understand what he said or thought.

But there was one sight guaranteed to make him pay attention – and that was if a girl walked down the lane. Then Fred's startling blue eyes would open wide and his young, monkey-like face would break into a gap-toothed, lascivious grin.

2

BRAIN DAMAGE

In 1957 John West left Marcle School and went to work on the farm with Fred and their father. Life as an unskilled labourer was poorly paid, but the West boys could expect nothing better. Their father had been a farm worker all his life, as had their maternal grandfather, William Hill, and his father before him; there was no reason to hope or think that John and Fred would ever do anything else. An acquaintance of Fred's at the time, Patrick Meredith, says that he fully expected Fred to be 'walking behind a cow with a stick for the rest of his life'.

It was hard, unforgiving work, and not without its physical hazards, as Fred found out when Walter suffered a serious accident shortly after the boys had started on the farm. The old man was lying under a tractor attempting to mend a part when the handbrake failed, allowing the machine to roll forward and trap his chest. He was freed, but was left with just one functioning lung.

Walter's eldest sons began to go into the nearby market town of Ledbury at weekends. The town represented Much Marcle's nearest 'bright lights', five and a half miles to the north at the foot of the Malvern Hills. Its high street featured a cinema, chip shop, milk bar and youth club. In the middle of the town, opposite the

clock tower, stood the Tudor Market House. Raised up on sixteen oak pillars, this offered a sheltered place for teenagers to
meet.

Some of the youths who gathered under the Market House
lived in Ledbury, while others, like John and Fred, came in
from the surrounding villages, travelling by motorcycle or push-
bike. Their average wages were little more than three pounds a
week, so entertainment was necessarily simple. Evenings were
spent chatting and smoking under the Market House, or loung-
ing in the cheaper seats at the Ledbury Picture House, where
Fred enjoyed watching John Wayne films. They did not go to
pubs, but drank coffee in the chip shop, which doubled as a
café.

One of the few places for teenagers to go in the evenings was
the Ledbury Youth Club, run by Ken Stainer, a veteran of the
King's African Rifles who persevered with the club despite considerable opposition. The view expressed in letters to the local
newspaper was that the club was part of the then fashionable
problem of 'delinquent youth', and should be shut down. Its
loud rock 'n' roll music, smashed windows and noise of motorcycles were apparently constant problems. But, in retrospect, the
entertainment was remarkably innocent: with nothing more
intoxicating than coffee and Coca-Cola to drink, the teenagers
played table tennis and billiards, watched television and listened
to records by Adam Faith and Elvis Presley. A few of the girls
attempted the jive while the boys, including Fred, slouched in
the background dragging on cigarettes.

Now that he was aged sixteen, Fred was taking more of an
interest in his appearance. He had started to shave properly,
combed his hair before going out and wore clean clothes. The
girls who attended the youth club considered him to be one of
the best-looking boys around town, and Fred's future
sister-in-law, Christine West, remembers that he was the talk of
her school. Fred was 'always chatting up girls', she says. But his

manner was crude. For every impressionable teenager who had a crush on Fred, there were many more who considered him boorish and unpleasant. These teenagers ridiculed Fred as a 'country bumpkin' and called him a 'dirty Gypsy', although, contrary to widespread belief, there is no Gypsy blood in his immediate family.

If Fred saw a girl he liked, at the club or at a local dance, he simply grabbed at her – it did not matter to Fred whether she was interested in him or not. He also took a perverse delight in trying to steal girls away from other boys. In the same way that he had goaded John by pulling faces at him through the parlour window, Fred went up to other boys' dates 'just for the hell of it', says his brother Doug. When it came to a fight, John would have to step in to defend his brother, because Fred would never hit back.

John's willingness to stick up for Fred, no matter how badly he behaved, was part of a fierce code of loyalty that the West family shared. An attack on one would always bring the wrath of the others. 'We could row amongst ourselves till the cows come home, but nobody else was allowed to pick on the family,' explains Doug.

FRED often visited H.C. Cecil's motorcycle shop off the High Street in Ledbury. He found motorcycles exciting and knew that, if he had his own transport, he would also have some freedom from Moorcourt Cottage. A small machine was within his reach if he saved carefully.

The motorcycle that took Fred's fancy was a 125cc James with a mauve-coloured tank. His mother was against the idea, but relented on the condition that Fred promise to sell it if he had a crash. He agreed and took delivery of a brand new James around the time of his seventeenth birthday. A photograph shows Fred proudly straddling his new machine, while his brothers and sisters gather round grinning: little Gwen perched on the tank between her brother's arms, and sister Daisy resting against his shoulders.

Brian Hill was a country boy who, like Fred, came into Ledbury at weekends and loitered around the Market House. Brian became one of Fred's few friends and was allowed to ride the motorcycle. At the chip shop, which was among their regular haunts, Brian remembers that Fred would ostentatiously park the James outside before sauntering in – 'he tried to be the big one for show'. When they were not riding the motorcycle, they often parked it in the alley next to the Plough public house, stripping it down to clean the engine.

On the evening of 28 November 1958, Fred was riding his James 125 home along the Dymock road when he had an accident. He was just a few hundred yards from Moorcourt Cottage when he collided with a local girl named Pat Manns, who had been cycling in the opposite direction, back to the neighbouring hamlet of Preston Cross where she lived with her parents.

There are a number of possible explanations for the accident: there may have been a car involved; the country road was not lit and the lights on both the push-bike and motorcycle were dim by modern standards; at the point where they collided there were also several potholes. It has even been suggested in village gossip that Fred deliberately rode into the girl. Whatever the cause, they were both sent sprawling across the road.

A labourer from Bridges Farm found the teenagers lying in the dark. The girl had cuts and scrapes, but was not seriously injured. Then the labourer turned to the boy. Fred was lying motionless; he was out cold and there was a fair amount of blood. When the ambulance arrived, the patient was judged to be in too serious a condition to be taken to any of the local cottage hospitals, so he was driven fourteen miles to the city of Hereford, in the west of the county.

In the early morning Fred's battered helmet and Wellington

boots were returned to Moorcourt Farm by a friend, who also delivered an alarming account of Fred's injuries. While an anguished Daisy sat mooning over her son's belongings, Walter walked up to Preston Cross to apologise to Pat Manns' family.

FRED lay unconscious in Hereford Hospital. His vivid blue eyes were unfocused, rolled back in their sockets as if he were dead. Daisy held his hand and tearfully blamed herself for allowing him to buy the motorcycle. The wait stretched into days, and there were fears that he would never come round. A full week passed, and then, on the seventh day after the accident, Fred roused himself from the depths of unconsciousness, his befuddled mind slowly cleared and he woke up. He later described the experience as like 'coming back from the dead'.

The relief felt by his mother was tempered by a sober appraisal of her son's injuries. Fred was a mess of lacerations and broken bones. He later claimed that a steel plate had to be fitted in his head to keep his shattered skull together. His nose was broken; injuries to one arm would give him trouble for the rest of his life; and one leg was so severely smashed it had to be held together by a metal brace while the bone mended. Fred was given callipers and a metal shoe. For months after the accident, he stomped about Moorcourt Cottage like Long John Silver, thumping the floor with his foot as he went. 'You could always tell when Freddie was coming back because he dropped one leg harder than the other. You could hear him coming at night,' says his brother Doug.

When, after several months, the leg-iron came off, he still had a marked limp and had to use crutches to get around. The accident also altered what good looks he previously had: his nose was crooked and one leg would forever be shorter than the other. The experience also left Fred with a lifelong dislike of hospitals.

Despite these not inconsiderable handicaps, he drifted back

into what social life he had enjoyed in Ledbury, hanging around the Market House building and the youth club. Bill Haley's 'Rock Around The Clock' was one of Fred's favourite records, but his leg was so stiff that his movements looked comical when he tried to dance. He was angry with himself, and for the first time in his life, became aggressive when other boys started making fun of him by saying that he 'wasn't any good'.

Fred was also finding life difficult at home. He told his friend June Ledbury that he was unhappy living at Moorcourt Cottage, that he 'couldn't hack it' any more and that his father was getting him down.

It was at this time that Fred met one of the most significant women in his life. Catherine Bernadette Costello, known as Rena or Rene for short, was the girl who would become his first wife. She was a pretty sixteen-year-old with blue eyes, auburn hair and a scar on her brow. They first met at a dance held at the Memorial Hall in Much Marcle, opposite the red-brick village school where Fred had been educated. Rena was staying with relations in the area, having moved down from Scotland in the summer of 1960.

RENA was from Coatbridge, an industrial town a short drive from Glasgow in the district of Strathclyde. Her mother, Mary, left home when Rena was a young child, and Rena's father, Edward, who worked in a scrap-iron yard, had to bring up his five daughters and their two orphaned cousins on his own. The family, who had little money, lived in Calder Street – a long, straight highway near the centre of the town. It is a grim area, dominated by a huge factory complex. Even the Church of Scotland near the Costello home is a monstrosity of dark stone, more depressing than inspiring. The men drank hard in the evenings and the streets glittered with broken glass after the pubs had closed.

Rena was a delinquent, in trouble with the police from a

very early age. Her first appearance at Coatbridge Juvenile Court was for theft, in May 1955, when she was only eleven. Rena was admonished and sent home, but she was back again the following year, also charged with theft. Rena made her third court appearance in 1957, and this time was given a two-year probationary sentence. When she was caught stealing yet again, in March 1958, the magistrates committed her to an approved school, but this served only to harden her character and make her even more reckless. When she reached the age of sixteen, Rena left home and moved to Glasgow, before travelling south to visit relations in England.

Her life had already been something of an adventure in comparison to Fred's, who had only travelled as far afield as Barry Island. He tried to impress Rena with exaggerated stories, including the colourful account of his recent motorcycle accident. He said that he had actually died after the smash, but had come back to life when his body was laid on the cold marble of the mortician's slab.

It was not Fred's fantasies which won Rena over. They came together because she was one of the few girls Fred had met who was prepared to accept his crude ways – and, crucially, his demands for sex. Rena was so coarsened by life herself that she must have been grateful for any affection, even Fred's. She agreed to sleep with him. The relationship became so intense that Rena tattooed Fred's name on her left arm, using a sewing needle and black Indian ink.

Probably because of her association with Fred, and the fact that she was staying out late at night, Rena had to leave her relations' house where she had been lodging. She moved into the New Inn public house in Ledbury High Street, sharing with a Scottish girlfriend. The girls were only there a matter of weeks, and are remembered by landlady Eileen Phillips only because they stayed out late and damaged the furniture in their room by being careless with bottles of hair lacquer.

By the autumn of 1960, Rena was struggling to find work and short of money. There had also been arguments with Fred, who was a jealous boy. She packed up and went home to Scotland.

With Rena gone, Fred turned his attention to the younger girls he knew around Much Marcle. It was at around this time that he began to pester a thirteen-year-old girl from the village.[*] It was later claimed that he seduced the girl, and continued to have sex with her secretly for the next six months, culminating in a scandal the following year.

He also continued to visit the Ledbury Youth Club a couple of nights each week. The club was held in a dilapidated former domestic science building in a part of the High Street known as the Southend. The building was on two levels, and both the ground-floor and first-floor rooms were used on club nights. An iron fire escape led from the first floor down into the yard. One evening, in the autumn of 1960, Fred made a grab for a girl who was standing near him on the fire escape steps, but instead of giggling or running away, as his victims invariably did, she turned and hit Fred. He lost his balance, toppled over the railing and fell headfirst on to the concrete below.

Teenagers rushed out of the club to look at Fred's stricken body. He lay perfectly still, and all efforts to revive him failed. He had fallen no more than ten feet, but had banged his head and was out cold, his blue eyes dilated, blood wetting his curly hair. An ambulance was called and he was taken to the cottage hospital in Ledbury. He was still unconscious when he was examined by the doctor, and was referred on to the main hospital in Hereford where he had been a patient just over a year before.

Once again Daisy had to wait by her son's bed and pray for his recovery. Once again his blue eyes lolled back in their sockets. This second period of unconsciousness, however, was not as long as the

---

[*] This girl cannot be identified for legal reasons.

first, and he came round after twenty-four hours. But there were lasting effects: Fred became more short-tempered and irritable. His family began to wonder whether he had suffered brain damage.

NOW that Rena was gone, and Fred had sold his motorcycle, he had little to do on his weekends in Ledbury, but Brian Hill was still a faithful companion and one day the boys turned to petty theft for excitement. In the spring of 1961, they were sauntering through Tilley and Son, a stationery store near the Ledbury clock tower, when Fred saw a display of ladies cigarette cases. He hissed to Brian, 'Christ, these are nice!' and on the spur of the moment put the cigarette cases into his pocket. The boys managed to make it outside without being caught and, flushed with success, Fred also snatched a gold watch-strap from a display in Dudfield and Gaynan's, one of the town's jewellers.

The boys slipped furtively along the High Street and turned into a toilet by the Plough public house. Fred said it would be safer if they hid what they had stolen until they were ready to go home. Brian, who was a year younger than his friend, agreed to do whatever Fred thought was best, so they stashed the cigarette cases and watch-strap on top of the cistern and then whiled away the hours until late afternoon.

The shopkeepers had worked out that the thieves must be the two scruffy boys who had been loitering around the shops earlier in the day. They gave the police a description, and when Fred and Brian attempted to leave the town, they were stopped. Fred had the merchandise in his pockets.

On a warm spring day in April 1961, Fred made his first-ever court appearance, standing alongside Brian Hill in the dock of Ledbury Magistrates Court. They were charged with stealing a rolled gold watch-strap, worth just over £2, and two cigarette cases. Brian and Fred pleaded guilty and were fined £4 each, plus costs. Outside the court Fred put on a brave show, grumbling about the size of the fine, which was more than he earned in a week. Brian Hill's mother was infuriated by the whole affair, and by Fred's devil-may-care attitude in particular. She told Brian that he was to have no more to do with his friend, whom she believed had led her son into trouble. The case earned Fred his first newspaper report: three paragraphs on page one of the *Ledbury Reporter*.

THE most significant event of Fred's youth came two months later, in June 1961. Moorcourt Cottage was thrown into turmoil when Fred was suddenly dragged before local police on a shockingly serious charge. He was bluntly told that he had been accused of having sex with a thirteen-year-old girl – the relationship which had allegedly started the previous December. A doctor had examined the child and discovered she was pregnant. It was suggested that Fred had had sex with the girl four or possibly five times, and emphasised that she was a full six years younger than him.

Far from being overwhelmed by the seriousness of the allegations, Fred was belligerent with the police, answering Detective Constable Baynham's questions as though they were completely unimportant. What was more scandalous to Daisy, when she found out, was that the family knew the thirteen-year-old well; Fred had been trusted in her company. 'She was disgusted,' says Daisy's sister-in-law Edna Hill.

Police, teachers and social workers became involved in the affair that followed. When Fred was questioned about his attitudes to sex, it emerged that he had been molesting young girls from his early teens, and that he did not consider his actions to be unusual or shocking. In fact, he was sulky and petulant, put-out that he had to talk about it at all. Of course it was right that he touched little girls, he argued, adding truculently, 'Well, doesn't everyone do it?'

The police charged him with having unlawful carnal knowledge of a child, and Fred was briefly kept in a cell while bail was arranged.

It was his complacent attitude to the charges that finally set him adrift from the normal world. After the accidents, the petty thieving and the grabbing at girls, he had now made it absolutely clear that he was not fit to live with civilised people. Daisy agreed that the boy could not spend another night under her roof. It was a turning point in his life, a rejection that Fred would remember with great bitterness. He was sent to live with his mother's sister, Violet, and her husband Ernie at Daisy Cottage in Much Marcle. None of the family back at Moorcourt Cottage would speak to him. The young girl had her child aborted and Fred's case was set down for trial in November.

Fred quit farm work, further distancing himself from his family. His decision was partly due to his father, from whom he wanted to get away more than ever. But he would have had to leave the land anyway. Machinery was replacing manual workers, and the life that Walter had led was dying out. Many young men of Fred's generation found they had to move away from the village. For Fred it would mean a lifetime of odd manual jobs, but he always returned to the first trade he took up – building. He started as a labourer, and then learned the rudiments of carpentry and bricklaying until he came to think of himself, rather grandly, as a fully-fledged builder. John worked alongside him for a while and then went off on his own to become a lorry driver. Building sites afforded Fred ample opportunities to steal. He was working on a housing estate outside the town of Newent, Gloucestershire, when he was arrested for stealing pieces of hardware from the site. When Fred appeared at Newent Magistrates Court he attempted to justify his actions by saying that other workmen took things, so why not he? Fred was fined £20.

He was still getting himself in trouble with girls, and one former girlfriend (who cannot be named for legal reasons) claims she was raped twice by Fred at this time. He had wanted to marry the girl, who lived in Newent, and had even offered her an engagement ring. But she was only fourteen, five years younger than Fred, and Daisy West warned them not to have sex – she did not want the police coming to the house again. Despite this, the girl claims that Fred raped her on two occasions after she had turned fifteen, and that, curiously, he collapsed on to his back after the first assault as if he were experiencing some kind of attack.

On 9 November 1961, shortly after his twentieth birthday, the scruffy labourer with piercing blue eyes appeared in court to face the most serious criminal charges of his young life. He stepped into the dock at Herefordshire Assizes, before Judge Justice Sachs, to be tried for the alleged sexual abuse of the thirteen-year-old girl. Despite Daisy's disgust, Fred was still a member of the family and she agreed to be called as a defence witness.

The other defence witness was the West family GP, Dr Brian Hardy. It was during the questioning of Dr Hardy by defence counsel that the possibility that Fred had suffered brain damage emerged for the first time. Doctor Hardy agreed with the defence that Fred had sustained head injuries through at least one motorcycle accident, and might be epileptic as a result.

A severe head injury is one of the most common causes of epileptic fits, and the longer the period of unconsciousness following an accident, the more likely it is that the victim will develop fits. Depending on the area of the brain scarred by the injury, there may also be personality changes. Brain damage was an explanation for Fred's behaviour that was seized upon by Daisy West. When it was her turn to speak, Daisy said that Fred took the blame for many misdemeanours which were not his fault – but her testimony proved unnecessary when, at the last minute, the child who had made the allegations refused to give evidence and the trial collapsed.

Fred walked free from the court, but he was not welcome at home and it is probable that this rejection marked his character. 'He thought he was the black sheep of the family,' says his friend, Alf Macklin.

AT the age of twenty, Fred was a convicted thief and widely believed to be a child molester. His moods were volatile and he may well have suffered brain damage. Shunned even by his own family, he had already become an outcast of society.

3

THE HELLER

THE GIRL WHO became infamous as Rose West was born in Devon in 1953, when Fred was twelve. To fully understand Rose, and her relationship with Fred, it is necessary to reach back several years before her birth to examine the lives of her mother and father. They were both unusual, deeply troubled people whose marriage was violent and profoundly unhappy.

Rose's father, William Andrew Letts, known as Bill, was born in 1921 and brought up in Northam, a small village near the town of Bideford on the North Devon coast. His mother, Bertha Letts, worked as a nurse at the Battle of the Somme and became a district nurse in Northam when the Great War ended. Bill's father (also called Bill) was a shiftless, lazy man who dabbled in a variety of jobs.

Northam was similar to Much Marcle, one hundred and twenty miles to the north-east, inasmuch as it is a small, quiet village cut off from the hurly-burly of the modern world. Northam is set upon a slight hill, on a lip of land which juts into the confluences of the rivers Torridge and Taw where their estuaries join the Bristol Channel. Laid out below the village is a rugged seaside park known as Northam Burrows, which ends in a sandy beach. The town of Bideford is within walking distance south of the village; Barnstaple is a few miles down-river to the east. The village was the scene of one great and violent historical event when, in the ninth century, a terrible battle was fought on the land where Northam now stands, between the men of Alfred the Great and an invading army led by Hubba, King of the Danes. By the time the enemy had been driven back into the sea, the Burrows were stained with the blood of eight hundred men.

There are several small hotels around Northam, but it is not a picturesque seaside village and there is only a small tourist trade in the summer. The church and the buildings around the central square are constructed of gloomy stone. Bill Letts' family lived in a terrace house in Castle Street, one of the narrow roads that lead off the square. This part of Northam is as dark as a Rhondda Valley mining village.

THE marriage of Bertha and Bill Letts was not a happy one. Neither wanted children, and they were initially disappointed when, despite their best intentions, Bertha became pregnant. They changed their view when Bill junior was born and came to dote on what would be their only child.

Bill was sickly, but his lack of strength only made Bertha love him all the more. She idolised her son, and spent hours knitting warm clothes to keep illness at bay. Bill was struck down by rheumatic fever shortly before he was due to start at Northam's Church of England Secondary School. He was kept at home for many months, and when he finally enrolled, his classmates were astonished to see that he was wearing girl's woollen stockings under his shorts. The stockings, together with Bill having missed the start of school, made him the butt of classroom jokes. 'We all thought it was very queer,' says Ronnie Lloyd, who later became a friend.

Bill was soon being bullied. When Bertha found out, she

took it upon herself to go to the school and deal with his tormentors. He was also lonely at home. Bertha played cards in the
evenings, leaving Bill with his father, but now the novelty of
having a son had worn off, his father lost interest in Bill and
often reminded him that he was only the result of an accident.

After leaving school, Bill first worked in an electrical shop in
Bideford and then for the Bristol Airport Company as a radio
engineer. He was a reserved and distrustful teenager, prone to the
notion that people were 'ganging up' against him. He experienced at least one unhappy romance, when a local girl he had
been courting moved away from the village to marry another
man, and the rejection added to his increasingly jaundiced view
of the world. This was compounded when his father began to
impose strict rules on Bill; for example, locking the front door
against him if he were not home by ten at night.

One of Bill's few friends was a Jewish boy named Lionel
Green, whose family were well-off people from London, where
they owned a business in the East End. The Second World War
had begun, and the Greens moved into a large house in Bideford
to escape the Blitz. Lionel had three sisters, and his parents
employed a young girl to help look after them. One day Lionel
introduced her to Bill.

DAISY Gwendoline Fuller was three years his senior, but so unas-
suming that she appeared to be much younger than Bill. Daisy
was from Chadwell Heath, Essex, a short train ride from East
London. Her father was a professional soldier, a decorated veteran of several famous battles who brought up his nine children
with Victorian-style discipline, giving them a 'good hiding' if
they misbehaved.

Daisy went into service after leaving school. During the late
1930s she worked at a public house in London's Brick Lane,
where she witnessed Oswald Mosley's Blackshirts march past the

door. Life there had been hard, and poorly rewarded; she was used to being up at six in the morning and often did not get to bed again until midnight.

After leaving the Brick Lane pub, Daisy was employed carrying out domestic work for the Green family, and was working for them when they decided to move to Devon.

The young man she met was not particularly prepossessing. He was small and slightly built, with stiff manners; a prim youth who hated bad language and did not smoke or drink, preferring grapefruit juice to beer when he went out. But Daisy was prudish herself, and was pleased that Bill did not manhandle her or chase after other girls. He was somebody she thought would meet with her father's approval.

They married on 18 April 1942, at St Mary's Church in Ilford, Essex, so that Daisy's family could attend the ceremony. Afterwards they travelled back to Northam, and Daisy moved in with Bill's parents in their tiny house on Castle Street. She was immediately struck by how obsessively neat and tidy the Letts were. It was also plain that Bill's father had little interest in his son and was not looking forward to becoming a grandfather, but because of his own unhappy experiences as an only child, Bill vowed he would not make the same mistake with his marriage and told Daisy that he wanted a large family. They were still living with Bill's parents when their first child, Patricia, was born in 1943. A second daughter, Joyce, arrived eighteen months later, shortly before Bill was called up to the services.

He joined the Navy as a radio operator, and was sent to the Philippines. While he was away, Daisy divided her time between his parents in Northam and her own family in Essex. When the war ended in 1945, Bill volunteered to stay on; he was proficient at his job and thrived on the discipline, becoming something of a martinet.

Their third daughter, Glenys, was born in 1950, and the Letts were granted a council property in Northam at 57 Morwenna

Park Road. The house was a newly-built three-bedroom end-of-terrace, on a small estate laid out between the old village square and the Northam Burrows. Built on a slight incline, there are views of the estuary and the Bristol Channel, although much of the time the sea is obscured by drizzling rain.

Bill remained in the Navy for the next few years, making infrequent visits home to Morwenna Park on leave, always immaculately turned out in his radio operator's uniform. When he was home, Daisy was struck by his Victorian ways. He demanded that the house be perfectly clean, and became angry if anything were out of place. When Daisy and Bill quarrelled, as they increasingly did, he accused her of being against him and worked himself into a rage. Daisy began to wonder what sort of life was in store for her.

He was reserved with the neighbours, even with his school friend Ronnie Lloyd, who now lived next door. Bill also discouraged Daisy from becoming familiar with the women on the estate, but Daisy took these oddities in her stride. She was so used to being ordered about by her father that she allowed her husband to make the decisions, no matter how unfair. Ronnie Lloyd and his wife Elsie were struck by Daisy's extreme timidity, and noticed she would only speak when spoken to. When Elsie tried to strike up conversation while the women hung out their washing in the adjoining back gardens, Daisy would address her neighbour formally by her surname, never relaxing enough to make conversation.

Bill's years in the Navy had been a happy time, but he could not raise a family being away from home so much, so when Daisy became pregnant with their fourth child, Bill returned home to Northam to settle down. He soon came to regret the decision bitterly, and never tired of telling his wife that he wished he had stayed in the services. The main cause of his unhappiness was the scarcity of work in Devon, and the poor wages for what little employment there was.

Bill worked for a while for Bernard Smith in Barnstaple, repairing television sets. The job came with a van, and Ronnie Lloyd said that it gave him a slightly above-average status in the village because television was so new. Unfortunately, Bill had little patience and invariably found a way of falling out with most people he knew. He did not stay a TV repairman for long.

When he did find employment, it was often casual work on the promise of payment when the summer season started. The money did not always materialise, and sometimes there were no jobs at all. One year Bill and Ronnie Lloyd tried to sell snacks to the few tourists who ventured on to Northam Burrows. 'Work was short and we would do anything,' says Ronnie. Daisy and Elsie Lloyd cut the sandwiches and Bill spent several dispiriting days trudging back and forth along the sandy paths by the sea looking for customers.

No matter how short money became, Daisy took a pride in turning her three daughters out smartly. She patched and mended old clothes to make do for the new ones they could not afford. They might be poor and hungry, but she would never let it show. The memory of her well-dressed children still makes Daisy proud: 'Neighbours complimented me on how smart they looked,' she says.

The neighbours also noticed that the children were set to work the minute they returned home from the village school. One might do the ironing, another would be told to look after whoever was the baby at the time. They were even sent out for Mrs Letts' shopping, and housewives found themselves standing beside the earnest-looking Letts girls in the village shop.

If Bill Letts were home, the house had to be made spotless. When he came in, he would run his finger across the furniture – and if he found dust, the house would have to be cleaned again.

The children were not allowed to play outside the house; instead, Daisy led her daughters on a long walk each morning. Sometimes they would march across the blustery Burrows down to the sea, where they could search for crabs in the rock pools. Other days they walked for miles through the peaceful country lanes, glad to be away from the oppressive company of their father. 'I wouldn't say that they had a natural childhood,' says former neighbour Elsie Lloyd.

It was noticed that the children had considerable respect for Bill's word. He never played with the children or gave them any of his time – but if he called to one of his daughters to do a chore, the child would go running without a moment's hesitation.

Arguments between Daisy and Bill were frequent, and became violent. Bill had started to hit Daisy during his tantrums, and she was often seen around the village with black eyes. One day a terrible scene unfolded outside the Letts home. The house was set down below street level, with a flight of five concrete steps from the gate to the garden path. Bill pulled his screaming wife down the steps by her hair and then slapped her. Neighbours were so shocked that they called the police. Daisy thought these outbursts had something to do with the phases of the moon; the abuse soon got to the point when she would tell herself that, if the moon were full, she would have to be careful.

The regime at home was terrifying; one of absolute obedience. Apart from their chores around the house, the children had to be perfectly behaved. They sat silently at dinner, waiting for their father to start eating, and watched him warily for any change in his mood. Any little thing would spark a row that could last for several days. The children looked up at their mother with earnest, worried faces as she implored them not to aggravate their father or get in his way.

Despite these lessons in survival, Bill Letts still found reasons to beat his children, hitting them across the face and thrashing them with the copper stick from the boiler. He had come to resemble the actor Donald Pleasance in looks, and was a truly frightening figure when angry. His eyes blazed, his face a picture of malevolence. He threw one of the girls down the stairs and banged another child's head against a brick wall. When Daisy protested, she too was beaten, as the children wailed for it to stop. Mad with his anger, Bill shouted that she was against him as well, and tossed boiling water over her. The sound of sobbing could be heard long after the screaming died down.

LOOKING back at those days, Daisy says sadly, 'He was a heller to live with. We lived under terror for years.' She was so ashamed, and confused, by her husband's extraordinary behaviour that she told nobody, not even her family, of the misery she lived with. 'We literally suffered hell behind locked doors,' she says. When some of the neighbours did challenge Bill about the way he treated his family, it only reinforced his belief that everybody was against him – and, when the front door to Number 57 was closed, he beat his family all the more. Daisy believes her husband took a perverse pleasure in hurting them. 'He was anything but normal,' she says. 'He was a tyrant to live with. I would say he was sadistic because he seemed to enjoy making you unhappy.'

WHAT she did not know was that Bill was hiding a secret from her, a secret she would only discover three decades later when she read his medical records after his death.

Bill was a diagnosed schizophrenic, suffering severe psychotic experiences. He had suffered with the illness from a very early age, but had never told his family and does not appear to have received treatment. Some days Bill was happy, planning surprises for Daisy's birthday or their anniversary; other days he walked in the front door spoiling for a fight. 'He was definitely two different people,' Daisy says; she compared his behaviour with that of Stevenson's character Dr Jekyll. Also, like many schizophrenics, Bill could be aggressive and had an irrational suspicion that people were plotting against him.

In 1952 Daisy gave birth to her fourth child, Andrew, the first of three sons. Daisy then entered into a long period of severe post-natal depression; at least, that is what she thought it was at first. But feelings of anxiety and an inability to cope deepened and lasted into 1953, when she suffered a severe nervous break-down. Strangely, Bill was sympathetic to Daisy's depression, perhaps due to the secret knowledge he had of his own mental imbalance. Daisy's doctor listened to her problems, and decided she should see an expert in mental health. He referred her to a hospital in Bideford, where she became an out-patient of the psychiatric unit. A psychiatrist there suggested to Daisy that her depression was so serious it might benefit from Electro-Convulsive Therapy (ECT). Daisy said she would try anything, and prepared to receive what was known as the 'electric hammer'.

Daisy Letts received her first ECT treatments in a small, coun-try hospital by the sea in 1953. She was given a muscle-relaxing drug and then strapped down like some lunatic in Bedlam. Clumsy electrodes were attached to her scalp and she was given a piece of rubber to bite on. When these preparations were complete, the power was switched on and an electrical current crackled through her brain. Daisy remembers biting on the rubber gag – and then blackness. When the power was turned on, she says, 'You didn't know no more.'

ECT is a mysterious form of medical treatment, the side effects of which can include confusion and memory loss. It is as contro-versial now as it was in the 1950s. The theory is that electricity passed through the brain redresses the balance of chemicals which govern mood. But scientists do not know exactly why it works, and some doctors believe it does more harm than good. It is an indication of how controversial ECT still is that the treatment is banned completely in the state of California.

After two treatments Daisy again saw a psychiatrist, who eval-uated her progress and decided she was a more serious case than had at first been suspected. More treatment would be needed. Daisy agreed, as nothing could be worse than the pain she already suffered at home, and went on to have a course of six treatments. During this time she continued to have a sporadic sex life with Bill, and became pregnant for the fifth time. The treatment finally ended, leaving her feeling battered and far from well, but there was no opportunity for recuperation. In the autumn of 1953, shortly after her last session, Daisy registered at the Highfield Maternity Home in Northam to have her fifth child, the daughter who would later become infamous as Rose West.

ROSE was conceived from the union of two mentally ill people. Her father was a violent schizophrenic; her mother a depressive recovering from a severe nervous breakdown. The children of schizophrenics have a 1-in-10 chance of becoming schizophrenic themselves, and the children of depressives are also far more likely than normal to suffer from mental illness. The child born to Daisy and Bill Letts at the Highfield Maternity Home that autumn had both these genetic dice loaded against her. What is more, she had grown in the womb while her mother's brain was slammed by the 'electric hammer' of ECT. Finally, the home that awaited Rose was one of almost Dickensian poverty and cruelty. A more troubled start in life is hard to imagine.

Rosemary Pauline Letts was born on the twenty-ninth day of November 1953. In the outside world, the young Queen Elizabeth II was touring the Commonwealth following her June coronation. Daisy could have no idea of the horrors that were to follow with this, her fourth and last baby girl. She held Rosemary – as the family would always call her – and loved the child as she had the others. Rosemary was a beautiful baby who 'never cried and was as good as gold'. Over forty years later, Daisy Letts smiles sadly at the memory.

Soon after bringing the baby home to 57 Morwenna Park Road it was clear that Rose was different to other children. She developed a habit of rocking herself in her cot; if she was put in a pram without the break on, she rocked so violently that the pram crept across the room. As she became a little older, Rose only rocked her head, but she did this for hours on end. It was one of the first indications that, in the family's words, she was 'a bit slow'. If a child with such a habit were taken to a doctor now, there would be great concern, as it is an early indication of learning difficulties. As Rose grew from a baby to a toddler to a little girl, she would swing her head for hours until she seemed to have hypnotised herself into a state of semi-consciousness. When Daisy called for her, Rose did not hear, and Rose's sister, Glenys, who had to share a room with Rose at one stage, complained that the incessant rocking kept her awake at night.

Rose was also marked out by her striking attractiveness. In the local phraseology of Northam she was described by mothers as a 'lovely young maid'. She had large brown eyes, olive skin and glossy brown hair. But there was a vacancy in those big, doll-like eyes that made the neighbours wonder. She would stand at the gate of 57 Morwenna Park Road and gaze at the world, almost as if she were not a part of it.

Rita New, who lived nearby on the estate, says it was clear that Rose was not like other children.

'It's the way her used to look; she used to stare a lot. I know her was different.'

4

DOZY ROSIE

ROSE WAS SUCH an unintelligent child that her older siblings nicknamed her 'Dozy Rosie'. Her elder brother Andrew says she was left out of their children's games because she was 'as thick as two planks'. As a result, Rose spent a great deal of time on her own during the first few years of her life, often amusing herself with her six pet hamsters. Then, in 1957, when Rosemary was four, Daisy gave birth to her second son, Graham. Rose played delightedly with her baby brother as if he were a doll, screeching with pleasure when she was allowed to help bathe him. It was with Graham, and other younger children, that she continued to play as she grew older, never being at ease with boys and girls of her own age; her mother says she was always 'babyish'.

Her eldest sisters, Patricia and Joyce, left home around the time that Rose started school, exhausted by their father's tyrannical behaviour. Because of the age gap, they never came to know Rose well.

IT was a plump girl, with ponytails dancing in the air, who ran along the road from 57 Morwenna Park to Northam Village

School each morning. Rose performed poorly at lessons: elementary mathematics, reading and writing were all a struggle. She stared uncomprehendingly at the blackboard, and was quite unable to master the spelling of even the simplest words. She did not join in with other children in the playground at break, and went straight home when school was finished, just as neat and tidy as when she had left that morning. Often she would have a number of smaller children filing behind her, and they would sit on the grass in front of the house having make-believe tea.

At home Rosemary was a 'cry-baby'. The other Letts children were used to working around the house. They were expected to clean it, often before going to school, and were also responsible for keeping up the garden. Fear of their father meant that they did not even consider skipping chores; the consequences were too awful. But Rose was different. When she was given a task, she whined until one of the others did it for her. The most surprising aspect of this laziness was that her father did not mind it – he considered Rose to be 'dense' or 'naïve' and thought her behaviour was funny. She became his favourite, and was the only child to escape physical punishment.

Dinner at Morwenna Park Road was eaten in silence, and then the children cleared away. Any misbehaviour was punished with a severe beating, yet Bill would tolerate Rose playing with her food while she stared vacantly around the table. Daisy says that Bill 'always saw the funny side of her'.

With the exception of his engagingly 'stupid' daughter, Bill found fault in everything. He could not find and keep a good job, and men in the village, even a member of Daisy's family, had started questioning him about the way he disciplined the children. When he passed down the village streets, children hissed 'schizo', little knowing how close to the truth they were. Daisy also presented Bill with another mouth to feed: their third son, Gordon, was born in 1960.

There was gossip in the village that Bill had an unhealthy

interest in children. The rumour became particularly persistent during one of his spells of unemployment when, despite his lack of patience with children, Bill decided to start a rock 'n' roll youth club for the local teenagers. It was held in a room behind the Kingsley Arms public house, overlooking Northam's graveyard. There was a tape player and some early Bill Haley and Elvis Presley music, although the few teenagers who attended found Bill's dour demeanour a deadening influence and the club soon closed. There was never any proven impropriety – and Ronnie Lloyd, who ran the club with him, was above suspicion – but it was said that Bill Letts had been overly attentive to certain young girls.

For all these reasons Bill was finding it difficult to continue living in Northam by the early 1960s. Supporting his family was a constant and losing battle; name-calling and innuendo suggesting he was a pervert represented the final straw. The Letts packed up their belongings and moved out of Morwenna Park Road.

They travelled south to the seaport of Plymouth, where they rented lodgings from a family named Scobling, taking the top floor of a large terrace house in Benbow Street in the Stoke area of the city. Bill found a poorly-paid civilian job at the nearby Devonport dockyards, and this brought him into contact with a pernicious asbestos-like material which would later cause him to develop a lung infection. Despite the money he earned from this job, the family were still poor and Daisy felt that she was on the verge of a second nervous breakdown. She became obsessed with the cleanliness of the flat. The Letts had to use an outside toilet and the neighbours watched in astonishment as Daisy bleached it out up to four times every day.

Bill's behaviour continued to be violent, but he had learned to conceal the worst excesses from neighbours. Only once did the façade crack at Benbow Street, when he attacked one of the elder girls, hitting her across the face and cutting her eye. The girl fled into the sanctuary of the Scobling flat, losing her shoes on the stairs.

Rose attended Stoke Dameral School and regularly ran home in tears at the end of the day. She was naughty, often in bizarre ways – cutting up her bedsheets to make clothes for her dolls, for example, and driving her family to distraction with incessant, nonsensical lies. One of Rose's school friends says she could see how easily Rose could be corrupted: 'She was sort of vulnerable.'

After the Letts had stayed in Benbow Street for two years, Bill became restless and the family moved again in search of work. He said he would do anything to make a living, and found a job in the kitchen of a children's home near Stratford-upon-Avon. For a short while the family lived nearby in the village of Mickleton, but it proved unsuitable in the long term so Bill travelled into Cheltenham at weekends in the hope of finding something better. He finally secured a relatively well-paid electronics job with the large defence company, Smith's Industries. When Rose was aged ten, the family packed up and moved again, leaving yet another school behind.

THE wire-ringed factory complex of Smith's Industries dominates the village of Bishop's Cleeve, five miles from the town of Cheltenham in Gloucestershire. Fred West's home village of Much Marcle is just a few miles away across the River Severn in the neighbouring county of Herefordshire.

Smith's is a philanthropic company, and had built a housing estate for the workforce in the village. The Letts family moved into 96 Tobyfield Road, a red-brick semi-detached house on what is still known as 'Smith's Estate'. A large garden wrapped around the house in an L-shape, and a brick wall divided it from a triangular area of common grass in front. A sign fixed to the wall warned: NO BALL GAMES.

Bill's new job meant that he was better paid than at any other time in his life. When he started at Smith's in the early 1960s, his wages plus overtime amounted to as much as £30 per week – meaning the family would not go hungry again. He was employed as an electronics engineer working on flight simulators, and gave the impression that it was top secret. Actually his tasks were quite mundane, low-grade electronics, but they demanded a high level of concentration. At the end of the working day, Bill was wound up tight like a spring. One wrong word from anybody in the family would make him uncoil violently.

'When he used to get angry, he went out of control. He would pick up a knife to you, an axe. He would beat us children up and not care how far he went,' says the eldest son, Andrew Letts. Bill seemed to take a delight in inventing new and unusual ways to torment his family: punching Andrew in the stomach and locking the boy in the coal shed, for example. Graham had his head battered against a wall. If any of the children returned home one minute later than their father had told them to be in, they would find the doors locked and would have to sleep outside, just as Bill's father had made him do back in Northam. He regularly turned off the electricity, plunging the family into darkness, and also turned off the gas so that Daisy could not cook. After Glenys had brought her future husband, Jim Tyler, home to meet her parents, Bill told her that he considered the young man to be a 'dirty Gypsy' and she was made to scrub and wash everywhere in the house he had been.

The family obtained a television set, but Bill would turn it off when the children had started to watch a programme they enjoyed. At other times, the children had to sit in silence while he watched his favourite western films. At ten o'clock the set was switched off and Bill went upstairs to bed. If any of the family were still up, they had to creep about in silence for fear of waking him. Before dawn each morning Bill woke his children and gave them a list of chores to do before he returned home; during winter evenings he selfishly surrounded himself with all the heaters while his children sat in the cold. Perhaps the most bizarre example of his behaviour was when he up-ended the dustbins simply so he could blame the mess on them.

He could also be antagonistic towards other adults. One of Daisy's sisters came to stay with them after the break-up of her marriage; she slept on the sofa in the living room until Bill took the door off its hinges, telling Daisy he did not want her sister becoming too comfortable. When his own father came to live briefly with the family, Bill ridiculed him in front of Rose and the children, hit the old man around the legs and angrily accused him of owing money.

ROSE attended Cleeve School, a short walk across the estate. It was not a happy time for her. Most of the other pupils had grown up together, and Rose was an outsider without the sort of friendly, engaging personality that would enable her to over-come this barrier. She was a loner, a tomboy and noticeably backward in lessons. Unfortunately for Rose, she had also become overweight, leading her to be mercilessly teased.

She reacted by becoming aggressive. The girl who only a couple of years before had regularly run home from Stoke Dameral School in tears, now lashed out at her tormentors with surprising ferocity, attacking both boys and girls.

By the age of thirteen, Rose had earned herself a fearsome reputation among the children of Bishop's Cleeve as somebody not to upset. But she did not stop there; she seemed to take plea-sure in her new, dominant personality. Her skinny kid brothers, Graham and Gordon, had their share of school problems as well, and when Rose heard about them being bullied, she strode across the estate to the homes of the boys who had fought with her brothers and hit them. 'A swipe from Rose and nobody messed again,' says Graham.

Rose's hold over her younger brothers strengthened when

Daisy decided to take a part-time job carrying out domestic work. Their mother was still desperately unhappy at home – even resorting to legal action to try and keep Bill away from her, but she failed to win a court order when Bill brought up her psychiatric history. At least a job would get her out of the house during the day, she reasoned. She had resisted going out to work before, but by now all three older children had left home, and she felt that Rosemary could be trusted to watch Graham and Gordon for the few afternoon hours between the end of school and when she and Bill came home from work.

Rose obediently promised to look after her brothers and get the housework done. But when her parents had left for work, the house degenerated into chaos, with the three children running wild and often not bothering to go to school at all. Rose passed all of her jobs on to Gordon and Graham, who did as she told them. When the work was done, the boys wandered around the village, stealing radios and other items. Bill called the police in when he found out, and it would not be long before Daisy saw her youngest sons in court.

ROSE became fascinated with sex as she entered puberty. She knew her father's expressed attitude: outwardly at least, he was an absolute puritan, a prim man whom the children nicknamed 'the Sunday School Teacher' because of his moral lectures. Sex was absolutely taboo in the house, and if anything Bill considered too suggestive appeared on the television, he would immediately turn the set off.

Daisy, too, was easily offended. As far as the marriage was concerned, it had been more or less chaste since the birth of Gordon in 1960. Bill had never been a particularly passionate husband, even when they were young. Daisy now slept downstairs most nights. 'He got on more with older, motherly women. He was a very cold man,' she says.

Rose's own sex education was extremely limited, and her mother never discussed the facts of life with her. Daisy did not explain pregnancy or contraception, or even what a period was, leaving Bill's mother to talk to the older girls (because she was a nurse) and the older girls in turn to talk to Rose, which they did when she was aged about twelve.

But Rose was curious about her body, and from the age of thirteen she was precociously sexual. When she was alone in the house with the boys, Rose indulged in exhibitionism, taking baths in the afternoon, leaving the door wide open, and parading naked around the house afterwards.

The children had to share bedrooms because the house was small, and Graham and Rose shared a bed. Graham, who is three years younger than Rose, claims that she masturbated him when they were together. Rose climbed into bed with nothing on and cuddled up to her younger brother. Graham was confused, thinking at first that it was just 'sisterly love'. The masturbation began when Rose was aged between thirteen and fourteen and Graham was ten, and would take place either early in the morning or late at night. It continued until she left home at fifteen. Graham was also suffering because of his parents' relationship, and was grateful for any affection. 'She knew I wasn't going to say anything,' he says.

IN January 1968, when Rose was fourteen years old, a young waitress disappeared in nearby Gloucester, causing great excitement. Mary Bastholm was fifteen, and was last seen standing at a bus stop in Bristol Road, Gloucester, carrying a Monopoly set. Mary had been on her way to visit her boyfriend. When she did not arrive the alarm was raised, but a search revealed only a few Monopoly pieces scattered in the snow. There had recently been two rapes in the area, and there was every reason to fear for her safety. A huge police operation was launched, involving more than three hundred officers, tracker dogs, a helicopter and a div-ing team, a member of which was a young officer named John Bennett. Twenty-six years later he would lead the investigation into the Gloucester murders.

Andrew, who travelled on the same route as Mary, told the family about the police search and how detectives were stopping people on buses. The warning to be wary of 'strange men' was added to the list of lectures that the Sunday School Teacher delivered to Rose and the other children.

Despite these admonishments to beware of strangers, Rose was eager to expand her sexual experience. She had tired of showing herself to her brothers, or touching Graham in bed at night, and the boys at school took little interest in her. Rose's weird alternating personality, combined with her plumpness, was enough to deter them from asking her out. Neither did she attend local dances — Bill thought she was too young — so she had little opportunity to form normal teenage relationships.

Older men were a different matter. In her childish way, Rose enjoyed the fantasy of pretending she was a grown woman, and was excited by the attention of adult men. When her parents were out of the house, she would wander around the village flirt-ing with men she met on the bus or outside the chip shop, where she went to smoke cigarettes.

Many years later, Rose told police investigating the Cromwell Street murders that she had lost her virginity at the age of four-teen, and that, a year later, she had been raped (although it is of course quite possible that she invented these stories to cover up what really happened between her and Fred). Rose claimed that she was first raped by a man who saw her at a Christmas party, not long after her fifteenth birthday. He had offered her a lift home, but instead took her up into the Cotswold hills behind Bishop's Cleeve and assaulted her. 'I felt threatened by this man,' she later said. 'I honestly felt he was going to kill me.'

*

THE abuse and misery at Tobyfield Road reached such a pitch
that, in the early spring of 1969, Daisy decided she could no
longer live with Bill. She collected fifteen-year-old Rose and her
younger children and left home, going first to her daughter
Glenys' terrace house in Union Street, Cheltenham. Bill did
not trouble to come after them.

Glenys had recently married her car mechanic boyfriend Jim
Tyler. They ran a small mobile snack bar together. Glenys usually
looked after the snack bar while Jim was at work, but she was
heavily pregnant with her first child and they needed another girl
to stand in. Rose, aged fifteen and a half, was just about to leave
school, and it was decided that she could help out for a while.

Each morning Jim Tyler rose early, hitched his fourteen-foot
Sprite Major caravan to the back of his car and towed it from
Union Street to a gravel pit at the hamlet of Seven Springs on
the Cirencester Road, just south of the city. Half the side of the
caravan opened up to make a serving hatch; a sign in the road
advertised REFRESHMENTS. Jim would then visit the cash-and-
carry wholesale store to buy provisions before going to his
mechanics job, leaving Rose in charge.

Jim worked for the Volkswagen-Audi garage in Cheltenham,
carrying out services and general repairs. After completing a job
it was his habit to test-drive the vehicle he had been working on
by taking it over to Seven Springs. In this way he could check on
the snack bar and have a coffee break at the same time.

The snack bar catered for lorry drivers and travelling salesmen.
It was parked in a half-acre of land, and there were usually several cars and lorries around when he returned in the middle of
the morning.

'On more than four occasions that I can recall, I arrived there
to find the shutters down, the caravan empty and Rose emerging from a cab or a lorry,' says Jim. 'One time some workmen
were laying the natural-gas pipeline across the Cotswolds, and
she emerged from their car on the pretence that they had just

taken her down the shops because she had run out of sausages for the hot dogs.' Rose's clothes were dishevelled and it appeared to Jim that she had probably been having sex. 'She was a hot-arsed little sod,' he says.

One night at Union Street Jim heard someone crying. He came downstairs to the living room, where Rose had been sleeping on a double bed. When he asked what was wrong, she sobbed that she wanted to go out with one of the men she had met at the snack bar, but the man was not interested in her. Jim, who was six years older than Rose, sat on the edge of the bed and put his arm round her, suggesting that she concentrate on boys her own age. Rose then slid her hand along the inside of her brother-in-law's thigh. She said how lucky her sister was to be married to him, and that she wished she could change places with Glenys. 'It could have gone a lot further, if I had allowed it to,' says Jim Tyler. It was also at around this time that Rose's association with another, much older man resulted in her being questioned by police. She had taken a job as a trainee seamstress, and met a thirty-year-old man with whom she began a sexual relationship. Rose later claimed that the police found out that she was under-age and took her into a local station for questioning, but no charges were brought against her lover and she soon stopped seeing him.

IN the summer of 1969, Daisy moved her family to lodgings at a chicken farm in the village of Toddington, north of Cheltenham. Daisy earned a pittance cleaning, and was allowed to live rent-free with her children in a tied cottage on the property. After a few weeks at the farm, Rose announced that she had decided to go back and live with her father at Tobyfield Road – an extraordinary decision as far as the other children were concerned. There was a special relationship between father and daughter that mystified the rest of the family, and it was understood that Rose was their father's favourite. When Bill flew into one of his insane rages Rose would take his side, agreeing with his tirades. Brother Graham thinks it may have been her form of self-preservation: 'It was like there was a bond between them,' he says. But for Rose to choose Bill in preference to their mother was incomprehensible.

There may have been a sexual aspect to the relationship between Rose and her father: it certainly seemed odd when Rose stood stark naked in front of him one day, and declared that she was going to have many children. There had already been rumours about Bill and young girls in Northam, and Jim Tyler believes that Bill showed an improper interest in his own daughters. 'He used to cuddle and tease and roll them around when they were three or four,' he says. 'I didn't like the way he did it. There was always something I didn't trust.'

It was at this time that Rose contacted Gloucester social services to report that her father was 'being restrictive'. A social worker called at the Letts home and mediated between Rose and Bill Letts, but it is unclear exactly what the cause of the problem was.

Years later, it was understood by members of the West family at 25 Cromwell Street that Rose had been sexually abused by her father.

5

THE SCOTTISH CONNECTION

Each Saturday evening Fred West's family put on their best clothes and ambled down the lane to the Wallwyn Arms public house in Much Marcle. They ordered tankards of beer from the landlord, Tony Davies, and went and sat in the corner of the bar, nodding hello to their neighbours when they came in, scraping their boots on the stone floor. Fred had been banished from Moorcourt Cottage since being charged with having sex with the thirteen-year-old girl. But after a year with his uncle and aunt at Daisy Cottage, his parents decided they wanted Fred home again. In the summer of 1962, before the harvest was brought in and the village lanes were filled with hay dust, Fred was reconciled with his parents and started to join them on these Saturday nights in the Wallwyn Arms. They sat together as a family and left together at the end of the evening, silent and united.

Fred was living at Moorcourt Cottage and working as a building labourer when he was reunited with his old girlfriend, Rena Costello. She returned to Ledbury from Scotland in the late summer of 1962, and was serving as a waitress in a café known as the Milk Bar in Ledbury High Street. Fred had not been alone in her affections in the two years she had been away, as a new tattoo on her right forearm showed. It read: 'Rena, John – True Love' and was accompanied by a heart and two arrows.

When she went back to Scotland in the autumn of 1960 Rena had moved to Glasgow, where she became one of the band of girls who walked the canyon-like streets around the Central Station. They were a pitiable sight, instantly recognisable as street prostitutes. They wore cheap, revealing clothes, no matter what the weather, and the white skin they displayed was often marked with sores. The girls smoked cigarettes as they dawdled along in the shadows of Glasgow's granite office buildings, stopping every few yards to look flirtatiously into the windows of passing cars. It was a miserable, dangerous occupation which inevitably ended in arrest. Rena was picked up by Glasgow Central police on 19 November that year, and was warned for importuning. She was still only sixteen years old.

A few weeks later Rena and a girlfriend were convicted of attempted burglary. Rena was sentenced at Airdrie Juvenile Court to borstal training, and served seventeen months until May 1962, being released shortly before her eighteenth birthday. She made an attempt to get away from petty crime, found new lodging in Glasgow's Florence Street and began training to become a nurse, but she was back in court in July, convicted of theft and fined £2. She then found work as a bus conductress in the northern suburbs of Glasgow. Rena had a brief affair with an Asian bus driver who worked out of her depot, becoming pregnant with his child, but there was no prospect of the relationship continuing further so she decided to travel back to England.

THE girl who returned from Scotland after these experiences was a wild and uninhibited delinquent, the perfect partner for Fred.

She had also changed her looks by dying her hair peroxide blonde.

Fred and Rena dated in Ledbury, sleeping together in the back of Fred's van. Fred soon discovered she was pregnant with a mixed-race child, and convinced Rena to let him try and abort it himself. A friend of theirs, Margaret Clarke, agreed to act as look-out while this was done. The three of them went up to a wood by Dog Hill near Ledbury, and Fred began his bizarre operation – but they were seen while he was at work, the police were called and Fred was forced to abandon the termination.

According to Margaret Clarke they then decided to marry, because Rena now had to keep the baby and they were 'besotted' with each other anyway. Rena had met Daisy West on two occasions, but Fred did not think his mother would approve of the match between him and this brash Scot. It would have to be done in secret. They decided to wait until Fred reached his twenty-first birthday, when they could have their wedding without needing his parents' permission.

On 17 November 1962, at Ledbury Register Office, Fred married for the first time. His bride, Catherine Bernadette Costello, wore a blue dress. Her hair was bleached almost white. The groom wore a white shirt, a dark tie and a suit jacket that was too big for him. The only guest was his younger brother, John, who acted as witness and took the one wedding photograph, which shows the grinning youngsters holding hands. Thirty-two years later, during the height of the murder inquiry, that same wedding photograph would be printed on posters labelled: MISSING.

Daisy was unhappy about the secrecy involved when Fred told her that he had married, but Walter was less concerned, telling his wife, 'It's up to Fred. He's got his own mind.' The newly-weds spent their wedding night, and the following few days, on the sofa at Moorcourt Cottage. They would have stayed longer, but with Fred's brother Doug and his sisters Daisy, Kitty and Gwen all still living at home, it was uncomfortably cramped in the cottage. Fred and Rena announced that they would start their married life in Scotland.

THEY moved into a small flat in Hospital Street, Coatbridge, near where Rena had been brought up. It was Fred's first experience of urban life, and the grimy industrial town was difficult to get used to after the slow pace of Much Marcle. Rena, on the other hand, was happy to see her sisters and friends again, especially now she was expecting her first child.

The marriage was in trouble from the beginning, partly because of Fred's sexual appetite. His lovemaking was short and brutal and he wanted sex at the most inappropriate times. Rena might be washing up or peeling potatoes when Fred demanded sex. He did so in such an insistent, uncaring way that the act which followed was more like rape than any normal form of intercourse. Sometimes Rena would be sitting reading a magazine when he would begin, often wanting oral sex. There was never any foreplay, and when they did have full intercourse, it would be over in seconds, with Rena often reduced to tears.

His brutal behaviour degenerated into sadism. Fred took pleasure from pinching intimate parts of Rena's body extremely hard while they were having sex. He also tried to tie her hands together, but Rena was frightened and would not allow him to do this.

Rena had already made her living as a prostitute. Years later, when Fred spoke about his time in Scotland, he said that he had encouraged Rena to go back on the game. He bragged that when she went out to work, she always left another girl in bed to keep him company, and that he made a lot of money from being a pimp. This conflicts with his complaints that Rena's prostitution brought him 'trouble'. The truth is that he probably felt he could not satisfy his wife sexually, but was powerless to prevent her from seeing other men. Her prostitution therefore both aroused and annoyed him.

Any rejection angered Fred. He slapped Rena around the face when she refused to perform a sex act with him. He also flew into a rage if his dinner was not ready on time or if there was something wrong with the flat. Rena was left with bruises and marks all over her body where Fred mauled at and beat her. Violence, and increasingly bizarre, frightening sex became part of daily life at Hospital Street.

ON the afternoon of 22 March 1963, at the Alexander Hospital in Coatbridge, Rena gave birth to a beautiful baby girl. The baby was coloured, and obviously of mixed race, with the dark skin and brown eyes of her Asian-born father. Some members of Rena's family were shocked and displeased by this, and it appears that Fred and Rena decided to concoct a story that would explain the baby to his parents in Much Marcle, thereby avoiding the wrath of the other side of the family. Shortly after the birth, Rena wrote to Daisy West, saying she had unfortunately miscarried Fred's child and they had decided to adopt a little coloured girl to take its place. They had chosen the name Charmaine Carol Mary; the name Mary was in honour of Rena's mother.

The letter Rena sent to Daisy West may have been instigated by Fred because he was angry and embarrassed that his wife had given birth to another man's baby. He took an immediate dislike to the child, and it appears that he briefly left Rena at this time. It was a crucial stage in the development of his attitude towards both women and the children that came into his care. In the years to come, Fred never mentioned the adoption of Charmaine, or how the child had come into the family. His sister-in-law Christine West says it was all 'swept under the carpet'.

Certain members of Rena's family were also intolerant of the scandalous birth, and it was partly because of their negative reaction that Rena moved from Coatbridge into the centre of nearby Glasgow. She rented a flat in the Bridgeton area of the city and, at first, lived there on her own with Charmaine.

NUMBER 25 Savoy Street was a one-bedroom ground-floor flat in a grey sandstone tenement block. There were three other blocks in Savoy Street of exactly the same design, each with six flats on three levels, most of them rented out by private landlords. The tenements dated back to the Victorian era and were primitive by the standards of the 1960s, forming one of the worst slums of Glasgow's South Side. Very few of the residents of Savoy Street owned cars, so the street in front of the tenements was used by the neighbourhood children as a play area. On hot summer days they forced open the pavement fire hydrants and danced about in the jets of cool water until the council workmen came to shut them off.

Despite the area's rudimentary conditions, there was still almost full employment, with the men mostly working in the local steel mills or as dockers at the busy shipyards on the River Clyde. A small sweet factory in the adjoining Ellsworth Street employed about twenty women from the tenements.

Savoy Street was the first of three addresses where Fred was to live for an extended period which were numbered twenty-five; the other two being the houses he would later occupy in Gloucester: 25 Midland Road and 25 Cromwell Street. The recurrence of this number is no more than coincidence. Although twenty-five is significant to numerologists (adding the two and the five makes seven, which is said to indicate an interest in the occult), Fred was neither adept at arithmetic nor particularly superstitious.

Each tenement had a central opening, or 'close', at the front of the building. The door of 25 Savoy Street was on the right side of the close as one walked in. Directly opposite was the front door' of steel-worker Archie Jackson and his wife, May. The Jacksons came to know Rena quite well and considered her to be an exceptionally good neighbour, but they never saw Fred and did not even know that Rena was married. 'As far as we were concerned, she was just a single parent,' says Archie Jackson. 'We never saw a man at the house at all.'

For a short while an older woman with an Irish accent stayed at the flat, looking after Charmaine while Rena went out at nights. It seems that Rena and Fred had temporarily split up, and it is likely that Rena was working as a prostitute in the evenings to pay the rent.

But the separation did not last long. At Christmas, Fred took his young family home to Much Marcle, boasting of how much money he was making and what an important man he was in Scotland. He hinted at associations with the underworld, talked about making money from dealing in hard drugs, and boasted that so much cash was coming in that he dressed in silk shirts. He became ostentatious with the little he had and bragged that he 'ran' a number of prostitutes. He never tired of talking about his time in Glasgow and, many years later, spoke darkly about it, saying 'I still have my Scottish connection.'

The reality was ridiculously far from this. Fred was not a gangster in silk shirts – he drove a Mr Whippy ice cream van for the Wall's company. Each morning Fred travelled across the city to a depot in Paisley, where he collected a yellow van decorated with four large blue beacons. He then spent the day touring the South Side of Glasgow selling the white whipped-up ice cream that was dispensed from a machine into sugary cones.

A large number of ice cream vans and other mobile shops worked Glasgow's sprawling estates, and there was fierce competition among the drivers for custom. Fred kept a selection of sweets to give to children, so they would remember him and buy a cone when he next came to their street. His van was also stocked with cigarettes, drinks and crisps, so the round could continue throughout the winter.

The ice cream van also allowed Fred to meet the sort of teenage girls he found most attractive. He told them elaborate stories about his adventures and tried to entice them to take a ride with him. Fred was licensed to work until ten at night, but if he had met a girl during the day he often did not return home to Savoy Street until the early hours of the morning.

IN 1964 Rena again became pregnant. She gave birth at the flat in Savoy Street in July, to a baby girl with the same luminous pale blue eyes as Fred. She named the child Anna Marie, after the romantic song of that name by Jim Reeves, one of her favourite entertainers. The child was given the middle names Kathleen Daisy, in honour of Fred's mother.

Fred doted on Anna Marie, his first child. He sat her on his knee and made a fuss of the baby, while Charmaine received only criticism and the brunt of his bad temper. Once, when Charmaine asked her father for an ice cream from his van, she was answered with a slap.

The family moved from Savoy Street to Maclellan Street, near Kinning Park. Maclellan Street was, at that time, one of the longest in Glasgow, an uninterrupted arcade of tenement buildings stretching for many hundreds of yards. The Wests took a flat in the last block at the southern end of the street, in a tenement opposite the Maclellan Steel Works. The flat was on the first floor and had its own inside toilet – a comparative luxury.

Beyond the tenements at the end of the street was an area of garden allotments, or 'plots' as they were known. Money was tight in the area, and men hired a plot to grow vegetables for their families. Fred decided to do the same, but it was noticed by the other plot-holders that the Englishman only cultivated a small section of his allotment, growing a few potatoes and cabbages. The rest of the plot had been raked over as if he were going to plant something, but he never did. When they asked why, Fred replied, 'I'm keeping it for something special.' He began to visit the plot late at night after he had finished work, and often took girls with him to have sex in the shed.

HUNDREDS of young women are reported missing in Glasgow each year. At least four young girls of the type that Fred was later accused of murdering disappeared at the time he lived in the city, and it is quite possible that Fred began his murderous career in Scotland. The allotment was a perfect burial ground for his victims, similar to those he would later use in England. It also had a shed, where he kept a collection of tools that could be used to dismember the bodies and dig their graves.

But it will never be known for certain whether Fred did bury any bodies here: the allotment and shed were bulldozed when the area was redeveloped. His plot has since been obliterated by the thousands of tons of concrete that form junction 22 of the M8 motorway, where it joins the M77 to Kilmarnock. Thirteen lanes of traffic now sweep relentlessly back and forth over the patch of earth that Fred said he was keeping for 'something special'.

FRED was having affairs with several women at this time. Years later he boasted about how many women he seduced in Glasgow and how many children he had fathered. Some of these stories are no doubt simply fantasies, like the night he claimed to have had sex with a girl in the middle of the Celtic football stadium. But there is some truth in a lot of what he said. One of Fred's most significant affairs was with a twenty-year-old girl from the Gorbals, who worked in a factory bottling mineral water. She became pregnant by Fred, and in July 1966 at Glasgow Maternity Hospital gave birth to a son she named Steven. There is also evidence that another of Fred's Scottish girlfriends became pregnant by him, and that they had a son named Gareth. But Fred's name did not appear on either birth certificate, and he had little to do with their upbringing.

Rena knew that Fred was being unfaithful, even catching him with another woman on one occasion, so she saw no reason why she should not see other men. She began an affair with a bus driver named John McLachlan, who frequented Telky's book-makers next to their tenement in Maclellan Street. McLachlan was married, but was about to divorce his wife. He and Rena had sex together while Fred was out on his ice cream round, and Rena told her lover of the violence and abuse she was suffering.

One night, Rena and John were kissing in Kinning Park when they saw the shadowy figure of Fred coming towards them across the grass. The lovers split up and John McLachlan watched as Fred came closer and barked at his wife: 'Up to the house!' He then punched her, making her scream. John McLachlan came out into the open and punched Fred, who drew a knife, or some other sharp instrument, and grazed it across his rival's stomach, drawing blood. When McLachlan realised he had been cut, he hit Fred again. Fred made no further attempt to defend himself. 'He couldn't tackle a man, but he was not so slow in attacking women,' McLachlan says.

Rena and her lover did not end their relationship there; if anything, it intensified. Using Indian ink and a needle, John tattooed Rena's name on his left wrist. He added his name to Rena's arm and scored out the tattoo: FRED. When Fred found out about this, he was eaten up with jealousy and insecurity.

McLachlan was playing cards in the flat below Rena's one night when he saw Fred's face pressed up against the living room window. A few seconds later he heard a door bang on the landing above, followed by shouting and screaming. McLachlan went upstairs and found Fred attacking Rena. 'He was kicking the shit out of her. She had bruises everywhere. It was sadism.'

When Rena went out of the flat it was often to go to one of the local cafés, such as the Bluebird or the Victoria, where younger people from Kinning Park socialised. It was in one of these cafés that Rena met a brunette named Isa McNeill, who had been working at the Livingston Industrial Clothing factory on the Dalmarnock Road, making knitwear, but was now unemployed and looking for a job. The Wests decided they wanted somebody to look after the children full-time while they were out. Isa was offered bed and board at Maclellan Street if she would care for Charmaine and the baby, Anna Marie, and she took the job.

Isa could not help noticing oddities in the West household, particularly the way in which Fred treated the children. Both Anna Marie and Charmaine were made to sleep in the bottom of a bunk-bed. Slats from a cot were secured across the space between the bunks, effectively penning the girls in like animals. If Fred were in the house, even during the day, he insisted that the children were put into this gaol-like space and only ever let out when he was at work. Charmaine, in particular, was caged in for hours on end.

Isa introduced the Wests to a childhood friend of hers, an attractive teenager named Anna McFall. Born in April 1949, Anna had grown up on Glasgow's South Side, and worked in the knitwear factory with Isa after leaving school. The girls were best friends, despite Anna being a Catholic and Isa a Protestant: a cultural and religious difference which was enough to divide whole sections of Glasgow's community. Like Rena and Isa, Anna had suffered an unhappy upbringing, did not get on with her mother, Jeannie, who was a cleaner, and was discontented and restless at home. It was not a happy household: Anna's parents were unmarried, and Tom McFall kept another family, including his legal wife, in another part of the city. Anna's brother,

'Scarface' McFall, was also frequently in trouble with the police. Anna's boyfriend, Duncan McLeish – whose nickname, 'Kelly', she had tattooed on her arm – had recently been killed in an accident at work, electrocuted while climbing into the cabin of a crane. The voltage was so high that the coins in his pockets were burned into his thighs. Anna was despondent partly because of this gruesome death, and, for company, began to spend a great deal of time visiting the Maclellan Street flat.

ONE day, during the first half of 1965, Fred was driving his ice cream van in the southern suburbs of Glasgow when he had an accident. His van had large blue beacons that lit up and a mechanical chime to attract children. As Fred was driving down one of the streets he often visited, he ran over a small boy, leaving him lying motionless on the road. A large crowd gathered, angrily accusing Fred of careless driving. The boy was dead.

Fred was interviewed by police, but fatal accidents involving children and ice cream vans were, curiously, fairly common in Glasgow. A three-year-old boy named Michael O'Keefe died outside his home in Linwood around the same time, when an ice cream van backed into him as it was trying to turn round. In light of this and other tragedies, it was decided that the boy's death was probably accidental and Fred was released without charges. But if it *were* no more than an accident, it was nevertheless strangely reminiscent of the autumn night several years before when Fred had run down Pat Manns. This time he had actually killed somebody.

Despite being cleared by the police, Fred was scared of the hostile reaction of local people, as he depended on their goodwill to make a living. Knowing he could stay in the city no longer, Fred gathered up his belongings and left Maclellan Street. But Rena would not go with him.

★

FRED and the children arrived back in Much Marcle tired and short of money, with nowhere to live. Fred told his parents about the death of the boy and asked if they could stay. (Years later, Fred adapted this story to explain why he did not see his illegitimate son Steven, saying that this had been the boy run over and killed by the ice cream van. This was a complete fiction, as Steven is alive and well. He also later told his daughter Anna Marie that the family had been 'thrown out' of Glasgow because of Rena's prostitution – yet another lie.) His brothers and sisters were still at home, including his recently married sister Daisy, who had brought her husband Frank Phillips home to live. Consequently there were only three bedrooms for ten adults and two children, and once again Fred had to sleep in the front room.

Some time later he collected Rena from Gloucester railway station, and the reunited family went to live at The Willows caravan site in the village of Sandhurst. Rena worked serving tea from a café on the newly-built M5 motorway, while Fred was hired to drive a lorry for an abattoir, calling at local farms to collect the carcasses of animals and their offal, stored in forty-gallon steel drums.

Fred and Rena's relationship was very unstable, and she only stayed at the caravan intermittently, spending much of her time back in Scotland. On one trip home to Glasgow she asked her friend Isa McNeill if she would like to come back to England with her. Isa agreed, since she was not getting on with her parents and the idea of moving away appealed to her. Her friend Anna McFall also asked to come, because she too was unhappy at home and felt she was at a 'dead end'. They also hoped to find work in England.

The three women and Rena's two children travelled south together, their destination being the bus station in Gloucester opposite the mainline railway terminal. They were met there by Fred, who invited them all to clamber into the cab of his blue abattoir lorry for the bumpy ride out of the city to Sandhurst. The lorry was loaded with bones and cow hides, and the stench was almost overpowering.

The caravan was claustrophobic with four adults and two children. Fred and Rena shared the main bedroom, which had a view over the fields; the children slept together in a tiny room next to their parents; and Anna McFall and Isa McNeill had to make do with the U-shaped couch in the dining area, taking an end each. It was not comfortable, and living in the country was a big change for the three city girls. They could not find work, became bored and soon wished that they had not come south at all.

The relationship between Rena and Fred continued to be tense and difficult. Before Fred set out each morning for the abattoir, he warned Rena not to venture off the site. Isa believes he was paranoid that Rena was going to leave him. While Fred was out at work, the girls whiled away the hours chatting and flicking through magazines. Isa looked after the children, leaving Rena and Anna with nothing to do other than occasional baby-sitting jobs for neighbours, for which they were paid in cigarettes and food rather than cash. When he returned home in the evening, Fred was still wearing his overalls and Wellington boots from the abattoir, by now splattered with blood and offal. His hands were scarlet and there was blood on his face where he wiped his brow.

His temperament was unpredictable; he was either full of vulgar good cheer or in a black and dangerous mood. After a few weeks in the caravan, the women learned to be nervous of this volatile personality. If his food was not ready on the table when he came in, Fred did not hesitate to slap Rena around the face. Isa bravely tried to intervene, but Fred snarled that he would kill her if she did not get out of the way.

Isa and Rena secretly planned to leave, and Rena sent a letter to John McLachlan's neighbour in Glasgow asking him to pass on the message that John should come and collect them. Rena's lover then telephoned the girls and said he would pick them up by the telephone box on the caravan site.

After a long overnight drive south in a hired Mini, John McLachlan arrived at the site shortly after dawn. The girls took the children for a walk, and when they returned, they saw McLachlan's car parked in the lane. McLachlan was with his friend, John Trotter. The plan had been to take the girls and children away while Fred was at work, but Fred returned home unexpectedly while they were still packing. Both Isa and John McLachlan now believe that Anna had told Fred of their scheme; she had become very friendly with him in recent weeks. When Fred saw his rival, a violent scene erupted. 'Everybody screamed and bawled at each other,' says John McLachlan. Rena went into the bedroom to put on her coat, and Fred went in after her. 'I heard him at it again, giving her a couple of slaps.' McLachlan asked Isa if she was coming with them and she said she was, quickly packing a bag. Rena turned to her young friend Anna McFall and entreated her to escape with them, but Anna was oddly calm. She said that she would stay and work as Fred's 'nanny'.

As the others were about to leave, Rena decided she could not abandon her children, but Fred held Charmaine in his arms and, no matter how hard Rena tugged at the girl, he would not let her go. McLachlan punched Fred in the stomach, but still Fred hung on. He hissed at Rena, 'I'll kill you if you ever show your face again!'

One of the neighbours had called the police because of the commotion, and as the Mini drove away, a police officer appeared on a bicycle. He called for them to stop, but the car kept going.

In the back seat, Rena was sobbing, desperately worried about leaving her children behind. She turned to her friends, wailing, 'But something might happen to them!'

6

THE MURDER OF
ANNA McFALL

THE TRUE NATURE of Anna McFall's relationship with Fred was revealed in the letters she sent home to her mother in Glasgow. 'Anna was infatuated,' says her friend Isa McNeill, who read the correspondence. Anna's affection was founded on the belief that Fred, who was eight years her senior, could give her a new life away from Glasgow. Fred encouraged these hopes, and although she stayed at the caravan as the children's 'nanny', Anna soon became his lover. She wrote to her mother that she and Fred had moved out of the caravan into a beautiful house, that they were doing well financially and planning to marry. This was all fantasy; they were still struggling to make ends meet in the caravan.

She tried to care for the children, taking them out on trips – including visits to Walter and Daisy West in Much Marcle – but Anna was only sixteen and not experienced enough to look after the girls properly. Fred placed both Charmaine and Anna Marie into the custody of Gloucestershire social services. They would be in and out of foster homes several times over the next five years, being sent away whenever Fred felt he could not look after them, or simply did not want them around.

Rena was attempting to make a new life for herself back in

Glasgow, but was unhappy without her children. She and Isa rented a flat together in Arden Street, Maryhill, and Rena found a job as a bus conductress, working in the same depot as John McLachlan. She went out with many of the depot workers and soon gained a reputation for promiscuity.

During the summer of 1966 Rena gathered enough courage to confront Fred again and come back to England to reclaim her children. Before leaving Glasgow, she asked friends, including Isa McNeill, to accompany her for moral support – but Isa was about to get married to John Trotter, who had helped rescue them from the caravan, and said she could not leave Scotland.

When Rena arrived back in Gloucestershire she discovered that Fred was conducting a relationship with Anna McFall. Rena took back Charmaine and Anna Marie and went to lodge on the Watersmead caravan site in the village of Brockworth, outside Gloucester. But even though she was reunited with her children, Rena was jealous of Fred and Anna; Fred was also uneasy that Rena had found out about the affair. Strangely, although both Rena and Fred had many affairs and Fred fathered at least two children by other women during their marriage, they always tried to keep their liaisons secret from one another. They had learned that the truth inevitably caused trouble.

Rena was so angry with her former friend that she spitefully stole some of Anna's belongings. Rena went on to commit other thefts and, on 11 October, stole an iron, some cigarettes and cash from another woman. The theft was reported and Rena hastily returned to Scotland hoping to evade the police, but was arrested there in November.

Gloucestershire police sent a young WPC named Hazel Savage to collect Rena from Glasgow airport and bring her back to Britain for trial. On the flight south Rena chatted readily to Hazel, who was a sympathetic listener. Rena demonstrated a strong dislike of her husband, saying he was having an affair and that she had committed the thefts 'in spite'. The meeting was the beginning of Hazel Savage's long involvement in the life of Fred West and his extended family: it culminated twenty-eight years later in 1994 when, as a Detective Constable, she fought to convince senior officers to excavate the back garden of 25 Cromwell Street.

Back in Gloucester, on 29 November 1966, Rena was convicted of house-breaking and stealing. Her defence counsel, John McNaught, pleaded for leniency, saying, 'This offence was the action of a jealous woman. If she goes to prison, her children must go into care.' Fred gave evidence, admitting to the court, rather guiltily, that he was still living with Anna, but that he intended to pay her fare back to Scotland immediately. Rena was put on probation for three years.

Following the trial, Anna moved to the Timberlands caravan park in Brockworth. Meanwhile, Rena came back and forth to Gloucestershire. She sometimes stayed with Fred, and sometimes lived on her own at the Watersmead site. Juggling relationships with Rena and Anna McFall was becoming overwhelmingly difficult for Fred to cope with.

IT is likely that Fred was involved in crimes committed during this period that have never been solved. There were a number of attacks on women at this time, and other mysterious events, that are of particular interest and have been looked at by detectives working on the murder inquiry. Eight violent sex assaults were committed on young women in the Gloucestershire area between December 1965 and January 1967 by men fitting Fred's description. These include a girl in Cheltenham who was struck on the head when walking near her home, a fifteen-year-old who was grabbed in Gloucester and a nurse who had her jaw broken during an attack.

Also, a fifteen-year-old boy named Robin Holt died in bizarre circumstances during this period. Fred became friendly with

Robin at the Wingate factory plant in Gloucester. The factory built farm machinery and had a large order in 1967/68, which meant that a number of extra men, including Fred, were hired as casual labourers. Robin, an amiable young boy who worked at the plant, also knew Anna McFall. On 20 February 1967, Robin failed to return to his home on the outskirts of Gloucester. The next day he was seen in Much Marcle. Nine days later Robin's half-naked body was found hanged in a disused cow-shed on a farm near his home. On a manger next to his body were porno-graphic magazines; nooses had been drawn on the necks of the models. The verdict of the inquest was that the boy had com-mitted suicide. In 1994, police working on the West case became interested in Robin's death, but could not establish a definite link.

By the spring of 1967 Anna McFall had become pregnant with Fred's child. She was very excited and wrote to her mother say-ing how wonderful Fred was; that she loved him and wanted to marry him. At the same time she was still looking after Anna Marie and Charmaine, when they were not in the care of their mother. This situation came to the attention of a probation offi-cer in July of that year, when Anna McFall was six months into her term; the officer wrote a report expressing concern about the situation. It read in part that the officer was 'extremely worried about these children, who are being looked after by Annie McFall who is expecting Mr West's baby'. A copy was filed with the social services.

Although Anna was no longer living full-time with Fred, it seems she was trying to persuade him to divorce Rena and marry her. This was not what Fred wanted. He was particularly concerned about the situation because Rena was living in Gloucestershire intermittently and he did not want her to find out that Anna was having his child. It seems the stress of dealing with these problems became insupportable for Fred, and reached a crisis as Anna's pregnancy entered its final weeks. Fred probably decided he simply could not allow Anna to have the child: it would give her too strong a claim over him, would cause more problems with Rena, and he could not afford to support another baby.

ANNA McFall was last seen in July 1967. She went missing from the Timberlands caravan site, where she had been living on her own for some time.

DURING police interviews in 1994, Fred denied he had murdered the girl he called his 'angel' (even though he knew where she was buried), and there has been a suggestion that he was not responsible for her death at all, and that Rena and another person killed her. However, Fred did discuss Anna's murder in private prison visits and it seems more likely than not that he was responsible. It is not known for certain where Fred committed the crime, but he later told one prison visitor that he had killed Anna at her caravan, stabbing her to death after an argument. It is quite possible there was a sexual element involved: when Anna's remains were finally discovered, there was a long length of dressing gown-type cord wrapped around the wrists and coiled under the rib bones in her grave, and this cord must have been used to restrain her. Perhaps Fred and Anna had been indulging in some form of bondage before she died; perhaps he tied her up so he could take pleasure from torturing her before committing murder. It is even possible that Fred got carried away as they performed a bizarre sex act, and killed Anna by accident.

Little of any certainty is known about her death. Although it comes first in the story of Fred's career as a murderer, it was one of the last crimes that he talked to police about, and by then his mental state had degenerated so badly that little of what he said made sense. Forensic examination was among the most difficult in the whole investigation. There are also hardly any witnesses to Anna's relationship with Fred in the last months before she died.

What *is* known is that Fred dismembered Anna's corpse.

To cut up a human body requires an enormous physical and mental effort. Dismemberment is not only extraordinarily unpleasant, but physically tiring and technically difficult. The corpse of the pregnant woman would have been heavy and unwieldy, literally a dead weight. It would have oozed large amounts of blood when Fred started cutting. Everything that Fred wore, and any clothes that Anna still had on, would have been sodden with blood (a round-necked, long-sleeved cardigan, coloured blue and black, was later found within two clear plastic bags in Anna's grave. There were also various pieces of blue and floral-patterned material, including a large sheet, or curtain). Human remains would have covered the floor, making it slippery. Blood may have got on the walls. For all these reasons, Fred must have carried out the dismemberment at a place where he felt confident he would not be disturbed – probably inside his own caravan. He would also have needed tools, several different knives, and facilities to wash himself, clear up the mess, and change his clothes afterwards.

Fred probably worked on the body for at least half an hour, but could have taken very much longer. It seems that he enjoyed the process; it was like performing an operation. Fred did not hack at Anna's body like a madman, but carefully disarticulated her limbs using the skills he had observed working for the abattoir.

The main task would have been the removal of Anna's legs. Fine knife marks found on the femur bones of her skeletal remains show that Fred mostly used a sharp, delicate blade for this.

He later said that he cut up his victims so that it would be easier to bury them. He explained that he only needed to dig a relatively small, square hole for a dismembered body, whereas an intact corpse would necessitate him digging a coffin-length grave, and would consequently involve far more work.

But this explanation does not tally with the mystery of the missing bones. When Anna McFall's remains were eventually discovered, a considerable number of small hand and foot bones, known as phalanges, were absent, as were ankle and wrist bones. It seems that Fred had sliced off Anna's fingers and toes. Possibly this was to make her body difficult to identify in case the corpse was discovered: there would be no way of taking fingerprints from a body with no fingers. But it is more likely that Fred mutilated, or *dehumanised*, Anna in this way because it sexually excited him and made him feel powerful. He also wanted a reminder of an act he had greatly enjoyed, so it seems he kept her fingers and toes as trophies.

WHEN Anna's remains were finally found, the skeleton of her unborn child was nestling by her side. The foetus may have been cut from her womb; it was not possible to know for sure from the forensic examination of the remains. It *is* known, however, that Fred had developed a bizarre interest by this time: he claimed to conduct abortions, and there is some evidence to back this up. Fred kept a collection of odd implements that he led friends to believe were used to carry out terminations. These included an oxyacetylene burner, a large knife, bottles of anti-septic and a ten-inch tube with a corkscrew at the end. He boasted to male acquaintances that he offered his services to teenage girls he met in pubs such as the Full Moon in Cheltenham. If anybody knew of a young girl in trouble, said

1. Gertrude Maddocks, the first wife of Fred West's father, Walter. She died in 1939 after being stung by a bee. Walter kept this photograph, and the Maddocks family bible, among his most prized possessions for the rest of his life.

2. Fred West's maternal grandparents, pictured here outside their home, Cowleas, were known within the village of Much Marcle as 'the Hillbillies'. Fred's maternal grandfather, William Hill, is on the far right, next to Fred's grandmother.

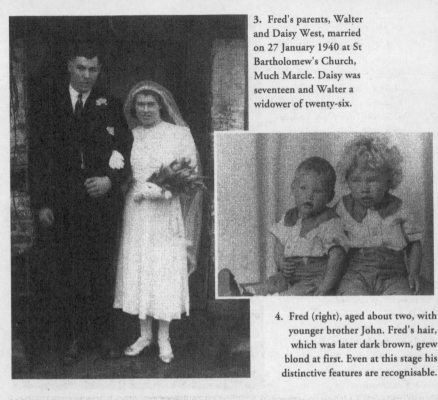

3. Fred's parents, Walter and Daisy West, married on 27 January 1940 at St Bartholomew's Church, Much Marcle. Daisy was seventeen and Walter a widower of twenty-six.

4. Fred (right), aged about two, with younger brother John. Fred's hair, which was later dark brown, grew blond at first. Even at this stage his distinctive features are recognisable.

5. Fred always appeared to be uncomfortable in the presence of his father, as in this picture, taken on a day trip to Barry Island in 1952. Walter and Daisy West stand behind; the children, from left to right, are Douglas, Daisy, Kitty (in front), Fred, Gwen (in pushchair), and John.

6. Fred loved his mother, and she in turn doted on her 'blue-eyed boy'. In this photograph from the early 1950s Fred (top left) laughs as he stands next to brother John, behind their mother who has her arm around a neighbour. The children in front are Fred's youngest brother, Doug, and sister, Kitty.

7. Mid-1950s school photo, Much Marcle. Fred, flanked by sisters Daisy (left) and Kitty (right), was slow and slovenly at school, often receiving a beating from his teachers.

8. Fred West in his late teens, with his prized James 125cc motorcycle. With him are Doug, Kitty, Gwen (between Fred's arms), and Daisy (behind Fred). He crashed the motorcycle near Moorcourt Cottage just over a year later, in an accident which almost cost him his life.

9. Fred's father, Walter, sitting on a tractor outside Moorcourt Cottage with his grandson, Christopher.

10. Having given birth to eight children, by the late 1960s Fred's mother Daisy was a heavy-set, unhealthy-looking woman. Standing with her outside Moorcourt Cottage are her husband Walter and younger sons Douglas (second from right) and John (far right). Daisy died not long after this picture was taken.

11. Rose West's mother Daisy Letts suffered such severe depression that she undertook a course of Electro-Convulsive Therapy (ECT). She is photographed here in 1950 in the garden of the family home at 57 Morwenna Park Road, Northam, Devon. With her are three of her daughters: (left to right) Patricia, Glenys and Joyce.

12. Rose's father, Bill Letts (left), was a violent schizophrenic who sadistically abused his family. He is pictured here shortly before his death, with his wife Daisy on the day of their son Graham's wedding in 1979.

MISSING
can you help?

CATHERINE   COSTELLO

Gloucester Police have asked the national charity the Missing Persons Helpline to try and make contact with Catherine Costello.

Relatives have not heard from her for over 20 years.

Catherine Costello may be living somewhere in Scotland, but could be anywhere.

WE WOULD APPEAL TO CATHERINE COSTELLO OR ANYONE WHO KNOWS HER OR HAS ANY INFORMATION TO CALL THE 24 HOUR MISSING PERSONS HELPLINE ON (081) 392 2000.

Posters suppoted by *Today*

 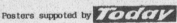

081-392 2000
24 HOURS
MISSING PERSONS HELPLINE

MISSING PERSONS BUREAU

13. This missing person poster appeared soon after the 1994 murder investigation began. The picture of Fred and his first wife, Rena Costello, was taken by Fred's younger brother, John, just after Fred and Rena's marriage on 17 November 1962.

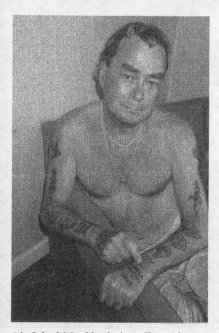

14. John McLachlan had an affair with Rena and later rescued her from Fred's caravan, where she was being physically abused. He is seen here pointing to the faded tattoo of Rena's name.

16. Anna Marie, aged six or seven, is seen here posing for a photograph at 25 Midland Road shortly before the murder of her half-sister Charmaine.

15. Charmaine (left), was Rena's daughter by an Asian bus driver. Anna Marie (right) was Fred and Rena's child, and is about one year old in this picture from the mid-1960s. Although both children were ill-treated by Fred, Charmaine suffered particular cruelty.

17. The intimacy and affection between Fred and Rose is obvious in this photograph, taken at 25 Midland Road in December 1971, after the murders of Anna McFall, Charmaine, and Fred's first wife, Rena, had all taken place. Rose is a strikingly attractive teenage girl, quite different in looks to the plain, overweight woman she would become.

18. Twenty-five Midland Road, Gloucester, where Rose murdered Charmaine. Flowers on the doorstep were placed there by police, who were searching the property when this photograph was taken in 1994.

Fred, they should refer them to him. He said he used a garage near the caravan for the work.

WITH the dismemberment complete, all that was left was to bury the remains. Fred probably put the chunks of Anna's corpse into plastic bags which were later found with her remains. He then drove towards Much Marcle. Fred parked in open country just off the Dymock road, less than a mile from Moorcourt Cottage. Finger Post Field is a thirteen-acre cornfield between Much Marcle and the neighbouring hamlet of Kempley. The field, which is just inside the Gloucestershire county border, takes its name from a white signpost by the gate. It was a familiar place to Fred because, apart from growing up in the area, he had worked the nearby land as a young farm labourer.

The grim job of burying Anna's remains must have been carried out in the dead of night. Fred was well-known locally, making it virtually impossible for him to do anything during the day, so he had to steal out across the darkened field, shovel in hand, listening to the rustle of the trees and darting looks at the silhouettes in the hedgerow.

Fred almost certainly chose to bury Anna's remains in Finger Post Field because it was familiar and because he felt confident his secret would be safe there. Criminal psychologists would say that Fred wanted total control over Anna, and all the other women in his life. When he failed to keep her in line, and she became pregnant and threatened the stability of his life, he killed her to exercise that control completely. By burying her remains somewhere familiar, virtually at home, he could continue to have power over her even in death. She was close at hand, and could never get away or disobey him again. Fred almost certainly enjoyed concealing her body. It would have made him feel good, even happy.

Murderers often fail at this, the last stage of their crime, because they do not dispose of the body with sufficient care. But Fred knew that, unless a carcass was deeply buried, it might be dug up by scavenging vermin or uncovered by farm machinery. So he went down for a good five feet. He carried out his work so thoroughly that twenty-seven years were to pass before Anna's remains were recovered from that lonely Gloucestershire field.

WHEN Anna's letters stopped arriving in Glasgow, her friends, including Isa McNeill, assumed that she had found a new life in England and had put the old days behind her. It was thought strange that she did not return home for the funeral when her mother Jeannie died of malnutrition, but even then Anna was not reported to the police as a missing person and nobody came to look for her, despite the anxious note left in the files of the local social services.

Not long after the murder Fred moved to the Lake House caravan site in the village of Bishop's Cleeve. Rose Letts, the girl who would become his second wife (and partner in crime) was then a thirteen-year-old living half a mile away in Tobyfield Road.

The caravan site was situated off the Stoke Road, and took its name from a large pond in the grounds. It was not a Gypsy encampment, but an established business with permanent and semi-permanent residents. Many were young families who could not afford to buy a house; others were single men who worked at the nearby Smith's Industries plant, where Bill Letts was employed. There were two substantial buildings on the site: Lake House, which took boarders, and Lake View, the home of the owner, Mrs Dukes. The caravans were grouped around the lake, upon which was moored a small boat. Fred rented Number 17, which, like most of the caravans, did not have wheels and was set on a concrete stand. It had a small garden surrounded by a low wooden fence.

The caravan itself was not the most modern or best-kept on

the site. It was slightly shabby, about twenty feet long, built of plywood and painted a cream colour. There were two bedrooms, a dining area, and a stove with a shiny metal chimney. A large septic tank on the site provided for the sewage and toilet facilities.

There was a marked change in Fred's behaviour in the months following Anna's death. He must have been in a state of intense anxiety, fearful that he would be discovered any day. This preoccupation was reflected in his behaviour. 'He was in a dark, strange mood at times. He seemed withdrawn,' says Michael Newman, a boarder at Lake House. Fred undertook odd jobs for the site-owner Mrs Dukes, and would often be found sitting in her lounge, lost in his own thoughts. Interruption brought a terse response. 'He was almost in a dream world,' says Newman.

Rena had moved back into the caravan, her relationship with Fred greatly improved. The Wests took their children out of care and they stayed together as a family for most of that year. Fred allowed his wife to be more like her gregarious self. Occasionally they even visited pubs together, she flirting with other men while he sat brooding over a half-pint of bitter.

Fred was hired as a labourer at Oldacres mill, a flour and animal feed manufacturer in Bishop's Cleeve, and was put on the night shift. While he was at work, men – always the same men – called at the caravan for Rena, and gossip soon went round the site that Mrs West was working as a prostitute. There is no doubt that Fred was told about this. He was known to grumble about his long hours and low pay at the mill, and he and Rena sometimes quarrelled over money, so he may have been content to see a little extra cash coming in. Fred and Rena were quite open about the sexual side of their relationship, showing friends pornographic pictures that Fred had taken of his wife. Fred was also seen to sexually abuse Charmaine in the caravan at this time, rubbing the semi-naked child over his groin.

*

AFTER returning from an arduous night shift, Fred would snatch the briefest amount of sleep before rising again. In the hours before he was due back at work Fred carried out general maintenance for Mrs Dukes, tried to fish in a small boat on the lake and worked on cars and engines for his neighbours. Obsessive hard work became one of his traits.

He enjoyed talking about motorcycles. Whilst working on his neighbour Michael Newman's Honda moped, Fred showed that his fantasy life was flourishing. He bragged that he was used to riding big British motorcycles of at least 400cc, and that he had ridden in the Isle of Man TT race. Fred said that if he got on the Honda moped he would 'blow it up after a hundred yards'.

Petty crime was second nature to Fred and, typically, his Vauxhall Viva car was seldom legally taxed or insured. It was common knowledge on the site that Fred dabbled in stolen goods. He was described as looking dishonest, with 'the sort of eyes that slid off you', and the police called regularly to question him over minor offences.

During the day, Fred sometimes visited the Pop-In café in Southgate Street, Gloucester. The street is one of the main artery roads bringing traffic into the centre of the city, and the café was situated on the ground floor of a tall building near a motorcycle shop and a camping centre. It was a seedy dive used as a gathering point for petty criminals and drop-outs. Pornographic photographs were circulated and stolen goods changed hands when the owner was not looking. One of the waitresses at the café was Mary Bastholm, the girl who went missing that January.

MARY was an attractive and slim fifteen-year-old girl. She was last seen at 7:15 P.M. on 6 January 1968, waiting at a bus stop in Bristol Road, Gloucester. Mary was on her way to visit her boyfriend, who lived five miles away in the village of Hardwicke. She wore a blue and white striped coat, lime-green pleated skirt, a navy-blue twinset, matching shoes and gloves and carried a royal-blue umbrella. She was also carrying her handbag and a Monopoly game in a white plastic carrier bag. Mary was not the sort of girl to run away, and the police feared she had been snatched off the street.

A major hunt was launched; Scotland Yard were called in; hundreds of officers scoured the ditches and fields around Gloucester in difficult weather conditions. Theories abounded in the Pop-In café – and right across the county – as to what had happened to Mary. Fred listened and said nothing. The mystery deepened shortly afterwards when Mary's family received an anonymous message instructing them to place an advertisement in the *Skyrack Express* of Tadcaster, Yorkshire, saying that they 'forgave her'. The advertisement appeared, but nothing more was heard of Mary.

There were a number of links between Fred and Mary Bastholm: he was a customer at the Pop-In and Mary often served him tea; Fred had been employed to do some building work behind the café; Mary had been seen with a girl fitting the description of Fred's former lover, Anna McFall; and one witness claims to have seen Mary in Fred's car. Her disappearance has never been solved, and the police file on the case remains open. In 1994, twenty-six years after she vanished, the case was reactivated when Gloucestershire police questioned Fred about Mary.

Several factors indicate that Mary was one of Fred's victims. It is likely that he murdered Mary after abducting her from the bus stop that January evening, just as he would go on to kill other girls picked up at bus stops. She was of the physical type and age that he found attractive. He also knew her habits.

But despite admitting to many other crimes, including some that he was not charged with, Fred refused to talk about this case. However, in private prison meetings with members of his own family and others, he did indicate that he had killed Mary just as the police suspected. His son Steve claims that Fred admitted to the murder, gloating that he would tell the police about it only when he was good and ready. 'There's only one person who will ever tell them and it's me,' he said. For all these reasons Mary's brother, Peter Bastholm, and police officers who worked on the West inquiry are almost certain that Mary was murdered by Fred, but there was never enough evidence to charge him.

There are a number of reasons why Fred decided not to talk about Mary. Fred enjoyed playing with the detectives working on his own case – killers often hold information back for a later date, when they want to interrupt the monotony of prison life. Another theory is that Fred did not murder Mary on his own, and was protecting somebody else. But the most likely – and the most alarming – reason for his silence is the location of Mary's body. She was clearly not buried with the other victims that were found, which means there must be another grave site – and possibly other bodies that he was not ready to talk about.

A month after Mary Bastholm went missing, Fred's mother, Daisy, was taken into Hereford hospital. She died on 6 February following complications after an operation to remove a gallstone. She was forty-four. Fred was the only member of the family who did not trouble to visit her. He claimed he could not bring himself to go into a hospital after what had happened to him as a teenager.

The funeral service was conducted three days later at Much Marcle's parish church. Fred stood at the graveside with his brothers and father: four stocky men in dark suits. Rena also attended. Fred's brother, Doug, and his sister, Gwen, were the only two children left at home, and did their best to comfort Walter, who reserved a plot next to Daisy for himself. He ordered a headstone engraved with a crucifix and inscribed with the words: 'In loving memory of a devoted wife and mother.'

Following the funeral Fred committed a series of thefts and

again fell foul of the law. In the summer of 1968 he was working at a private house in Cheltenham when he stole a blank cheque. He used the cheque to buy a record player for £10, was caught and convicted by Cheltenham magistrates on one charge of theft and another of deception, and was fined £20. Shortly afterwards Fred was dismissed from Oldacres mill on suspicion of stealing money. He then worked for a while emptying septic tanks, before becoming a delivery driver for a village bakery.

It was while he was working at this last job that Fred met Rose.

7

ROSE LOVES FRED

It was several weeks before Bill Letts came to enquire after his family at the Toddington farm. In the end, he made a number of visits, but he never actually brought himself to ask them back to Tobyfield Road, where he and Rose were living on their own. 'He never said sorry. He wouldn't belittle himself,' says Daisy Letts. She finally decided to return home for the sake of her children, whom she could not support on her wages as a cleaner, and the family were reunited at Bishop's Cleeve in the late summer of 1969.

Bill had been telling Rose for some time – she had by now left the seamstress shop – that she had to find a proper job, something better than helping out at her brother-in-law's snack bar, although he admitted he did not expect much of his 'dozy' daughter. Rose surprised him by finding regular work as a waitress at a tea shop in Cheltenham High Street, a five-mile bus journey away. At the end of her first week at work she delighted Daisy by bringing home left-over cakes for the family. Rose had also agreed to contribute to the housekeeping now that she was earning a wage, and dutifully paid her mother some money.

It was after work one night, when Rose was waiting to catch a bus home, that she claims to have been raped for the second time – a fantastical story that is almost certainly part invention. According to her story, a man tried to chat her up at the bus stop, and then made a grab for her when she said she was not interested in him. Rose fled, and found herself in a park where her attacker caught up with her. They came to a pair of padlocked gates. Rose recalled that he 'just smashed the padlock off with his fists. He said he had been in the army and was very strong.' He then dragged her down under some trees by the side of a lake, and raped her.

After this second attack, Rose decided she would catch the bus home from the central station in Cheltenham in future, because it was safer there. It was at the station that she met another man, distinctive-looking and much older than herself. He had wild curly hair like a bird's nest; bushy sideburns down almost to his collar, merging with dark stubble that swarmed across his swarthy face; his hands were covered with marks and cuts, as though he had been in a fight or was used to rough work; he was not very tall, walked with a limp and had surprisingly blue eyes. The man also attempted to chat to her, speaking in a guttural accent like a farm hand, but was so dirty and poorly dressed that Rose took him for a tramp at first and ignored him. But he would not be dissuaded, and asked her out – with a leering smile that revealed dirty teeth later described by Rose as 'all ganky and green'. It was an openly sexual gesture, and must have reminded her of the men she had met working at Jim Tyler's snack bar. Despite herself, Rose felt a little excited.

His name was Fred, and despite his rough appearance he proved to be a charming man, talkative and full of compliments. He told Rose that they had a lot in common: she worked in a bread shop, while he was a delivery driver for a bakery in nearby Gotherington. He said he might have delivered to her very shop; anyway, he was sure he had seen her somewhere before. Then Fred found out that she lived in Bishop's Cleeve, only a short walk from his caravan.

It was true that Fred flirted with every young girl he met; that is why he enjoyed the delivery job. Like the ice cream round in Glasgow, it gave him an opportunity to travel around and meet girls. He stopped to chat with teenagers he saw as he passed through the villages. Some of the girls he took an interest in were no more than children, like ten-year-old Barbara Ann White, who lived in the hamlet of Stoke Orchard. Years later Barbara was to marry Rose Letts' brother Graham, thereby becoming a sister-in-law to Fred. But in the summer of 1969 she was a village child happy enough to accept a lift in the delivery man's van. 'He used to chat everybody up,' she remembers.

But Fred was particularly interested in this young girl at the bus stop. She was quite attractive, if a little plump, with sleek brown hair, full breasts and brown eyes. He asked her out three times, and climbed on to the bus with her – after all, he said, they lived in the same village, so why not travel together?

The journey to Bishop's Cleeve led through the crowded shopping streets of Cheltenham, past the grand Victorian buildings on the outskirts of town and into the country. On the way, Fred told Rose exaggerated stories about his life and times, and although she stared fixedly out of the window as he spoke, Rose must have found herself smiling – he was a funny fellow after all, and a 'good talker'.

One day Fred came into the bread shop in Cheltenham and asked Rose to meet him later, in a pub near her home in Bishop's Cleeve. She agreed, and when she arrived for the date he presented her with extravagant gifts (no doubt stolen) of a lace dress and a fur coat. She wanted to hand them back at first, but Fred was insistent that they were hers.

She could not help being flattered by the attention. She had never had many friends. Both the boys and girls at school had avoided Rose, considering her slow and odd, and in her last years there she was despised as the school bully. Even at home with her family, Rose's older brothers and sisters tended to leave her out of their activities. Her parents, too, were contemptuous of her low intelligence. But, at last, here was somebody who seemed interested in her, in much the same way as the workmen she had met at Jim Tyler's snack bar, but much more intense. Rose also enjoyed playing at being an adult, and flirting with men like Fred was just such a pretend game. 'Her idea of being grown up was going out with somebody a lot older,' suggests her eldest brother, Andrew.

Fred was adept at probing for secrets, and must have been excited when he realised that Rose was so sexually aware. She was flirtatious, and did not flinch when he spoke about sex in his crude way or made advances to her; indeed, she seemed to welcome them. Her obvious unhappiness at home, and willingness to keep secrets from her family, must have made her even more attractive to Fred. She was not likely to talk about anything that they did together.

He tried to excuse his disreputable appearance by saying that he had only just returned from Glasgow, where he had been sleeping rough. He said he had left Scotland in a hurry because his wife was working as a prostitute, and had caused him a great deal of trouble. The truth was that he and Rena had broken up after yet another row, and, far from being back in Glasgow, she was living there in Gloucestershire – in fact, in March that year she appeared at Cheltenham Magistrates Court, where she was found guilty of attempting to defraud the Department of Social Security. But Fred kept all this from Rose, portraying himself as the abandoned husband.

AFTER Rena had left, Fred briefly shared the caravan with another man, a fashion-conscious pot-smoking hippy named Terry Crick, and his girlfriend, Cathy. It was with Terry Crick that Fred demonstrated just how out of step he was with the mood of the late 1960s. Fred had asked his friend where he could meet girls, and was directed to a pub in Cheltenham that was popular with young people – but these were not the same as the young people Fred had known in Much Marcle, Ledbury and Glasgow. They wore tie-dyed T-shirts, smoked drugs, and their conversation and attitudes were completely beyond his experience, even though Fred was of their generation. He spent a frustrating evening at the pub trying to pick up one of the sophisticated young girls, but finally left alone. 'The next day the girls asked me who that creep was,' says Terry Crick.

Fred also boasted to Crick about his proficiency as an abortionist, and showed him pornographic pictures he had taken with a black-and-white Polaroid camera, claiming they were of women he had operated on. He wanted his friend to find him more girls who had 'got in trouble', but Crick was so alarmed by the photographs that he called the police. Fred was questioned, but the photographs were not illegal, and no charges were brought.

FRED told Rose that his wife had left him with two small children to look after, and that he could barely manage. When Rose heard this she became very interested in Fred, for Rose had a fascination with young children. 'She was always playing with them,' says her mother, Daisy. It was the attraction of Charmaine and Anna Marie that persuaded Rose to visit Fred's caravan.

Conditions at the caravan could not have been more different to the almost clinical environment in which Rose had been brought up. Her parents' house at Tobyfield Road was scrubbed daily, because any dirt or disorder enraged her father. Fred's home, by contrast, was so filthy it took her breath away. Apart from the shabbiness of the place, the caravan smelled strongly of cigarette smoke, sweat and unwashed dishes, and the floor was strewn with dirty clothes, children's toys, work tools and an accumulation of dust balls and dried mud. It was particularly chaotic as Fred had been living as a bachelor for the past few months since he and Rena had split up.

In the weeks that followed, Rose became a frequent visitor to the caravan, a playmate for the two girls. Fred was relieved to have found somebody who enjoyed looking after his children, and he also found Rose sexually exciting.

Rose discovered that Anna Marie and Charmaine were quite different in temperament, as well as looks. Charmaine was now six, just ten years Rose's junior. She was strikingly pretty, with Asian colouring, a very intelligent and lively child who loved bright colours, especially reds and greens. Despite the years of neglect and punishment, her spirit had not been broken.

Her half-sister, Anna Marie, who was five, had a pale complexion and the blue eyes, broad nose and wiry dark-brown hair that were characteristic of the West family. She was treated much more kindly than Charmaine and was a quiet child inclined to do as she was told.

Fred's relationship with the children was contradictory. On one hand, he had a very strong image of himself as a father and a provider. He always referred to himself as 'Dad' and truly believed that he loved the children, often sitting Anna Marie on his knee, ruffling her bushy hair and saying she was 'Dad's girl'. Rose enthusiastically joined in, turning the business of caring for the children into a kind of game. They took the girls out into the fields to collect wild flowers, just as Fred had done as a child, and Fred spoke to Rose about wanting to have more children. He lay in the long meadow grass and told Anna Marie stories about when she was a baby in Scotland. Fred said he had made her a crib out of a wooden box and put her under the counter of his ice cream van as he drove around the streets of Glasgow. He said that he and Anna Marie were a 'team' and she was his 'big girl'. Anna Marie naturally basked in the attention. 'I idolised my

dad,' she says, even telling her father she wanted to marry him
when she grew up.

At the same time, Fred was capable of extreme cruelty, beating Charmaine for no reason. He generally neglected the
children, did not take any part in their daily care, and, if there
were no women around to look after the girls, thought nothing
of bundling them into the car and driving them to Gloucester
social services.

THE fact that Charmaine and Anna Marie were taken into temporary foster care meant that they *should*, even at this early stage,
have been identified by the authorities as vulnerable children.
Two important new documents, the Children Act of 1958 and
the Children and Young Persons Act of 1963, had been published by this time. They were largely concerned with improving
and developing protection for fostered or adopted children, and
Charmaine could have qualified for special attention under both
these categories.

Fred's family should have been known to Gloucestershire
Children's Department as a 'problem family', and might be
expected to have had a 'family card', upon which was recorded
confidential information. This in turn should have led to health
visitors making random checks on the family to make sure the
children were well. The 'At Risk' register had also been in
operation since 1967, and Gloucestershire County Council
employed full-time Children's Officers to examine families like
the Wests.

Yet it seems that Fred was not scrutinised carefully enough.
In one of its internal reports on the background to the later
murder case, Gloucestershire County Council admits that
checks on children in the area during the 1960s were rudimentary. In one passage of the 35-page document, the council
says, 'Incredible as it may seem today, child abuse cases were

unlikely to be recognised. Child care agencies and legal agencies concentrated on child neglect and delinquency, and were reluctant to believe that parents would deliberately harm their children.'

WHEN Fred first met Rose, he was increasingly in trouble with the police. In June he had been fined £22 by Cheltenham magistrates for motoring offences, including stealing a tax disc to use on his van. He attempted to excuse his misdemeanours by telling the court a fabricated hard-luck story: he said he had been left with debts of £2,000 after his 'business' in Scotland failed, adding that he had been paying his creditors off in instalments, but still owed £300.

Fred knew that Rose's mother would become suspicious if she did not receive her housekeeping, so he gave Rose a few shillings a week to give to her mother. In this way, the pretence of Rose being at work was kept up for some time – the first of many secrets that Fred and Rose shared.

ONE day Rose astonished her parents by bringing Fred home. She had never had a boyfriend before – even of her own age – and yet, suddenly, here was a fully grown man standing beside their daughter in the living room of 96 Tobyfield Road. Daisy, who had heard gossip in the village that Rose was not going to work at all, began to think that something was seriously amiss. 'Immediately we thought he was an older man,' says Daisy. 'He was twenty-seven, but he did not look young for his age.'

It was Fred's habit to be silent and moody in company, but on this day he was quite animated, telling a string of boastful stories in an excited, gabbling speech that was at times almost surreal. The theme of his conversation was how successful he was and the possessions he owned. He again told the lie that he had only

just returned from Scotland, where he said he owned property
including a number of mobile homes, a fleet of ice cream vans,
a house and a hotel. But it was plain to Bill and Daisy that he
'obviously didn't have anything'.

Daisy noticed an ugly scar on the bridge of Fred's nose – one
of the injuries he had sustained when he crashed his motorcycle
into Pat Manns as a teenager. But, instead of simply telling Daisy
the truth, Fred launched into a weird story. 'He babbled on that,
in Scotland, some woman had chased him and that he fell down
a manhole, and this woman smashed him across the face with a
chain,' says Daisy, who took the story to mean that Fred was on
the run from another woman.

Rose listened in silence to Fred's stories. When he finally left,
Bill and Daisy were united in their dislike of her new friend. Bill
told his daughter that Fred was a liar and a 'dirty Gypsy' and that
she was to have nothing more to do with him. Daisy agreed.
'What he was saying didn't add up,' she says.

It was shortly after this that Rose's parents discovered she was
spending all her time with Fred, and not going to work at all.
Rose admitted as much when Bill confronted his daughter, saying there was no one else to look after the children. She said she
was working at the caravan between eight and six, that nothing
improper was going on between her and Fred, and that Fred was
going to pay her for her work. This glib reply infuriated her
father and he ordered her to stop seeing Fred. 'There was no
way Dad was going to allow her, at her age, to go down to a
caravan with a man who had two children,' says Daisy. She was
especially alarmed when she worked out that Rose was visiting
that 'eerie' place by the lake. Daisy often passed the caravan site
on the bus, and the dismal lake made her shudder. She thought
it exactly the sort of place where the type of men her own
mother had warned her about might live, and wondered
whether the missing teenager Mary Bastholm was drowned in
the grey water.

But Rose's relationship with Fred had already gone beyond looking after Charmaine and Anna Marie. She had become his secret lover, just like Anna McFall, the 'nanny' who preceded her.

By this stage in his life Fred had developed perverse ideas about sex. He was particularly excited by aggressive, sadistic sex and had begun to collect extreme sado-masochistic pornography. It was difficult to find a girl who would allow herself to be tied up, a girl who would also allow Fred to beat her and who would beat him when he asked, because Fred enjoyed receiving punishment as well as giving it. Rena had flatly refused to take part in his sex games, but in Rose he probably found a willing partner to all his perversions, a pretty teenager who did not have to be *forced* into doing what he wanted.

Rose accepted Fred's behaviour because she was craving affection. She had also probably been abused herself as a child, and placed little value on her own body. Rose was also excited by the company and attentions of an older man and was naïve enough to accept whatever she was told to do. After all, Fred was twelve years older than her. 'The way Rose was, she could have been influenced by anyone,' says her brother Andrew.

From deviant sex, Fred introduced Rose to prostitution, and she began to entertain men in the caravan just as Rena had done. Fred was used to the idea of his women selling themselves; indeed, he found it exciting. He was also grateful for the money it brought in, and knew that a young girl was more valuable because she could pretend to be a virgin. Several of Bill Letts' workmates at Smith's Industries lodged at Lake House, and he soon became aware of the rumours surrounding caravan 17.

Rose's brothers Andrew and Graham Letts believe it was because their father knew about Rose being a prostitute that he first considered placing her into care. Before taking this step, Bill led his errant daughter into the living room at Tobyfield Road and lectured her on the fate that awaited girls who associated with older men. He explained exactly what he thought of Fred, emphasising how dishonest he considered him to be and dared Rose ever to visit the caravan site again. Rose listened in sullen silence.

Bill despaired of getting through to Rose. He visited Gloucestershire social services and explained that his fifteen-year-old daughter was seeing an older man. As a result, the social services suggested that Rose be taken into care to keep her away from Fred.

TOWARDS the end of the summer of 1969, Rose was taken to a large converted house near the centre of Cheltenham, which was home to a number of troubled teenagers. She was only to be allowed out under controlled conditions, to visit her parents or go to work. She was not allowed to see Fred. There was also a curfew. Rose hated the home, which she described as being like a prison. In the three months she stayed there, she did not receive a single visit from either her parents or any of her brothers or sisters; neither could she speak to them on the telephone, as the Letts family were not connected. Rose felt that she had been forgotten and completely rejected. It naturally seemed that her only friend in the world was Fred. She escaped from the home on one occasion to see him, and when she was legitimately allowed out for the weekend to visit her parents, Rose went instead to the caravan site. They went to considerable trouble to keep these assignations quiet.

In one love letter from Rose to Fred – which was written at around this time – it is clear she was already taking a dominant role in the relationship, insisting that she be told everything about Fred's past:

Dear Fred,

I am glad you came to see me. Last night made me realise we are two people, not two soft chairs to be sat on . . . about us meeting this week, it could be Sunday afternoon. I will have to get Lynda to say I'm going with her. You know we won't be able to meet so often, that's why I can't get the idea out of my head that you are going with someone else . . . You told my aunt about Rena. But what about telling me the whole story even if it takes all day. I love you, Fred, but if anything goes wrong it will be the end of both of us for good. We will have to go somewhere far away where nobody knows us.

I will always love you,

Rose

When Bill Letts found out that Rose was still seeing Fred, despite being in care, he marched down the road to warn Fred off. Fred, who had recently finished at the bakery and was about to start a new job at a garage, was at home when Bill came into the small, fenced-in garden that surrounded caravan 17. The older man worked himself up into a rage, shouting and waving his finger at Fred, who listened without any significant reaction as he was warned to leave Rose alone. He did not even register a grim smile when Bill threatened he would 'cut [Fred] up into little pieces' unless he heeded the advice.

Fred was facing more serious problems with the police. On 23 August he was reported for failing to produce documents for his car, and was also warned about unpaid fines from June. He was told he could go to prison unless he paid. Five days later he appeared at Cheltenham Magistrates Court, charged with the theft of fence panels from one of his employers. He was fined £20 and given a suspended prison sentence. On the same day he was also reported for not having a test certificate for his car.

While Fred's criminal problems were mounting, Rose learned

that her time in care would soon be over. When she reached her sixteenth birthday the authorities would no longer be empowered to detain her and she could go back to her lover, but eleven days before Rose was due to be let out of the home, Fred was sent to gaol for the first time in his life. He was given thirty days for failing to pay his fines.

HER Majesty's Prison Gloucester is a grim fortress-like building behind the law courts on the western side of the city. It is near enough to the docks to be within reach of Herring gulls, which perch on top of the gate house. In 1969, when Fred first lined up for his 'kit' of rough prison clothes and toilet equipment, the prison was already more than 150 years old. It was not a high-security gaol, but was still a depressing institution where inmates were disciplined by being put on a diet of bread and water. The cells are lined along landings, under a curved Georgian roof which echoes with the noise of men trudging up and down the steel stairways. Fred did not cope well with prison life. He was not a 'hard man' inside, and was a victim of 'taxing', the term used for bullying by other inmates. He could not wait to leave.

On 28 November, while Fred was still inside, Charmaine and Anna Marie were taken into care yet again. The next day was Rose's sixteenth birthday, and she duly left the Cheltenham home. Her father gave her a final lecture, which ended with a familiar ultimatum: if she ever went to see Fred again, then he would disown her, but if she stopped seeing him and found a good job, then she could stay with her family. There must have been an argument over this because a policewoman was called to the house, and later a social worker as well, who appears to have calmed the situation and wrote in an official report of the visit that the family 'presented as quite reasonable'.

*

ONE morning a few weeks later Rose came downstairs with her bags packed. It was the first her parents knew of her decision to leave home. Daisy and Bill were surprised, as they thought that Rose had decided to see matters their way. In fact, Rose had only been waiting for Fred to finish serving his thirty days in prison.

Rose had decided that she loved Fred, and that her future lay with him – the first and only man ever to have taken such a strong liking to her. She was excited by him sexually, intoxicated by his attentions and relished the prospect of uninterrupted days spent playing with his children. The relationship also freed her from the constraints of Tobyfield Road, where she was forced to live like a child, answering to her mother and especially to her oppressive father. Fred was her means of escaping all this; her graduation to adulthood.

Daisy asked if she really intended to leave, not quite believing such a thing possible of her simple-minded daughter. Rose airily replied that, yes, of course she was going, and laughed about it. Without saying another word, she slipped out of the front door and walked gaily down Tobyfield Road in the direction of Fred's caravan, carelessly swinging her bags as she went.

But Bill Letts was not about to give up on his daughter just yet, and made another attempt to curb her, contacting the police and requesting that they 'pick Rose up' because of her association with Fred. This happened at an address in Cheltenham. A police surgeon then examined Rose, and, on 21 February, discovered she was pregnant. Bill Letts refused to have her back at home, so Rose was again placed into care.

She was discharged only days later, on 6 March, on the understanding that she would return home and have her pregnancy terminated. Instead Rose went back to Fred's caravan, and Bill Letts washed his hands of his youngest daughter once and for all.

8

THE TRAGEDY OF MIDLAND ROAD

WHEN ROSE LEFT home to live with Fred, he collected Anna Marie and Charmaine from the social services, intending that they should all live together as a family. At first Rose was pleased to have two little girls to wash and feed, but she was soon exasperated by their demands for attention – her mother, Daisy, describes the relationship between them as 'like a child looking after children'. Fred had nothing whatsoever to do with their care. Rose's brother Graham remembers: 'It was her job to look after the kids. He was quite strict about it.'

After a few months living at Bishop's Cleeve, Fred decided they should move to another caravan site, at Sandhurst Lane, just north of Gloucester, where he was working as a labourer. Faced with the enormous problem of becoming a mother at sixteen, Rose showed remarkable self-reliance, refusing to ask her mother for help and insisting that Fred move the family to a proper house.

Rose found it increasingly difficult to cope with the children. Charmaine in particular was a wilful girl who did not take kindly to being told what to do by somebody only ten years her senior – and a girl who, in many ways, was less intelligent than herself. Because of the situation, Fred sent Anna Marie and

Charmaine to live with foster parents in the town of Tewkesbury, although they were soon home again.

Rena reappeared the following month, demanding that the girls be returned to her. It was almost certainly at this time that Rena and Rose first met. Rena cared little now about her own relationship with Fred, and their troubled marriage was effectively over. Her only concern was that he did not harm the children, and she may have come to the conclusion that they were safer with Rose looking after them. Whatever she felt about Rose, and whatever happened when they met, she did not regain custody of her daughters.

Fred had found a house for Rose and the children to live in, and in June 1970 he led his ragamuffin family into the city of Gloucester – the place which would be their home for the next twenty-four years.

A small city, with a population of under a hundred thousand, Gloucester lies approximately one hundred miles west of London in the foothills of the Cotswolds. Much Marcle is fourteen miles to the north-west.

Gloucester was first established as a Roman fort, and later became a colonised Roman town known as Glevum. For centuries it was the lowest crossing-point on the River Severn, the gateway to Britain's West Country and an important trading centre.

Until the mid-nineteenth century, the land south-east of Gloucester's ancient Roman walls had been left as pasture and orchard, sometimes burial ground. But the city boomed during the reign of Queen Victoria with the expansion of the railway, the building of a canal system and the enlargement of the docks. Between the mid-1700s and 1871, the population had increased sixfold and hundreds of brick houses had to be constructed to accommodate these new people.

A formal park, known simply as The Park, a bandstand and

cricket ground were laid out on the site of a natural spa just out-side the city walls. Streets of generously-proportioned houses were built around the perimeter. These middle-class develop-ments included Midland Road and Cromwell Street, the two addresses where Fred and Rose were to live in their twenty-four years in the city. Both were built at about the same time, a few hundred yards apart, on side streets just off The Park. Midland Road had the slightly larger houses: semi-detached villas with walk-up steps at the front, and an attic room facing on to a light railway line raised on an embankment. The street took its name from the Midland Railway company which owned the track.

The residential area around The Park began to decline after the Great War. The spa in nearby Cheltenham was a more fash-ionable place to visit, and Gloucester increasingly faded in comparison with its sophisticated neighbour; a decline hastened after the Second World War by the exodus of people out of the city centre to modern housing estates in the suburbs. Gloucester changed further in the 1960s, when many of the ancient tumble-down buildings which had crowded the city for centuries were torn down to make way for a shopping centre, multi-storey car park and one-way system.

The handsome houses of Midland Road fell upon hard times. Front gardens became parking bays. Scrubby grass and nettles grew where the Midland Railway line had run, and the parallel Trier Way was widened, bringing more traffic, exhaust fumes and dirt. This was the faded street that Fred and Rose came to in 1970.

They lodged briefly at Number 10 before moving to 25, the second of Fred's homes to bear that number. The property was then owned by a Polish immigrant named Frank Zygmunt, who had bought up several city-centre houses and converted them into low-rent flats.

Twenty-five Midland Road is a large semi-detached building clad in grey concrete, divided into three flats. There is a neglected front garden and a small flight of steps leading up to a black front door. Fred and Rose moved in to the ground floor, which had a small living room facing the road, a bathroom, kitchen and two bedrooms. A door in the central passageway led down to a cellar where the coal was kept for open fires. Light came into the passageway through a window of coloured glass.

WITH rent to pay on the flat, and Rose and the children to provide for, Fred soon resorted to petty crime. He went to work as a fitter for Cotswold Tyres in Albion Street, Cheltenham. It was a hard, dirty trade and he was frustrated by his poor pay. One day he told his boss that he was delivering an order of five new tyres – instead, he stole them.

He later left the tyre-fitters and went to work for Frank Zygmunt, carrying out odd jobs on the various houses that the entrepreneur owned in Gloucester. Fred was an industrious worker, almost to a fault, but he was also hopelessly light-fingered. When the tax disc expired on his car, he stole one from a pick-up truck belonging to his boss and forged the details. He was later stopped by traffic police and arrested.

In the early autumn Rose gave birth to her first child, a girl they named Heather Ann. She was born at the maternity unit of the Gloucestershire Royal Hospital on 17 October 1970, a pretty baby who soon had the distinctive dark hair of the West family, although her facial features were closer to those of her mother. Rose bottle-reared Heather, trying her best to care for her daughter under difficult conditions.

The simple fact of Rose's tender age should have brought her under the scrutiny of social services at this time. The Register of At Risk Children, introduced in 1967, specified that 'very young parents' should be monitored. To this end, there was supposed to be communication between midwifery services and health visitors in Gloucester – Rose's case should have been discussed by them, and follow-up checks should have been made on her well-being and on that of her children. Such checks would have revealed a worrying domestic situation; Rose, who was already known to Gloucester social services because she had been in care, was struggling to look after two young children and a baby. Gloucestershire County Council's own report into the background of the West case admits that vital communication between departments occurred 'less frequently [then] than [it does] now'.

Just as Fred was wondering how he could afford to support his growing family, Cotswold Tyres discovered that Fred's 'order' for five tyres, worth a little over £50, had been bogus. He was arrested and charged with theft. Before the case was heard, Fred was called before Gloucester magistrates and pleaded guilty to four motoring offences, including stealing Frank Zygmunt's tax disc. He blamed the offences on Rena, who he said had given him the forged disc. This time the full weight of the law came down on Fred: he was jailed for three months, and was also ordered to serve a six-month suspended sentence imposed in August 1969 for stealing fence panels from a building site. It came to a total of nine months behind bars.

A few weeks later, on New Year's Eve 1970, Fred was taken from his cell to Cheltenham Magistrates Court to be tried for the theft of the car tyres. Once again, he pleaded guilty and blamed Rena. His defence counsel said he had been left with two small children to care for and had been short of money after being deserted by his wife, but now his 'family affairs had pulled round'. The magistrates took a cynical view of this excuse. The prisoner before the bench was a seasoned petty criminal, a recidivist. He was sent back to gaol with an extra month to add on to his sentence.

IT was a forlorn New Year for seventeen-year-old Rose. Snow had been falling across the county that week. It settled white and crisp out in the countryside, but turned to brown slush in the streets of Gloucester. The cold wet seeped into Rose's shoes as she trudged back from Fred's court hearing. Inside Midland Road, she stared sadly at an unmade fire grate. Horns honked out on the river; revellers skidded past the window calling out: 'Happy New Year!' The *Andy Stewart Hogmanay Show* was on the television in a nearby house, but it was a joyless scene inside Number 25. Nappies and clothes were strewn about the flat, Heather would not stop crying and there was rent to pay.

In the bleak months following Fred's imprisonment, Rose turned her frustrations on the children. She did not have the strength of personality to command the girls' respect or love, so she attempted to 'curb' what she considered to be their inability to behave by beating them, soon contriving punishments as sadistic as those her father had used.

As the children lay in their beds at night, Charmaine tried to comfort her younger half-sister by whispering that their real mother would come back and rescue them, and everything would be all right. But their childhood had been so chaotic that Anna Marie could barely remember what Rena looked like, and despite the terror they both faced, Charmaine and Anna Marie were not particularly close anyway. 'It was like there was a void between us,' explained Anna Marie.

There was bad feeling between Rose and Charmaine, and Anna Marie felt that she suffered because of it. 'Charmaine disliked her and was antagonistic. Rose would retaliate by taking it out on me,' she says. Rose lost her temper with frightening violence. The children were in the kitchen washing up one day when Rose decided that Charmaine was taking too long. She snatched a cereal bowl from the child's hand and smashed it over Anna Marie's head.

A young family named Giles lived in the flat at the top of the house: Ronald Giles, his wife Shirley and their two daughters, Tracey and Janet. Shirley Giles often complained to her husband that Midland Road was eerily quiet. She said that it was 'like a morgue' – a prophetic description. Her daughter Tracey was nearly eight, the same age as Charmaine, and the two girls became best friends, playing together on the communal stairs. Tracey's sister Janet also joined in the fun, but Anna Marie was quiet and 'seemed like Charmaine's shadow'. Tracey also played in the downstairs flat. She noticed that Rose always seemed to be telling Charmaine off and frequently accused her of being 'guilty'. But no matter how cruelly she was treated, Charmaine refused to cry. 'She felt like if she cried, she was giving in,' remembers Anna Marie, who also concedes that Charmaine was a stronger character than her.

The Giles family were about to have breakfast one morning when Mrs Giles realised they had run out of milk. Tracey was sent down to the bottom flat to ask Rose if she could spare a cup. The little girl, excited with her errand, ran helter-skelter down the stairs, and, without knocking, barged into Rose's kitchen. The scene that confronted Tracey brought her to a sudden halt. Charmaine was standing on a kitchen chair, her hands behind her back with the wrists crossed and tied together with a leather belt. Rose held a long wooden spoon in her right hand, which she had obviously been using to hit Charmaine. Anna Marie was standing by the door with a blank expression on her face. It seemed that such sadistic punishments were a regular occurrence. (Years later Anna Marie had a dim memory of seeing Charmaine tied to a bed.)

Tracey came back upstairs very distressed and told her mother what she had seen. When Shirley next saw Rose, she asked about what had happened, but Rose was neither embarrassed nor apologetic; she said she was punishing Charmaine to curb her naughty behaviour. 'Rose would say that she couldn't cope with Charmaine,' says Shirley Giles. 'She ruled Anna Marie and Charmaine with a steel rod, but Charmaine had a rebellious nature which she didn't like.' Mrs Giles discovered that Fred was in prison and that Rose was just looking after Anna Marie and Charmaine. She said she was having particular problems with the eldest girl and that her natural mother was coming to collect her. (Rena was having problems of her own at this time, for example being picked up by police in Bristol for soliciting.) Rose added that she 'had had enough of Charmaine'; she was 'at the end of her tether' with the girl and could not wait to get rid of her.

AT 6:50 P.M. on the evening of 28 March 1971, Rose took Charmaine to the casualty unit of the Gloucestershire Royal Hospital. It was six days after the child's eighth birthday, and she had an ugly puncture wound in her left ankle – hospital records show that Charmaine had sustained the injury at Midland Road. There had either been an accident or, in retrospect, Rose had gone too far in her attempt to correct the child.

One might have thought that such an odd and serious injury to a child, sustained at home, would have been brought to the attention of the local social services. But, at this time in Gloucester, health visitors had no official liaison whatsoever with the Accident and Emergency department of the local hospital, and consequently never knew what had happened to Charmaine.

AFTER months without news from their daughter, Bill and Daisy Letts decided to visit Rose. They took their younger children Graham and Glenys along, and were all astounded by the squalid conditions in which they found Rose living. The floors of 25 Midland Road were bare boards and there was hardly a stick of furniture, yet the tiny flat was cluttered with children's clothes, soiled nappies, toys and dirty plates. The fastidious Bill Letts was so appalled by what he saw that he did not want to sit down. 'The place was a shambles. You wouldn't want your dog to live in it,' recalls Graham Letts.

Rose was upset. Daisy well knew that the only way in which

Rose expressed unhappiness was by crying, and it was clear that she had been doing just that. 'Her eyes was red and you could see she'd been crying. Dad said that he'd like to know what was going on.' But Rose, whom they noticed was also thin and unkempt, did not explain her unhappiness – other than to tell her sister Glenys that she did not like Charmaine because the child wet the bed. Rose said she smacked Charmaine when she did this. 'Rosemary couldn't cope with it,' says Graham. 'It hit her all of a sudden and she got run down.'

The family were surprised to find another little baby crawling about in the dirt, for Rose had never told her parents that she had given birth to Heather. Now they met their new granddaughter for the first time. Daisy made two more visits to Midland Road, and on one occasion was surprised to discover that Rose had gone out leaving Charmaine completely on her own in the house.

FRED and Rose were writing each other passionate letters which, in retrospect, speak volumes about both their own obsessive relationship and the callousness they showed towards Charmaine. The following letter was received at Leyhill open prison, Wootton-under-Edge, in the south of the county, on 4 May 1971. Rose had drawn a heart at the top and written the words 'From now until forever' and 'That ring that means so much' in the right-hand corner. The body of the letter (with its original errors of grammar and spelling) reads as follows:

> *To My Darling,*
> *What was you on about at the beginning of your letter. I just can't make it out for trying. Hey love thats great, three more visits, it'll take up half the time I've got to wait for you. Blinking base people get's on my nerves. Darling, about Char. I think she likes to be handled rough. But darling, why do I have to be the*

one to do it. I would keep her for her own sake, if it wasn't for the rest of the children. You can see Char coming out in Anna now. And I hate it.

Love, I don't think God wan'ted me to go to that dance. Because I didn't go after all. Darling, I think from now on I'm going to let God guide me. It always ends up that way anyway (As you may know) Ha! Ha! Oh! Love! about our son. I'll see the doctor about the pill. And then we'll be safe to decide about it when you come home.

Well, Love, keep happy, Longing for the 18th.

Your ever worshipping wife,

Rose

This letter is fascinating for many reasons. Rose agrees with Fred that she has to be 'rough' with Charmaine, but is tired of taking all the responsibility for the children. She is clearly only interested in seeing Fred again, the man she 'worships'. She writes of a 'ring that means so much' and of being his 'wife' even though Fred was still married to Rena at this time. As to their 'son', it appears that Rose was pregnant and had assumed the baby would be a boy. The letter reads as if she is considering terminating her pregnancy, and as there is no record of a baby having been born to her in 1971, it seems this is what she did.

On 7 May Rose took the children to visit Fred at Leyhill Prison. He was delighted to see her. When they met, he presented his beloved with a painting he had made in his cell, showing Rose, naked, kneeling down and silhouetted before a burning sunset.

Fred wrote to Rose from Leyhill on 14 May. He refers in the note to a model Gypsy caravan he made for her out of plywood. The model was cleverly designed so that it opened up to make a jewellery box; a wooden heart suspended from the front by a chain was inscribed 'To Rose Love Fred'. He also mentions a table, which was presumably built in the prison workshop. Across the top of the note he scrawled: 'Our family of Love'; underneath this Fred wrote, in an illiterate hand which mimicked his countrified way of speech:

To My Darling Wife Rose.
   Darling be at home Tuesday for your table Will be cuming so be at home all day untill thy cum it will be in the morning if thy do cum then cum see me but don't cum to thy cum Darling.
   Darling you for got to write agen. Darling your caravan is at the prison gate for you I have put your assisted visits form for the 18th or 19th and for the 15th of June. Will, it wont be long be for the 24 now Darling so get the pill if you want it or will be a mum for or son to son Darlin. I love you darling for ever my love. Your has you say from now until for ever. Darling. Will, Darling, untill I see you. All my love I sind to you.
   Your Ever Worshipping Husband
                          Fred.

Fred then decorated the letter with the words 'for Heather', 'ANNA', 'CHAR', 'For Rose' and a number of crosses representing kisses. Then he wrote:

And more, 100 more,
   Mr and Mrs West for ever

Again Fred writes as if they are husband and wife, although they would not marry for some time.

Rose wrote another letter to her 'husband' on 22 May,

putting 'FROM NOW UNTILL FOR EVER' with a heart across the top of the note, which read:

To My Dearest Lover,

Darling, I am sorry I upset you in my previous letters I didn't mean it (NO joking). I know you love me darling. It just seems queer that anyone should think so much of me. I LOVE you. Love I don't mind what you make me, because I know it will turn out beautifull. Darling I would like to get a horse for our caravan & put it in a showcase. We've got a lot of things to do darling in the next couple of years. And we'll do it just loving each other. Well Love, see you on the 31st, Better not write to much incase I go putting my big foot in it. (Ha! Ha!) Sending all my love & heart your worshipping wife,

Rose

Then there are a number of crosses representing kisses, and:

PS. Love I've got the wireless on and it's playing some lovly romantic music. Oh! how I wish you were hear beside me. Still remembering your love & warmth, Rose

ROSE, Anna Marie and Charmaine made another visit to the prison on 15 June, and Fred told Rose excitedly that he might be granted parole in a few days.

It was on a day shortly after this visit, while Fred was still in prison, that Charmaine went missing. The girls usually walked to St James' Junior School together, but one morning Charmaine was kept back by Rose. While Anna Marie was at her lessons,

Rose murdered Charmaine in that squalid little flat in Midland Road.

ROSE has never said what she did that day, but the explanation is not difficult to imagine: it seems likely that she finally lost her temper with the spirited but sad eight-year-old girl who wet the bed at night and dreamed of being rescued by her real mother, the girl whom Rose could not wait to get rid of and who had already been to hospital with a curious injury. It seems likely that she lost her temper, and either battered or stabbed to death the child who Rose believed liked to be 'handled rough'.

After the murder, Rose began to face questions about what had happened to Charmaine, questions which would be asked again and again until they were ultimately asked in a Crown Court. They started that very day, when Anna Marie returned home from school and wanted to know where her half-sister was. Rose already had the story prepared, the same story she would doggedly tell friends, neighbours, family and the police for the next twenty-four years. She told Anna Marie that, while she was at school, Charmaine's real mother, Rena, had come to the house and taken Charmaine away to live with her in Bristol. Anna Marie was pleased for her half-sister, because she knew she had wanted to go back to her real mother and thought that maybe the 'smacking and hitting would stop now and Charmaine [would be] happy'.

A variation on this rather flimsy story was also sufficient for Charmaine's school. St James' was informed, probably by Rose herself, that Charmaine had left the area to live with her real mother – but the school did not check that this was true. In the school register, the reason for Charmaine having left was given as 'moved to London'.

Amazingly, under a system still in effect to this day, schools have no obligation to verify that a child leaving their care has arrived safely in a new area and been properly registered at a new school. St James', like all state schools then and now, simply waited for the child's new Head to write requesting the file. If nothing is heard, the file, including the child's attendance register, is kept for the statutory three years and then destroyed. This is exactly what happened in the case of Charmaine.

Easter brought more awkward enquiries, and some awkward visitors. Rose was not pleased to see her former neighbours Shirley and Tracey Giles smiling in the doorway of her flat one day. They had dropped by because Tracey was missing her 'first best friend' Charmaine so much. Could they see her, if it was not inconvenient? Rose told Tracey coldly that no, it was not convenient, because Charmaine had 'gone to live with her mother and bloody good riddance!' Tracey was so upset by the news that she sat down on the hall stairs and cried. Anna Marie comforted Tracey, while Mrs Giles spoke to Rose. She discovered that Fred was still in prison, and asked if he could make her a caravan like the model Rose had displayed in the living room.

Fred was released from prison on 24 June. One of the first pieces of news Rose gave him was that she had murdered Charmaine. There is no evidence that Fred was angry with her; after all, Charmaine was no blood relation of his – she was only the child of his estranged wife, fathered by another man. He had never liked Charmaine, and besides, Fred had committed murder too, so he was reconciled to the idea of killing as an expediency. It is likely that Fred told Rose about his other crimes at this time, explaining that he had killed Anna McFall because she was a threat to him, and possibly telling her about the other girls, such as Mary Bastholm.

Now both Fred and Rose knew terrible secrets about each other. Sharing those secrets brought them closer together, because provided they covered up for one another, they knew they would be safe from justice. It was a pact made in blood, more binding than any marriage ceremony, and one which would keep them together for over twenty years.

BUT first they had to dispose of the body. Rose led Fred down to the cellar, where she had kept Charmaine's body dumped among piles of coal. He carried the corpse of his stepdaughter up the stairs and dug a grave for her in the yard near the back door of the flat, similar in size and shape to the one he had dug in Finger Post Field for Anna McFall. He laid Charmaine on her back in the pit with her arms stretched out. After his arrest in 1994, Fred told police that he could not bring himself to dismember Charmaine because she was so 'young and pure' – it would not have been an easy job in any event, now that rigor mortis had set in. Yet he may still have cut up this tiny child.

When the Home Office pathologist Professor Bernard Knight came to reassemble Charmaine's bones in the mortuary of Cardiff Royal Infirmary in 1994, he was faced with a considerable problem. The skeleton had collapsed inwards, leading him to believe that her grave may have been disturbed by building work in years past. (Some time after Fred and Rose had left Midland Road, Fred was hired to come back to the house and build an extension for the landlady. He used the opportunity to conceal Charmaine's remains further, under the foundations of what became a new kitchen.) When Professor Knight attempted to place the bones of her skeleton in the correct order, many were unaccounted for, just as in the case of Anna McFall. Small finger and toe bones, in particular, were missing, as were her patellae, or kneecaps – an odd detail which would be repeated in later crimes. Parts of her wrists and ankles were also absent. It is possible that Fred had removed these body parts for a special purpose, even though Charmaine's corpse must have been stiff by the time he set to work. It is also possible that Fred had cut Charmaine's legs off at the hip.

Despite their pact of silence, Rose began to feel the strain of her crime as people continued to ask after Charmaine. The pressure became too much for Rose and she decided to leave Fred – one of only two occasions on which they ever separated.

She picked up baby Heather, walked out of Midland Road and travelled to Bishop's Cleeve, a difficult journey for a young mother with a baby in her arms, involving catching two buses. When she arrived at 96 Tobyfield Road, Rose told her father that she was finished with Fred and wanted to come home. But Bill was still angry that she had ignored his orders in the first place – he told her she had 'made her bed' and now must lie in it.

Later that same day, Fred appeared at the back door. In his excited way, he beckoned to Rose and repeated the same coaxing sentence: 'Come on, Rosie, you know what we've got between us.' He also added that unless Rose came back within ten minutes her place in his bed would be occupied by another woman. This seemed to unnerve Rose. When he stopped talking, she spoke to her parents with a passion and self-possession that was entirely new. Pointing to Fred, she declared, 'You don't know him! You don't know him! There's nothing he wouldn't do – even murder.'

Having revealed the truth, and fundamental secret, of their relationship, Rose allowed her lover to lead her away from the house. She had tried to escape, but it was no use.

When she had gone, Bill and Daisy discussed what Rose had said and decided that she was simply 'highly-strung' – a woeful misunderstanding of the situation. Rose had turned to her father for sanctuary and forgiveness, but he had failed her dismally, as he had all her life.

9

CROMWELL STREET

THE MAN ON top was West Indian and the woman was white, very young with wavy brown hair and large breasts. She urged her lover on until he reached a bellowing climax; then they fell back and relaxed on the bed. Rose turned to face the wall of her shabby room, focusing on a detail in the pattern of the paper. There was a quick movement, something like the scuttling of an insect. It was perceptible to Rose only because she knew what it was: the blink of a startling blue eye, Fred's eye, leering at her through a spy-hole in the wall.

Rose regularly entertained men at their flat in Midland Road in this way, and Fred derived great pleasure from watching her, only complaining if he thought she had not been enthusiastic enough with the customers. He liked her to yell out and scream her enjoyment. If she had sex with a man while he was out, Rose had to tell Fred about it when he returned. Voyeurism stimulated him far more than the act itself.

He referred to sex with Rose as 'going off to bunny-land', because rabbits 'did it all the time' and their couplings were bestial. They had sex almost every day – brief episodes in which Fred penetrated Rose for a few moments and then ejaculated.

Normal sex did not stimulate him greatly. He only became

truly aroused if a fetish was involved, like bondage, defecation or sadism. He was excited by Rose's developing interest in lesbian sex and threesomes, where he would usually be happy to watch. Fred also liked to use a vibrator on Rose, and was extremely excited either by being tied up himself, or by tying her up. It was bondage, above all else, that turned him on.

On the other hand, however, there were certain ordinary activities in which he would not take part. Rose often complained that there was never any foreplay with Fred – he just mounted her and came. Also, he flatly refused to perform cunnilingus and was squeamish about her period.

Many of Rose's customers were from Gloucester's large West Indian population. Thousands of Caribbean islanders had settled in Gloucester in the 1950s and early 1960s, tempted by advertisements for work placed by the British government. A typical advertisement in Jamaica's *Daily Gleaner* enthusiastically invited 'Come to England!', and went on to promise good jobs and homes. The reality was very different. Many found Gloucester a hostile city where life was depressingly hard. There was a deep prejudice against blacks and an unofficial colour bar preventing them from finding work, renting homes or even drinking in the pubs. 'For Sale' boards on houses sometimes had the words NO BLACKS added.

One of the few landlords to welcome the West Indians was Frank Zygmunt, the owner of 25 Midland Road, who was himself an immigrant from Eastern Europe. And one of the few English families to make friends with the new arrivals were the Wests, who often had coloured men as guests in their home.

In fact, Fred's closest friends were Jamaicans: he trusted and respected them more than white men. One such friend was Ronalzo Harrison, a house painter, who came to Britain from Jamaica in 1958 at the age of twenty-two. They met when Fred carried out some repairs on Ronalzo's car, and went on to work together on building sites, often borrowing tools from each other and helping with home improvements. The bond between them was strengthened because Heather West and Ronalzo's daughter, Denise, had both been born in the same month at the same hospital and were growing up together.

Fred had much in common with the immigrants. He was a countryman from a little village in Herefordshire, and therefore an outsider in the city. Fred's neighbours and colleagues often laughed at him, calling him a 'country bumpkin', just as they mocked the blacks, thinking them slow-witted. As Ronalzo puts it, 'Fred was different to Gloucester people.' Also, like many of the immigrants, Fred had limited reading and writing skills. He did not like paperwork and always preferred to be paid in cash. Fear of being conned was an insecurity which Fred shared with many West Indians.

Rose liked West Indians for a different reason. She was sexually excited by coloured men and considered them to be the best lovers. Many of her customers were coloured, and these were the encounters that Fred most enjoyed spying on through the hole in the bedroom wall.

AFTER Fred had disposed of Charmaine's body and settled back into a domestic routine with Rose, he turned his attention to the problem of his wife. Rena was becoming an intolerable threat to his well-being because of her natural desire to see her eldest daughter. She had always worried about Fred mistreating the girl, and had kept in touch with Midland Road in case anything was wrong. It is therefore probable that Rena quickly found out that Charmaine was missing. This must have alarmed her and caused her to ask Fred and Rose questions about Charmaine's whereabouts. It was, of course, of the utmost importance that Rena did not discover the truth: that her daughter was in fact dead and buried behind the back door of the flat.

The air was scented with the smell of cut hay when Rena

knocked at the front door of Moorcourt Cottage in August 1971. She was met by the jolly figure of Christine West, who had recently married Fred's youngest brother, Doug, and who was now living at home in Much Marcle with her husband and father-in-law. Christine had her baby son, Christopher, with her – he had been born the previous year – and was pregnant with her second child, due the following January.

It was very unusual for Rena to turn up unexpectedly at Moorcourt Cottage; indeed, Christine had never met Fred's wife before, understanding them to be separated. Rena explained to her sister-in-law that she was looking for Walter. It was harvest time, and the old man had been down at Moorcourt Farm since dawn, helping to bring in the corn. He would not be back home until the evening. Rena said she would go down and see him at work, but did not explain what she wanted to talk about. Later on that day she came back to the cottage, and, because she had helped with the harvest, had a bath before leaving again. Neither Rena nor Walter offered any explanation for the meeting, or what she had wanted, but it is likely that she asked Walter if he knew where Charmaine was. It is an indication of her extreme anxiety and desperation that she turned to Fred's father for help: after all, she hardly knew him.

Some time later, in an apparent attempt to placate her, Fred agreed to take Rena to see Charmaine. She got into his car expecting to be reunited with her daughter. But first Fred took her to a pub, where he made sure she got staggering drunk. Then, when she was incapable of resisting, he strangled her to death.

IT is not known exactly where Fred murdered Rena, but he probably killed her in the car, while she was helplessly intoxicated. Strangulation was the most likely cause of death; it was also an aspect of sadistic sex that excited him. He may have constricted her breathing by inserting a pipe in her throat: a short length of narrow chromium tubing was later found with her remains, together with a child's toy – a small red plastic boomerang. It is also possible that both these items were used to abuse Rena's body in other ways. Eventually she died. Fred then wanted to dismember her body, just as he had Anna McFall's. To do this, and to be able to enjoy it, Fred needed a place where he would not be disturbed, a place where he could take his time, wash afterwards and change his clothes.

Fred probably took Rena back to 25 Midland Road, where he could make as much mess as he wished. He cut up Rena's body carefully, exactly like Anna McFall: disarticulating her legs at the hip, removing her left kneecap and a total of thirty-five finger and toe bones. When Fred had finished, he put her remains into bags and put the bags into the car.

Late at night, Fred drove out towards Moorcourt Cottage. He stopped the car a few hundred yards away by Letterbox Field, so-called because a red mailbox is attached to the fence. Fred was near to the spot where he had crashed his motorcycle into Pat Manns when he was a teenager, and next to Finger Post Field, where he had buried the remains of Anna McFall. Letterbox Field is on a slight hill, so Fred could see the lights of Much Marcle in the distance, and, with the engine switched off, could hear crickets chirruping in the fields.

Once he had negotiated the five-bar gate, Letterbox Field rose up ahead of him in the gloom. He struggled a little under the weight of the sacks containing Rena's remains as he climbed towards a cluster of trees known as Yewtree Coppice. He chose a spot next to the hedgerow, where he felt he would not be disturbed, and dug a deep pit, placing sections of her corpse into it together with pieces of her clothing. He then refilled it and crept back to the car.

In the months following Rena's death, nobody reported her to the police as a missing person, and, just like Anna McFall, there is no record of anyone looking for her – not even health visitors, who should have known about Rena and checked on her welfare, because of her children being fostered and the struggles she had experienced with Fred in trying to get them back. It might also be expected that Rena would have appeared on the 'At Risk' register, if only because of her criminal history. Yet her disappearance, if noted at all, was never seriously investigated at the time.

Fred had got away with another extraordinary crime.

IN November 1971 a young mother named Elizabeth Agius moved into a flat at 24 Midland Road, the house adjacent to Fred and Rose. Elizabeth Agius was married to a Maltese man, but was bringing up their child on her own. Fred first saw this pretty young woman as she struggled to get a pushchair up the steps to her flat next door. He gallantly offered to help, and had soon charmed her into coming in to meet Rose and have some tea, adding, 'My name's Fred.'

The good neighbours asked a series of personal questions about Elizabeth Agius' family. Fred and Rose were both sexually attracted to her, but they did not want an angry husband or father coming to cause trouble. They were pleased with what they found out: with the exception of her mother, their neighbour had few relations in the area.

With her husband living many hundreds of miles away, Elizabeth was naturally lonely and began to pay regular visits to Number 25, finding Fred and Rose to be most solicitous hosts. Fred explained the domestic arrangement to her frankly: Rose was his girlfriend, and his wife had moved back to Scotland. Elizabeth got on well with Rose, who looked to her to be no more than fourteen, and began to drop in on her neighbours almost daily. Fred often went out at night, saying he wanted to 'see what I can find to bring home'. But Elizabeth thought little of it, and did not hesitate when Fred and Rose asked her to baby-sit for them. She did this on two occasions.

The first time Fred and Rose returned at a normal time, but on the second occasion they did not get back until the early hours of the following morning. Elizabeth naturally asked where they had been: 'I said, "Did you go anywhere nice?"' The answer astounded her. Fred said they had been 'driving around looking for young girls'. He said it was easier if Rose was with him because the girls would think it was safe to get in the car. 'If he could get a young girl between fifteen and seventeen, hopefully she would be a virgin, and he could get more money for a virgin. [The girls] had the opportunity to come and live with [Fred and Rose] and be on the game if they wanted to,' says Elizabeth Agius. Fred and Rose added that they preferred to pick up runaways, because they had nowhere to go.

They claimed to have travelled all the way to London and back looking for a girl to pick up – a six-hour round trip in their small car – and that they frequently drove down the A38 beside the Severn estuary to Bristol. Here they parked the Ford Popular by the bus station. Fred used a callous logic in choosing this place to look for girls; he told Elizabeth that teenagers passed through the city on the way to the bright lights of London, and that they would do anything for money.

Elizabeth now says she did not believe what she had been told, because Fred and Rose were 'such a nice couple' and because Fred was always laughing and joking. She therefore continued her friendship with her neighbours, but several months later made another shocking discovery about them.

She was alone with Rose in the kitchen at Number 25 one day when a direct sexual proposition was put to her: Rose confided that Fred was in love with her and wanted to have sex. In fact, Rose continued, Fred wanted to have sex with both of them, together in the same bed. Rose went on to tell her neighbour extraordinary details about her unconventional life with Fred. She said that she was a prostitute, and boasted of the large number of men she entertained on a regular basis, showing Elizabeth the condoms she used and the special pills, shaped like sugar cubes, that she believed would prevent her from contracting venereal diseases. Fred was 'all for' this and would watch Rose through a spy-hole in her bedroom wall. If he were out when she was with a man, she had to describe what had happened when he got home.

Elizabeth's husband returned from Malta, and one evening the couple visited Fred and Rose together. When Mr Agius put an affectionate arm around his wife, Fred leapt up from his seat and stormed into the kitchen in a rage. Elizabeth followed and asked what was the matter. Fred was enraged because he had not succeeded in seducing her and did not want another man to have her, even if that man were her husband. He pointed to the floor and yelled, 'Your husband should be six feet under fucking there!' Fred ranted that if he could not have her, then why should any man. 'I told him he was nuts,' says Elizabeth. Fred then produced a pair of handcuffs and snapped them roughly around her wrists, snarling, 'Now I've fucking got you!'; but Rose pulled him off and freed her neighbour, realising that Mr Agius was in the next room.

It was several days before Elizabeth visited Fred and Rose again. When she did, Fred was still insistent that they go to bed. 'Fred said he would like to tie me to the bed [or] I could tie him to the bed, burn him or whip him, anything I wished.' Rose encouraged her to carry on. 'They were really close. They were the type of people who didn't hide anything from one another,' she says.

Each time she visited, Elizabeth was given her customary cup of tea, but on one of these visits she began to feel drowsy and soon passed out. When she woke up, she was in bed with Fred and Rose, who were both naked. She was told that Fred had raped her while she was unconscious. Fred and Rose helped their groggy neighbour dress and then took her, and her baby son, home.

Anna Marie and toddler Heather were always within yards of these extraordinary scenes, and Elizabeth noticed that the children were also badly neglected. The baby in particular was often wet and left in soiled nappies.

Rose's prostitution, Fred's voyeurism and all sorts of bizarre and violent sex were so open at 25 Midland Road that the children became precociously knowledgeable.

Anna Marie was now coming up to eight, and her adored father started to ponder the pleasure she could give him. Fred and Rose told Elizabeth that Anna Marie had lost her virginity in an accident, when she fell off her Raleigh Chopper bicycle. They said that one of its handles had entered her vagina, and she had needed to attend hospital because of it. Whether they were testing their neighbour, to see if she too were interested in paedophilia, or whether they were deliberately introducing a story that could excuse later abuse, is unclear.

ROSE had been agitating for marriage for some time, and in January 1972, Fred and Rose finally became man and wife. They did not tell their families about this, and the service was conducted secretly, just as Fred's first marriage had been. The ceremony took place at Gloucester Register Office on 29 January 1972. Fred described himself incorrectly as a bachelor on the certificate, and there was no reference to his first marriage, which had never legally ended. None of their family or friends were invited.

The happy couple went away on a short, and unconventional, honeymoon. They visited various places in the West Country that Rose had known as a girl. One evening they appeared in the Golden Lion public house in Northam, the Devon village where Rose had been born. She had not been back for over ten years. In the crowd at the bar that night was Rita New, who had grown up in Morwenna Park Road with the eldest Letts girls, Joyce and Patricia. Rita was drinking with

friends when two young women and a man were brought over
to be introduced by a young man named Barry Seathe, who had
formerly dated one of Rose's elder sisters and happened to be in
the pub that night.

'It was Rosemary with her husband. They were on honeymoon,' said Rita New. But there was a second young woman
with them, a blonde girl who was obviously intimate with the
couple, and was, no doubt, a bisexual whom the Wests had asked
along on their honeymoon so they could indulge in three-in-a-
bed sex. Her identity remains a mystery; Rita and her friends
were told that she was a girlfriend of Fred's. The idea of bringing another woman on honeymoon astonished everybody. The
strange threesome stayed long enough for just one drink, but
behaved so oddly during those few minutes that the evening left
a deep impression on all those present: both Fred and Rose
talked in a fevered, disconnected fashion, gesticulating excitedly
with their hands as if they were high on drugs, or insane. 'It was
weird,' said Rita New.

Fred and Rose also appeared in Benbow Street, Plymouth,
outside the house owned by the Scobling family where the
Letts had lodged. The Scoblings' daughter, Joan, was at home,
and she came out to talk to Rose. She was introduced to Fred
and two small children, probably Heather and Anna Marie, but
Fred did not seem to want to get out of the car so Joan brought
out glasses of orange juice and passed them through the windows for the girls. Rose stood on the pavement and chatted for
a few minutes, then said that they had to be going. As Joan
Scobling watched them drive away, she thought about the huge
responsibility her friend had taken on.

BACK in Gloucester, Fred and Rose started to plan their future
together. They decided that they needed a house large enough
in which to raise a family, but which would also have separate

facilities to enable Rose to continue her work as a prostitute. A broken-down place for Fred to renovate and modify to their own requirements would be perfect. To help pay for it, they would take in bed-and-breakfast lodgers. It was not long before Fred found exactly what they were looking for.

NUMBER 25 Cromwell Street is a large, semi-detached house in a faded residential street on the opposite side of The Park, just a few hundred yards from where they already lived, and like their present home, was also owned by Frank Zygmunt. The Wests agreed to rent the property at first. On the day they moved in, they simply packed up their belongings in suitcases and walked to their new home. Fred did not bother telling his family in Much Marcle that he was moving. (When his brother, Doug, called at Midland Road a few weeks later, he had to be redirected by neighbours.)

From Midland Road, Fred and his family crossed into The Park and then strolled for about five minutes along the path that curves between an avenue of mature trees. This path led them to the weathered statue of Robert Raiker, founder of the Sunday School movement and one of the city's most famous sons. The Wests crossed Park Road by the statue, with the United Reform Church on their right, and turned into Cromwell Street.

The street is straight and quite short, with rows of small, three-storey terrace houses crowding in on either side. These are slightly shabby homes with small areas in front and cars parked on the kerb. About two-thirds of the way up on the left stand a pair of box-like semi-detached houses; the one on the right was to be their new home. Next door was a prefabricated building made of tin, used as a church by the Seventh-Day Adventists. The road ends in a cul-de-sac, and beyond this is a large car park for city centre shoppers. Most of the locals use the Wellington Stores corner shop in the next street.

Cromwell Street had once been a very desirable address. Until 1964, the car park at the end had been the playground of a famous public school, Sir Thomas Rich's School, and many of the teachers had lived locally. But by the 1970s, Cromwell Street had fallen into the same state of decay as Midland Road: a seedy back-way of the inner city. Most of the houses had been sub-divided into flats and bedsitters, often used by students from the nearby campus of the Gloucestershire College of Art and Technology (GLOSCAT). The flats had been allowed to deteri-orate, and the street was noisy at night, especially in summer. There was a lot of petty crime.

Number 25 is larger than many of the neighbouring houses. It also had its own garage, which was unusual. This was behind the house, but could be reached from the front via a narrow drive that ran between the house and the church next door. Behind the garage was a long thin garden, fenced in with wire, with three trees. An alley at the bottom of the garden leads into St Michael's Square, which could be seen from the upstairs rear windows. The square had been turned into another car park for shoppers.

The house itself was relatively spacious, with two upstairs floors and a ground floor, all with open marble fireplaces. There was also an attic room and an extensive cellar. Compared with their little flat at Midland Road, it seemed quite enormous, especially to little Anna Marie who could not quite believe that they had the whole house.

From the outside, Number 25 was a featureless brick building. There were three sash windows at the front, one to each floor, with simple white pediments above them. There was a doorway below street level for the cellar, and this opened on to a small area. The main entrance to the house was at the side of the building. Because street lighting was poor in Cromwell Street (the nearest lamp was three doors away) the doorway to Number 25 was particularly dark at night.

Shortly after they moved in, Elizabeth Agius paid a visit. Fred showed her the cellar, which was divided into separate rooms. He said that he was thinking of using it as a special area for Rose's clients. 'I could soundproof it and use it as my torture chamber,' he smirked. Fred and Rose also invited Elizabeth to come and live at the house, saying that she could go on the game and that 'the soshe' (social security) would pay her rent. But Fred made it clear that she would have to leave her husband first.

To help pay the bills the Wests took in lodgers, installing a cooker and washbasin on the first-floor landing so the tenants would not have to come downstairs to where the West family lived. The family had also grown in size again, as one of Fred's illegitimate children from Scotland, the boy named Steven, had come south to stay with his father.

One of the first lodgers was an eighteen-year-old youth named Benjamin Stanniland. He shared a room on the top floor of the house with Alan Davis, who was about the same age. On the evening that Benjamin and Alan moved into the house, they were both taken out for a drink by Fred and Rose, and were amazed by the open way in which they discussed sex. They returned to Cromwell Street later that evening, and Rose changed into tight leggings and a revealing Spandex top. When Benjamin was in bed that night Rose slipped in beside him and they had sex together. She also had sex with Alan, who shared the room. In the morning the boys were worried about meeting their landlord, but apparently it was not a problem: 'She discussed it with Fred and he didn't seem to mind,' Benjamin said.

The young lodger began to bring a brunette named Lynda Gough back to the house. Lynda was a short, buxom girl, who wore National Health Service spectacles and pieces of jewellery she bought at Woolworths. She was the daughter of fireman John Gough and his wife, June, who also had two younger children. Lynda was a difficult adolescent, and had recently left a

private school in Midland Road for children with learning problems. Aged sixteen, with no qualifications, she went to work as
a seamstress for the Co-op store in Barton Street, where she was
employed when she started to see Benjamin Stanniland.

By the time Lynda reached the age of seventeen, her parents
had noticed a change in her behaviour. 'She made it clear to us
that what she did was her business,' said her mother. Although
she and her husband loved and cared for Lynda, they felt that
they should allow her some freedom.

Lynda conducted relationships with both Benjamin Stanniland
and, after the break-up of their relationship, other male lodgers at
the house. As a result, Lynda became friendly with Fred and
Rose, who explained that they needed a nanny for their children.
It would later prove to be a fateful meeting.

Rose was in need of extra help about the house because she
was heavily pregnant. In June 1972, Rose gave birth to her second child by Fred, a baby girl they initially named May (but
would later change the spelling to Mae). There were now four
children in the household.

It was later claimed at Rose West's trial that she had come
back from hospital to find that Fred was sleeping with their former neighbour Elizabeth Agius. Mrs Agius strenuously denies
this, but it is clear there was a sexual free-for-all at the house
during this time.

ONE day, during the summer of that first year at Cromwell
Street, Anna Marie was led down to the cellar by her father and
stepmother. Fred had soundproofed the cellar, as he had told
Elizabeth Agius he would, creating his 'torture chamber'. The
first victim would be his own eight-year-old daughter.

It was so warm that day that Fred wore shorts. Outside,
Cromwell Street was filled with light and heat. But when Anna
Marie came down into the cellar she found it damp, illuminated

by electric light. The door was closed and locked behind her. Fred told his daughter that he was going to help her; he said that what he was about to do was his duty as a father.

Anna Marie saw a Pyrex bowl, some cloths, a vibrator and tape on the floor. She asked what they were for, but there was no response. Rose removed Anna Marie's clothes. Anna Marie started to cry, and again asked what was happening. 'I was told that I should be very grateful and that I was lucky I had such caring parents who thought of me. They were going to help me and make sure that when I got married I would be able to satisfy my husband and keep my husband. I was led to believe that all loving parents were the same,' she says.

Rose sat on Anna Marie's face while Fred forced his daughter's legs open; her hands were bound and she was gagged. Fred then raped his daughter while Rose watched. Anna Marie could see the Pyrex bowl, and watched as her father removed strange red-coloured matter from inside her and put it into the bowl. She thought it looked like red frogspawn. The pain was so excruciating that she wished she were dead, but Rose was clearly having fun: 'She was laughing, smirking and saying to me it was for my own good and to stop being silly.'

When the ordeal finally ended, Rose took Anna Marie to a bathroom, where she helped her clean herself. Anna Marie was in considerable pain, and would be kept home from school for several days. Rose said that if she ever spoke about what had happened, she would 'get a hitting'. She added that what they had done to Anna Marie happened in other families, too.

One day Fred brought home to Cromwell Street a curious metal object: a long bar, bent into a U-shaped frame and fitted with handles. He had made it at the Wingate factory, where he was now employed as a machinist, and at first the children played with the frame as a kind of toy, rocking back and forth on it. But Anna Marie felt uncomfortable about the object.

Some time later Rose told her to go and tidy up in the cellar, which was also used as the children's play room. Anna Marie was apprehensive because of what had already happened down there, but she did as she was told. She saw that the U-shaped frame was against the wall and, because this scared her, turned to go back upstairs, but Rose was blocking her way. Anna Marie was ordered to undress by her stepmother, who was becoming 'somewhat agitated and annoyed'. She was strapped to the frame naked with her legs apart, and gagged. Rose lifted her own skirt up, and underneath Anna Marie saw a belt with a vibrator in it. Rose removed the belt and started lashing Anna Marie, swearing at the child and calling her names. Then Fred entered the room. 'I looked at my dad, pleading with him with my eyes.' But it was no good. Fred raped his daughter. He was quick about it because it was his lunch hour, and he had to be back at work.

When he had gone, Rose abused Anna Marie with the vibrator and then left her tied to the frame for a while. Later in the afternoon, Anna Marie, who was cut and bruised, was made to take a bath. Rose poured salt into the water first, saying it would sting, but that this was good for her, too.

10

THE SPIDERS' WEB

LATE ONE CHILLY November evening in 1972, Fred and Rose were driving through the outskirts of Tewkesbury when they came to the Gupshill Manor public house, a large half-timbered inn on the Gloucester Road. The pub had just closed for the night and the car park was emptying. On the opposite side of the highway, the Wests noticed a pretty teenage girl huddling for warmth in the cold night air as she thumbed for a lift.

They stopped and asked where she was going. She said that she was on her way home to the town of Cinderford, twenty-three miles to the south-west, beyond Gloucester on the other side of the River Severn. Despite the fact that Cinderford was a considerable detour, the Wests offered her a lift all the way home. The girl assumed they were a respectable married couple and that it was therefore safe to accept. Rose smiled and stepped out of the coupé so she could pull the passenger seat forward and let the girl into the back.

Her name was Caroline Owens. She was seventeen years old, and regularly hitch-hiked from Cinderford to Tewkesbury to see her boyfriend, Tony Coates. When it was time to go home, she waited opposite the Gupshill Manor because she knew a telephone engineer who would always give her a lift if he was passing on his night shift.

Caroline lived with her mother, Elizabeth, and stepfather in a council house in Hill Dean, an estate at Cinderford, a small mining community set high up on a hill just inside the northern border of the Forest of Dean. Caroline, who was one of fifteen children, disliked her stepfather, 'Pickles' Harris, and was looking for a job and somewhere new to live. Fred and Rose said they needed a girl to help look after their children. Would Caroline like to come to Gloucester and work as their nanny? They could pay £3 per week and would give her a lift home every Tuesday. Fred and Rose visited Caroline's home, taking their children with them. They told Caroline's mother that they would 'keep an eye' on her, and that she would be 'all right living with them'. Caroline thought the West children were 'cute'.

A few days later, having discussed it with her mother, Caroline arrived at Cromwell Street to take up the job. She shared a bedroom with the eldest girl, Anna Marie, who was very affectionate, but seemed to be frightened of her parents. 'She was withdrawn when they were around,' said Caroline.

Fred was out at work most of the day, as were the lodgers, Benjamin Stanniland and Alan Davis. There were few visitors to the house – just Rose's younger brothers; Fred's brother, John; and the coloured men Rose regularly entertained – so Caroline and Rose were often alone together. Caroline was petite, with a pretty face and long brown hair – she was later crowned Miss Forest of Dean 1977 – and Rose found her very attractive. She took strands of her hair and stroked it while they were talking, and also touched her legs. She admired Caroline's eyes, and would often barge in when she was taking a bath.

When Fred was at home he talked about sex incessantly. One evening he told Caroline that he carried out medical operations, including abortions. This led on to comments about Anna Marie, with Fred claiming that his daughter had already lost her virginity. Caroline was astonished to hear this, as Anna Marie was only eight years old. She asked what Fred meant. Seeming to realise his indiscretion, Fred hurriedly explained that Anna Marie had not lost her virginity to a man, but by falling off her bicycle – the same extraordinary lie he had told Elizabeth Agius at Midland Road.

In the evenings there was a great deal of activity at the house. The lodgers, who were mostly young men at the time, brought back friends and girlfriends; cannabis was smoked and impromptu parties held in the lodgers' quarters – often ending in a sexual free-for-all. It was after one of these sessions that Caroline had sex with Benjamin Stanniland, and then Alan Davis. Her regular boyfriend, Tony, and another young man also spent the night at the house with her. Rose too had sex with the lodgers, and was seen around the house wearing skimpy, see-through clothing. One lodger at the time, David Evans, says, 'She was the landlady, but she came upstairs now and again because she liked sex.'

Caroline decided she disliked Fred. She was not frightened of him, but rather pitied him and thought him inadequate. 'He was a little man with a big head. He was so cocky, a know-all,' she says. Life was made more difficult at the house because Fred and Rose were arguing between themselves. Together with Fred's distasteful conversation and Rose's lesbian advances, Caroline decided that the job was not working out. After several weeks at Cromwell Street, she announced that she was leaving.

ROSE had wanted to have sex with Caroline and was frustrated by her departure. She told Fred they would have to 'get' her – and, over the next few days, they formulated a plan to abduct and rape Caroline. When he was interviewed by police in 1994, Fred made it clear that murder was the likely outcome. He said the attack on Caroline Owens had been a test to see if Rose could help abduct a girl.

The plan was put into operation on 6 December 1972. They

knew Caroline's routine and chose a day when she would visit Tony Coates in Tewkesbury. Earlier in the day, Caroline was walking in Barton Street, Gloucester, when she saw Fred and Rose driving in their grey Ford Popular. In retrospect, it appears that they were stalking her. By 10:30 that evening, she had said goodbye to her boyfriend and was back at her usual hitch-hiking position opposite the Gupshill Manor. It was dark, and the Gloucester Road was quiet. She had not been standing there long when the Wests pulled up. Caroline had no particular reason to be scared of them, so she accepted a lift. Rose told Fred that she wanted to have a 'girl's chat' with Caroline and clambered into the back beside her.

They drove south through the suburbs of Tewkesbury until they were in pitch-dark countryside. After twenty minutes or so, Gloucester's cathedral spire rose in the distance, illuminated by floodlights. Fred bypassed the city centre and crossed the River Severn on the A40. During the journey, Caroline had become increasingly uncomfortable in the back seat. Rose had turned the conversation round to sex, and had slipped her arm over Caroline's shoulder. When Caroline looked at Rose, she saw that she was grinning at her in a maniacal way.

Fred barked from the front, 'You had sex tonight with Tony?' Caroline was embarrassed and replied that she had not. Rose was now touching her breasts and thighs and caressing her face. She tried to kiss her on the mouth and Caroline had to push her away. 'What's her tits like?' growled Fred.

They came to the Highnam roundabout, two miles outside Gloucester. Instead of taking the A40 to Huntley and then Cinderford, which was their normal route, Fred steered the car on to the A48 road to Chepstow. Caroline asked where they were going, and Fred said that he just wanted to 'have a look'. Fred turned the car towards a five-bar gate, and parked so that the Ford's yellow headlights illuminated the wooden slats and muddy field. Caroline was still fending off Rose's hands and

kisses, and noticed that Rose was 'looking at [her] in a nasty
way'. Fred turned round in his seat to face the women. He told
Caroline that she was a 'bitch', and then punched her in the face
several times, making her black out.

WHEN Caroline came round she was still in the car. Her arms
had been tied behind her back with her scarf, Rose was holding
her and Fred was winding brown adhesive tape around her head,
gagging her. 'My reaction was terror and panic. I couldn't open
my mouth even if I tried.' She was forced to breathe through her
nose. Fred started the car up again and they began moving; she
was being held down with her face pressed against the back seat
of the car and could hear Rose cackling with pleasure. All
Caroline could see from her awkward position were the tops of
street lights. She guessed they were back in Gloucester, and felt
tears running down her face.

The car came to a stop and the engine was switched off.
Caroline was pushed inside 25 Cromwell Street and bundled up
the stairs, while Fred and Rose pawed at her, laughing. They
entered a room on the first floor which contained a sofa and a
mattress. Fred then produced a knife and came towards her,
making Caroline cringe. The blade was laid against her cheek.
Fred turned it under the tape and cut. He ripped the tape
roughly from her face, yanking out some of her brown hair.
The knife had cut her slightly and Fred apologised.

They tried to calm their captive, and then removed all of
Caroline's clothes apart from her shoes. Fred tied Caroline's
hands behind her back with rope, blindfolded her and gagged
her with cotton wool. Caroline's eyes swivelled around, searching for light. She felt hands touching her, entering her vagina.
They were smooth and the fingernails were long. Then a
rougher, larger hand touched her; it was as if 'they were carrying
out an examination'.

She heard Fred talking about her genitalia. He said, 'She is big inside, but the lips are too fat. They will get in the way of the clitoris.' Caroline remembered what Fred had said about performing operations. Rose held Caroline's legs apart, and Fred started to beat Caroline's vagina with the buckle end of a leather belt, saying that he wanted to flatten her clitoris. Caroline counted ten strokes; the pain was appalling. Rose then performed cunnilingus on Caroline, while Fred fondled Rose's breasts and had sex with Rose from behind.

Fred had not yet made any attempt to penetrate Caroline himself: Rose had been the one who was directly involved in the sexual assault. But in the early hours of the morning, Rose briefly left the room, leaving Fred and Caroline together. Furtively, obviously anxious that Rose should not catch him, Fred raped Caroline. It seemed to last for no more than a minute, then Fred withdrew and got dressed. He turned to Caroline and made her promise not to tell. She saw that he was crying.

Fred and Rose finally exhausted themselves and fell asleep. Caroline attempted to get out of the house through a window, but was unable to escape because of her tied hands.

At about seven in the morning, there was a knock at the front door of the house. Fred went and let the visitor in, bringing him quite near the room where Caroline was being held. She could hear their voices and tried to make a noise to draw the man's attention, but Rose placed a pillow over her head to smother her. When the visitor had gone, Fred came back into the room. He was furious, snarling, 'I'll keep you in the cellar and let my black friends have you, and when we're finished we'll kill you and bury you under the paving stones of Gloucester.' Hundreds of girls were already buried there, he added, and nobody would ever find her.

In the morning Fred said he was sorry for what had happened, and that it was Rose's idea that they 'get' her. He started crying again and said she had been brought to the house for

'Rose's pleasure'. He added that Rose was like this when she was pregnant. Would Caroline forgive them and come back to work as their nanny? Caroline knew that her only hope of survival was to pretend she would. 'I thought I was going to be dead,' she says. She helped clean up the house, even doing the vacuuming, played with Anna Marie and Heather, had three hot baths, at Fred's insistence, to wash away the brown gum marks that had been left on her face by the masking tape, and then got ready to go out. They all left the house and got in the Ford, intending to visit the launderette together. But when they arrived at the launderette, Fred had trouble parking, so he let Caroline and Rose out while he went to find a space. Caroline saw her chance to escape, and told Rose she would see her tomorrow.

When she got home to Cinderford, Caroline's mother Elizabeth noticed the bruising on her daughter's face. At first Caroline refused to tell her what had happened, saying that people would come and kill her if she spoke about it. But gradually the truth came out, and her mother contacted the police.

DETECTIVES went to Cromwell Street and interviewed Rose, who demonstrated a belligerence which belied her innocent appearance and youth. When DC Kevan Price asked if the allegations were true, Rose mockingly replied, 'Don't be fucking daft. What do you think I am?' But her hardness of character was not complemented by any criminal common sense. When the police asked if they might search the Ford Popular, Rose replied, 'Please your bloody self.' This was a mistake, as inside the car was a button from Caroline's coat. A partially used roll of brown adhesive tape was found in the lounge, and a search of the house also uncovered a collection of pornographic photographs.

Fred and Rose were arrested. Rose told the police that she would not talk 'because I told my husband I would say nothing', but then went on to admit performing lesbian acts on Caroline.

Fred also admitted assault. During questioning, it emerged that Rose was supposed to have psychiatric help for her lesbian tendencies, but Rose probably invented this story, hoping it would mitigate what she had done to Caroline. In any event, Rose never received any such psychiatric advice or counselling.

To press rape charges against Fred and Rose would have meant Caroline Owens giving evidence in court. Partly because of her reluctance to go through with such an ordeal, it was agreed that the Wests would plead guilty if they were charged with the lesser offence of assault.

Gloucester Magistrates Court is a bland building of sand-coloured brick, built in 1965 and furnished primarily with linoleum and fold-back plastic chairs. The case was heard there on Friday 12 January 1973. Fred was thirty-one years old and well-used to the criminal justice procedure. His wife, in her first court appearance, was nineteen and had just found out that she was pregnant again. They were jointly charged with indecent assault causing actual bodily harm; Police Inspector William Kingscott presented the prosecution case.

The horror of Caroline Owens' ordeal was then steadily undermined by the defence, until it sounded as if she had practically asked to have sex. The court heard that Caroline had offered 'passive co-operation'; that the door had remained unlocked throughout but she made no attempt to call for assistance, or to get away. The Wests, on the other hand, were portrayed as a sympathetic young couple with several children to care for; it was also suggested in court that Rose was seeking psychiatric treatment. When Fred came to give evidence, he readily admitted assault and said, 'I don't know why I did it, it just happened.'

The magistrates retired to think the matter over in chambers. Although Fred had several previous convictions, they decided that his past offences had no relevance to this case. As a man, Frederick West struck the magistrates as a 'docile' sort who did not look capable of violence. The police who had handled his arrest agreed. As for Rose, she had no criminal history at all and was pregnant. It seemed inappropriate to gaol either of them. It was up to the chairman of the bench, John Smith, to deliver the verdict. He would live to regret his words.

Mr Smith returned to the modernist courtroom, sat and turned to the dock. 'We do not think that sending you to prison will do you any good,' he told the Wests. They were fined £25 on each of the four charges, and were allowed to walk free. When Caroline heard the verdict, she was bitterly disappointed. 'It made me feel like I wasn't worth anything,' she says. Shortly afterwards she attempted to take her own life.

As Fred and Rose wandered back through the shopping centre to Cromwell Street, it must have dawned on them what a very narrow escape they had enjoyed: they had set out to abduct, rape and murder Caroline Owens and had made the potentially disastrous decision of letting her go because they thought she would come back for more. Yet, even though she had gone to the police, they had still got away with only a fine. They might not be so lucky the next time. The next girl would have to be killed.

THE Wests had been cultivating the friendship of Lynda Gough, the Co-op seamstress who had conducted sometimes tempestuous relationships with several of their lodgers and occasionally helped out by baby-sitting. When Caroline Owens left Cromwell Street, Fred and Rose suggested that Lynda step in to look after their children permanently, and come to live with them at the house. Soon afterwards Lynda told her parents that she was planning to move to a flat in the centre of the city. A week later, in March 1973, while Lynda was still living at home, a woman called round to invite her out for a drink. Mrs June Gough thought the woman was a little overweight – she was in fact five months pregnant.

On 19 April, two weeks before Lynda's twentieth birthday, June Gough returned home at lunchtime as usual to find that Lynda had gone. She had taken most of her possessions with her, and left a short note which read:

Dear Mum and Dad
   Please don't worry about me. I have got a flat and I will come and see you sometime.
                                                  Love Lin

Lynda was a rebellious, headstrong girl who did not take kindly to being given advice by her parents. When Mr and Mrs Gough read her note, they were concerned about the daughter they loved, but decided to wait a while before going after her. 'Her father and I felt, "Let her have her head for a bit; she'll be back,"' says June Gough.

Rose was sexually attracted to Lynda, just as she had been to Caroline Owens. The girls were of a similar type: petite brunettes of the same age group. It was no coincidence that both Lynda and Caroline Owens had been offered work at Cromwell Street as nanny to the West children. If Fred and Rose were spiders, this was the web they used to trap their prey.

Lynda became involved in a sexual situation with Fred and Rose. It may have started in much the same way as with Caroline Owens, or Lynda may initially have been willing to have sex with them. However it began, what Fred and Rose did with Lynda went far beyond what she had expected, and even beyond the abuse that Caroline Owens had suffered.

LYNDA was gagged with brown adhesive parcel tape two inches wide, together with white surgical tape which was wrapped around her head to prevent her screaming. Gagging was also a form of extreme sado-masochism which Fred and Rose found sexually exciting. They possessed magazines featuring women with complete rubber head-masks breathing through tiny tubes.

She was almost certainly tied up, probably with binds made from her own clothes. In the form of bondage that excited Fred and Rose, the victim had to be completely helpless, then tormented to see how much pain they could endure. Lynda either died during this sexual torture, or was murdered because Fred and Rose could not afford to let her go after what they had done to her — they certainly did not want to give her the chance to talk to the police, as they had with Caroline Owens.

When Lynda was finally dead, the Wests turned to the job of covering up their crime. Rose sorted through Lynda's possessions. She threw away some of her clothes and may have tried to burn others. Those clothes that she liked, Rose kept for herself. Fred disposed of the corpse.

There was an old inspection pit in the garage behind the house, a rectangular concrete hole for working under cars — a ready-made grave. Fred claimed in police interviews that he only dismembered his victims because it meant he could bury their remains more easily. This time the grave was quite big enough to lay Lynda's body out full-length. However, cutting women up must have excited Fred, because he went ahead and dismembered her body anyway, even though there was no practical reason for doing so.

From examining the marks on Lynda's femur bones, it seems that he used a sharp knife for the work, and, feeling secure in his own home, where he would not be disturbed and where there was no need to rush, Fred went further than ever in the dismemberment. He disarticulated her legs at the hip, dissected her hands and feet, cut off her fingers at the joints, and removed many of her toes, her kneecaps, a breastbone, seven ribs and twenty-five wrist and ankle bones. Fred later said he wanted to 'make sure she was dead', so he almost certainly cut off her head as well (although because some of the cervical vertebrae were never recovered, it is not possible to know for sure whether this happened).

Five cervical vertebrae bones, fingers, toes, kneecaps and parts of the wrist were kept aside, probably as mementos. Fred placed the rest of Lynda's remains into the inspection pit. He dropped her decapitated head in with a band of tape still wrapped around it. He also put into the hole the other bits and pieces of torture: loops of string and fragments of her clothes, some burned and some knotted, and then filled the inspection pit with earth and debris.

TWO weeks went by, and Lynda's parents had heard nothing. On the third Saturday after she had left home, her mother went looking for her. Mrs Gough asked around the town, talking to Lynda's friends, and her supervisor at work, until her enquiries led her to a tall narrow house in Cromwell Street. A young couple came to the door. June Gough recognised Rose West as the woman who had taken her daughter out for a drink a few weeks earlier. She asked if they had seen Lynda. At first Fred and Rose were reluctant to admit knowing anything about her whereabouts. Then, as they were chatting on the doorstep, Mrs Gough noticed that Rose was wearing Lynda's slippers. When she pointed this out, Rose admitted that Lynda had stayed with them briefly, but had now gone.

June Gough looked behind Fred and Rose to the back garden. Hanging on the washing line were several items of clothing belonging to Lynda. Rose said that she had left them behind. They then said that she had been looking after Anna Marie, but that she had hit the child so hard that they had told her to leave. (The truth, of course, was that Rose was the one who continued to abuse her stepdaughter. A few months after this, in July 1973, Anna Marie fainted at a swimming baths. During a medical check-up afterwards, scratches and bruises were noticed around both her breasts. Anna Marie explained the marks by saying: 'Mummy does this.') Fred and Rose maintained that Lynda had been talking about going to Weston-super-Mare, the seaside resort near Bristol.

June Gough walked away from Cromwell Street not knowing what had happened. Some time later she and her husband went to Weston-super-Mare to look for their daughter. They asked at the job centre to see if she was registered, but were told that that was confidential information. It would be twenty-one years before she discovered the truth. During that time she contacted various organisations, including the Salvation Army, in the hope that she would find her, but Lynda was never officially registered with the police as a missing person, and, again, there was no organised search for her.

In those years Mrs Gough often walked past 25 Cromwell Street on her way to the shops. One day she noticed that the front entrance to the cellar had been bricked up, and found herself shuddering, not really knowing why, but experiencing an intuitive feeling of dread. She never went past the house again.

Within Number 25, Lynda's disappearance was explained to the lodgers by Fred and Rose. One morning Rose came and sat on David Evans' bed. She said that Lynda had hit the West children and that, because of this, she would not be coming back to the house again.

FOUR months after Fred and Rose had walked free from court for abducting and assaulting Caroline Owens, a crime punished only by a small fine, they had murdered a young girl and escaped with no penalty at all.

11

THE CHARNEL-HOUSE

CAROL ANN COOPER was not a very happy fifteen-year-old. Her parents separated when she was three. She lived with her mother at first, but when Mrs Cooper died, Carol went to live with her father, Colin, in Worcester. He had been in the Royal Air Force, had remarried and was working as an insurance salesman, but soon found that he was unable to look after Carol and placed her into care. By 1973, she was living at the Pines Children's Home in Bilton Road, Worcester, and had the distinct feeling that nobody loved her. A pretty, intelligent teenager with bright blue eyes, she was known as 'Caz' and had used a needle and ink to tattoo that nickname on her forearm.

On Saturday 10 November 1973, Carol, her boyfriend Andrew Jones and a large group of friends visited the Odeon cinema in the Warndon area of Worcester. After the film, they all had fish and chips and then went to a pub, where Carol drank bitter orange. At around 9 P.M. Andrew took Carol to the bus stop: she was spending the weekend with her grandmother and he was going to see her off. 'Carol and me had been getting a bit niggly with each other,' he said later. 'She put her arms around me and asked me to kiss her, but I wouldn't. I was still feeling a bit niggly. She was standing opposite me. I think she was crying and I went over to her and made it up.' Andrew then gave his girlfriend eighteen and a half pence to pay for her bus fare and to buy some cigarettes; Carol climbed aboard a number 15 bus and the teenagers waved goodbye to each other, looking forward to their next date. It was 9:15 P.M.; Andrew never saw Caz again.

IT is not known for sure how she vanished; Carol did not live to tell the story. But it seems likely that a young couple offered her a lift that winter night. What happened next can be deduced from the condition of Carol's remains, found at 25 Cromwell Street more than twenty years later.

If there were strange noises that night from the cellar of the house, then the lodgers who lived upstairs thought little of it. The landlord, Fred, was an industrious man who often worked at odd hours. He had recently been enlarging the cellar, and had dug down past the foundations to the main drain. Now a man could stand upright in the cellar without banging his head. He had carried out all the work himself, using just a pick and shovel to move literally tons of earth. He was also in the process of pulling down the garage behind the house to build an extension using, among other oddments he picked up, a railway sleeper as part of the foundations. To save time and work, he also built directly on to the wall of the Seventh-Day Adventist Church. Fred never seemed to stop, and loud noises were common at all hours of the night.

WHEN the cellar door was closed, a band of surgical tape was wrapped around Carol's head, gagging the terrified girl. Her limbs were bound with cord and pieces of braided cloth were fastened under her arms. Heavy wooden beams supported the ceiling, and in one of these were a number of neatly drilled holes. Fred later claimed that he fixed hooks into the holes and thereby suspended the bodies of his live victims. Carol may well have been strung up on a hook so that she was suspended above the floor. How long she dangled there, and what manner of torture she suffered, can only be imagined. She was undoubtedly used as a sexual toy by Fred and Rose, and subjected to extreme sado-masochistic perversions. She eventually died, probably by suffocation or strangulation, either as a result of what had been done to her, or because Fred and Rose could not risk setting her free.

THERE are two theories as to where Fred dismembered the bodies of his victims. Fred's son Steve claims his father told him this was done at a derelict farmhouse outside Cheltenham, explaining that he could make as much noise and mess as he liked there. Steve further claims that Fred said he transported the corpses between Cromwell Street and the farmhouse in large fibreglass water tanks stolen from the Wingate factory where he worked. There has also been an unproved allegation that he committed sex acts on the bodies at the farmhouse.

But the police, and their forensic advisers, believe the victims were killed *and* dismembered at Cromwell Street, over the holes that had been dug for their burial. This is what Fred himself said in contradictory conversations while in custody.

The 'farmhouse theory', if it can be called that, is an interesting one, however. Like much of what Fred said, it is probably part fact and part fiction, and therefore contains an intriguing element of truth. The victims found at Cromwell Street, including Carol Cooper, were almost certainly murdered and dismembered at the house, but it seems likely that a farmhouse did figure in Fred's crimes in some way, and may indeed have been the scene of other murders that have never been discovered.

★

HE removed her legs at the hip, leaving deep gouge marks in her left upper thighbone, and cut off her head between the fourth and fifth cervical vertebrae. An unusual gouge mark in the skull suggests that Carol was stabbed in the head – this could have happened either before she died or while Fred was dismembering her. He had already dug a pit on the right-hand side of the cellar, three feet deep with a step halfway down. He placed her jumbled remains, and the means of her torture, into this hole. The gag that had prevented her screams was still wrapped around her head; pieces of rope and knotted binds were also buried. As with the earlier victims, Fred did not bury all of Carol's remains: parts of her hands and feet, one of the cervical vertebrae and a breastbone were kept back.

Carol's sudden disappearance was suspicious. She had run away several times before, as her stepmother told the police, but it was odd that she had not taken any of her belongings with her this time. Carol was properly registered as a missing person, and West Mercia police made extensive enquiries in the Worcester area, but they found no trace. There was no reason to think she had met her end almost thirty miles away in Gloucester.

LUCY Partington was from an upper-middle-class background, very different to Carol Ann Cooper's. Her father, Roger, was an industrial chemist and her mother, Margaret, worked as an architect. One of Lucy's uncles was the novelist Kingsley Amis, later Sir Kingsley, and she had played as a child with his son, Martin, who also became a famous writer. By the Christmas of 1973 Lucy was aged twenty-one, and in her final year at Exeter University where she was studying medieval English. She was a serious, pious young woman who had recently converted to the Roman Catholic faith. She did not have a boyfriend. The only factor that Lucy had in common with Carol Ann Cooper was that both sets of parents had separated.

That Christmas Lucy returned home to spend the holiday at her mother's house in the picturesque Cotswold village of Gretton, near Cheltenham. She went to a party at a neighbour's house, watched a rugby match with her family, and attended midnight mass, but mostly Lucy spent her evenings at home, curled up in front of the log fire, reading *Wuthering Heights* and savouring the peace and quiet. On the morning of 27 December 1973, Margaret Partington briefly looked in on her daughter before leaving for work. Lucy was asleep, enjoying a lay-in. Her mother never saw her again.

Later that day Lucy rose and dressed in pink flared denim jeans, a pink shirt, sweater, brown shoes, knee-length socks and a rust-coloured raincoat, and went into the centre of Cheltenham with her brother, David. They split up, and at about eight o'clock that evening, Lucy went to visit her friend, Helen Render, at her home in the suburb of Pittville, not far from the Cheltenham racecourse.

Helen had been disabled from birth, and was confined to a wheelchair. She and Lucy, whom she knew affectionately as 'Luce the Moose', had been close friends since meeting at Pates' Grammar School's history group four years earlier. Lucy had been very active at Pates', appearing in the school's 1968 production of Arthur Miller's *The Crucible*.

Lucy thought of Helen's house as her second home, and had been going out of her way to see Helen during the holidays because her friend had not been feeling well. On the evening of 27 December, the girls talked about their shared interest in medieval art, and Lucy composed a letter of application for a postgraduate course at London's Courtauld Institute, admitting that she did not expect to be accepted. Helen's mother gave her a stamp, and Lucy left the house at 10:15 P.M. to walk to the bus stop on the Evesham Road, planning to post her application on the way. It was understood that if she missed the bus home to Gretton she could come back to the house and Lucy's father would give her a lift home.

The bus stop was only a three-minute walk from the Render house, but it was a lonely spot next to Marle Hill Park and Lucy was often the only person waiting there. Sometimes the bus drivers did not see her in the dark and drove straight past. Lucy could have gone back to the house and asked Helen's father for a lift, but it was late and she did not want to bother him.

As fate would have it, she was waiting on the A435 trunk road, the route Fred and Rose used when they travelled between Gloucester and Bishop's Cleeve. They often visited the village, especially during Christmas week, and were probably driving home with their children when they saw Lucy standing at the bus stop. It is unlikely that Lucy would have accepted a lift unless she felt confident they were a normal family group. She was a cautious girl, and would have been particularly wary of lone men because another of her old school friends, Ruth Owen, had been frightened a few years earlier when a dark-haired man fitting the general description of Fred tried to lure her into his car.

Neither was she the sort of girl who would have gone to Cromwell Street willingly, so what happened to her in that car is probably similar to what happened to Caroline Owens: she may have been knocked unconscious and then gagged and held down by Rose as they drove into the city. She was then no doubt quickly bundled inside. It was not a very festive house that Lucy found herself in, nothing like her own cosy home at Gretton. It was a seedy sort of place, decorated in a hodge-podge of half-finished alterations distinctly lacking in Christmas cheer.

Lucy was pushed down into the cellar, where she was bound and gagged with lengths of adhesive surgical tape, three-quarters of an inch wide, together with pieces of cloth. The surgical tape was wrapped around her head until it formed an oval mask over her face. Her limbs were restrained with cord, knotted in place. There is little doubt that Lucy was sexually tortured, as the other girls had been, and again died either as a result of her injuries or because the Wests could not risk letting her go.

Lucy's ordeal may have carried on for a very long time. Part of the Crown's case against Rose would later be that she and Fred kept Lucy tied up in the cellar, and used her as a sexual plaything, for anything up to seven days before she was finally murdered. The cellar at the time was a dark, dank hole; the floor was earth and there were puddles of water dotted about. There was no electricity and the only natural light came from a small metal grille.

The evidence for this long period of captivity is that a week after Lucy's abduction, at twenty-five minutes past midnight on the morning of 3 January 1974, Fred walked into the casualty unit of the Gloucestershire Royal Hospital with a serious laceration to his right hand. It was extremely unusual for Fred to attend a hospital; he feared hospitals, even refusing to visit his own mother when she was dying. 'It was very rare that you could get him inside [one] because of his motorcycle accident,' says his younger brother, Doug. Also, as a builder, Fred was used to cutting himself, so it must have been a major injury for him to voluntarily attend, and one wonders what he had been doing at midnight to cut himself so badly. The most likely explanation is that he had been dismembering Lucy's body.

Before he set to work, Fred had dug a hole in the part of the cellar later described by police as the 'nursery alcove', because of the nursery-style pattern of the wallpaper. Then, when the rest of the household had gone to bed, he began to cut up the corpse, using a knife from the selection he kept on a kitchen shelf.

The knife he used was a cheap stainless steel kitchen model with a riveted wooden handle, manufactured by Richards of Sheffield as part of a set given away to mail order customers. The blade had been worn away by vigorous sharpening until it ended almost in a point, and had come to look like a flexible dagger. Fred used this, and possibly heavier knives, to decapitate Lucy, disarticulate her legs and remove other body parts including her toes (a total of sixty-six foot and hand bones), ribs, vertebrae, the left kneecap and left shoulder blade.

The shoulder blade would have been particularly difficult for a non-surgeon to remove, and it was probably while Fred was struggling with this that he cut himself, gashing his hand so badly that he dropped the knife into the grave. After being treated at hospital he filled in the grave, forgetting to pick up the knife again. There it remained until 1994. (Rose later admitted in court that she had probably been the one who had sharpened the knife.)

Lucy was quickly reported to police as a missing person and an extensive search was launched. It was clear to detectives that this was not the sort of girl to run away, and as the days went by without word from her, it seemed increasingly likely that she had met a violent end. Teams of police officers, divers (again, including John Bennett) and sniffer dogs were all used in the search; there was even a reconstruction of Lucy's last trip to the bus stop. Her mother, Margaret, said at the time, 'How anybody could disappear and just vanish completely in three minutes baffles me.' Television appeals were made, some of which were no doubt seen by Fred, who made a point of watching the news every evening. But nothing was found, and the police had no reason to look in the direction of 25 Cromwell Street, where Lucy had died just one month after Carol Ann Cooper.

WHILE the newspapers and television reported daily on the mystery of Lucy's disappearance, Fred and Rose continued to live a remarkably ordered life and seemed untroubled by the fuss they had caused. Rose was nursing their first son, Stephen, who had been born the previous August, bringing the number of their genetic children to three (Fred's illegitimate son, Steven, and Anna Marie were also still at home, making five children in all).

Fred was busy negotiating a £5,000 mortgage to buy 25 Cromwell Street from Frank Zygmunt, becoming the first member of his family in several generations to own his own home. The mortgage was guaranteed by Fred's Jamaican-born friend Ronalzo Harrison, who had no doubts about trusting the Wests.

They continued to take in lodgers to help meet the financial burden of the repayments. These were now almost exclusively young women, attracted by the low rents on offer. One tenant was a teenager named Juanita Mott, who would soon play a larger part in their lives.

THERE were now the remains of two bodies in the cellar of Cromwell Street, and a third in the inspection pit by the kitchen, all victims of Fred and Rose's lust. But still they were not satisfied.

THÉRÈSE Siegenthaler was born in Trub, Switzerland, and had been brought up in the German-speaking Bern area. In 1974, Thérèse was a 21-year-old sociology student at the Woolwich College of Further Education in South-East London, living in a flat five miles away in Caterham Road, Lewisham. She had a weekend job in the Bally shoe shop at the Swiss Centre in London's West End. Thérèse was a strongly-built brunette of medium height, who wore glasses and little make-up. She was a highly principled and intelligent woman, with firm political beliefs and considerable self-confidence. She was fluent in English, but spoke with a distinct Germanic accent.

In April 1974 Thérèse attended a party in Deptford, South London, and the next day left to hitch-hike to Holyhead in North Wales. She intended to catch the ferry to Ireland and there meet a Catholic priest with whom she shared an interest in South African politics. As she prepared for her journey, a friend warned Thérèse about the perils of hitch-hiking. She laughingly replied,

'I can look after myself. I'm a judo expert.'

But Thérèse met her match on that journey between London and Holyhead. She was picked up, probably by Fred and Rose together, and taken to Cromwell Street. Fred misunderstood her accent and decided she was Dutch, so he nicknamed her 'Tulip'.

They gagged her with a brown scarf tied behind her head and fastened with a bow, bound her arms and legs with rope and raped her. When they had killed her, Fred set to work slicing at the hip joints, leaving distinct cuts on her left upper femur. He also cut off her head, again 'to make sure she was dead'. Other parts of her body, including a collarbone, fourteen wrist and ankle bones, and twenty-four finger and toe bones, were also removed. Thérèse's remains were jumbled into a sump-like hole in the cellar; Fred later disguised the grave by building a false chimney breast over it.

Her disappearance was reported to London's Metropolitan Police, and it was obvious to Scotland Yard that she had not intended to run away. Thérèse's bank account, containing 3,600 Swiss francs, was untouched. She had also written to her father, Fritz, in Switzerland, saying she would spend Easter in Ireland but would return to London after a week. Thérèse had even booked West End theatre tickets and an airline ticket to Zurich to see her family later in the year. Her family and the police made vigorous efforts to trace her, but they were not to know that she had gone missing, not in London or Ireland, but in an obscure back street of Gloucester, a city she did not even have to pass through on her projected journey.

FOUR months later Rose was admitted to the Gloucestershire Royal Hospital with an unusual wound – reminiscent of the injury Fred had suffered while dismembering Lucy Partington. Rose arrived at the hospital at 10:55 P.M. on 13 August with a deep laceration across the ring and middle fingers of her right hand. On admission, the cause of the cut was given as 'playing about with knives', but by the time Rose had been transferred to a ward, this had changed to 'cutting wood'. Her wound was treated and she was kept in hospital for two nights.

If Rose had been helping Fred to dismember a body, or had been involved in torture, it is hard to see who the victim might be, as months had elapsed since their last known murder. It is possible that the injury was caused during a game, or a row, with Fred; Rose intimated to her mother, Daisy, that she had been cut in this way on at least one occasion. But maybe there was another victim at this time, the details of whom have never been discovered.

Incredibly, Fred and Rose still did not stop killing. Three months after Rose's hospitalisation yet another young girl found her way into their cellar.

BORN Shirley Lloyd in Birmingham in 1959, Shirley Hubbard was a strikingly attractive teenager who had been taken into care at the age of two, following her parents' separation. When she was six she was fostered by council workman Jim Hubbard and his wife, and went to live with them in their large, double-fronted villa in Ombersley Road, Droitwich. It was from this family that Shirley adopted the surname Hubbard, although her name was never legally changed.

Shirley was a rebellious girl, who knew she was attractive to men and often flirted with them. She attended Droitwich High School, and first ran away from home in October 1974 – on that occasion she was found camping in a field with a soldier. A short time after this Shirley met a boy named Daniel Davis at a funfair. Daniel was a salesman at John Collier, the tailors. He made a date to take Shirley to the cinema. (Coincidentally, his older brother Alan, who worked on the fair, had formerly dated Carol Ann Cooper, but the two girls did not know each other.)

They ate ice cream while the film played, and kissed and cuddled. Afterwards they had hot dogs. Other dates followed: Daniel
went shopping with Shirley and she had tea with his parents. On
14 November 1974, when Shirley was aged fifteen and a half
years old, she spent the day working at the make-up counter at
Debenhams in Worcester, where she had been employed for a
month on work experience. Shirley left the store in high spirits
because she had a date. She met up with Daniel, they bought a
bag of chips and went and sat by the River Severn in Worcester,
watching the boats go by. At 9:30 P.M. Daniel saw his girlfriend
on to the Droitwich bus, arranging to meet her the next day at
the bus stop.

But when the next day came, Shirley was not on the bus she
said she would catch, or the next one, or even the one after that.
Daniel decided she had probably made other arrangements and
walked away, slightly upset. He never saw her again.

It is not known how Shirley came into the clutches of Fred
and Rose. She was not acquainted with the Wests, and had no
connection with Cromwell Street. She was probably picked up at
a bus stop, offered a lift in the same way as Lucy Partington, and
must then have been taken to Cromwell Street where she
became a toy for Fred and Rose's sexual games. In their search
for excitement, Fred and Rose subjected this slight fifteen-year-
old to an even more extreme form of bondage.

They wrapped tape around her head eleven or twelve times
to create a shiny brown mask which stopped just beneath her
eyes, with a strap of tape under her chin. A transparent plastic
tube with an internal diameter of one eighth of an inch was
inserted through the mask. It extended for three inches up
through one of her nostrils into the nasal cavity, while twelve
inches extended outside the mask. This device was an extreme
variation on the bondage pornography that Fred and Rose collected. In this unusual fetish, women are strapped into rubber or
plastic suits with tiny holes, or constricted, often zipped,

openings. Invariably they are also tied up. Sometimes the mouth and nostrils are covered over and tubes inserted through the masks to allow breathing. The idea is to confine the victim and sexually excite the participants by making the victim helpless to resist the sex act that follows. In Shirley's case, the device had a secondary purpose of keeping her absolutely silent, and yet still alive. Without the tube, Shirley would simply have been suffocated by the mask.

After her inevitable death, Shirley's naked body was dismembered and her remains concealed in the cellar, her decapitated head, which had been cut off from front to back, still encased in its mask with the tube lolling out. She was buried – minus a section of her trunk, including the third thoracic vertebrae, seven wrist bones and thirteen finger and toe bones – in what became known to police as the 'Marilyn Monroe' area of the cellar, so named because of the wallpaper which featured pictures of the film star. The cellar had now become a charnel-house, with four dismembered corpses buried within feet of each other.

Shirley's disappearance was reported, and enquiries were made, but the police could not pick up the trail. There were several 'sightings' of Shirley in later years, but it is now apparent they were tragically inaccurate.

To kill and cut up a human being is, as has been stated, no easy task, and one wonders why nobody noticed four young women being murdered in the house within a space of twelve months. Professor Bernard Knight estimates that a non-medical man like Fred might be able to remove a head and legs fairly easily within half an hour, and would become more adept at the work with practice. But the problems of disposing of the bodies would be formidable. Even if the victims had been left for several hours, or days, after death (which is very unlikely), the amount of blood caused by dismemberment would have been considerable, and not all of it can have soaked into the ground. The professor confirms that, when cut up, corpses ooze blood even after the heart has stopped pumping. This blood would have been on Fred's hands and all over his clothes, and there would have been stains in the cellar. The smell of rotting human flesh is also distinctive.

At the same time there were also the victims' clothes and personal effects to dispose of. The remains of Lynda Gough, Carol Ann Cooper, Lucy Partington, Thérèse Siegenthaler and Shirley Hubbard were all found virtually naked, and there were neither purses nor handbags in their graves – in fact hardly any personal possessions at all.

Several people, including children and lodgers, continued to live at 25 Cromwell Street while this mayhem was going on. It is true that Cromwell Street was badly lit at night, and that Number 25 was in a particularly dark part of the street, but it seems odd that nobody noticed young girls being forcibly bundled into the house, no doubt kicking and struggling to get away. Nobody saw women's clothes being burned on the bonfire, as they probably were, or strange items of jewellery appearing in the house. The only complaint by lodgers was of a slight fusty smell, and of bangings and crashings in the cellar late at night. In retrospect, it is all too clear what those noises were.

12

BETRAYAL OF TRUST

JUANITA MOTT, WHO had been staying at Cromwell Street as a lodger, was another teenager from a broken home. The daughter of a US Army serviceman, Juanita's parents had split up when she was a child. She went to live with her mother, Mary, who had remarried. Juanita left school at fifteen, and in her search for an affordable bedsitter to rent, found her way to Cromwell Street, where the Wests were offering very cheap accommodation at the time – as low as £7 per week. They advertised in the *Gloucester Citizen* evening newspaper, but most of their lodgers heard about Cromwell Street by word-of-mouth, and several young women were already living in the top two floors of the house. Juanita was a regular visitor over the next couple of years, eventually retaining her own door key.

By the spring of 1975 Juanita was eighteen years old: a pretty, brown-haired girl of average height who bore a striking resemblance to Carol Ann Cooper. She had worked briefly in a bottling factory, but was now unemployed and lodging with a friend of the family, Jennifer Baldwin, at her bungalow in the small Gloucestershire town of Newent. Jennifer was due to get married on Saturday 12 April 1975, and Juanita had offered to look after her children during the ceremony.

Juanita often hitch-hiked into Gloucester at weekends, and it seems that this is what she intended to do when she left the bungalow on the evening before the wedding. To catch a lift into the city, she normally stood beside the B4215. This quiet country road also happens to be the most direct route between Gloucester and Much Marcle.

Fred and Rose would have known Juanita's habits and the place where she picked up lifts. They were probably waiting, and offered her a ride in much the same way as they had picked up Caroline Owens outside the Gupshill Manor pub two and a half years before.

At Cromwell Street Juanita was gagged with a ligature made from two long, white nylon socks (similar to those often worn by Rose), a brassière and two pairs of tights one within the other. She was then trussed up with lengths of plastic-covered rope, of the type used for washing line. The rope was used in a complicated way, with loops tied around her arms and thighs, both wrists, both ankles and her skull, horizontally and vertically, backwards and forwards across her body until she could only wriggle like a trapped animal. Then the Wests produced a seven-foot length of rope with a slip-knot end forming a noose. This was probably used to suspend Juanita's body from the beams in the cellar.

Restriction of breathing – one part of the extreme bondage Fred and Rose found exciting – probably led to Juanita's death. It is also possible, however, that she was killed by a blow to the back of the head with an implement like a ball-headed hammer. There was an unusual fracture at the base of her skull suggesting this, but it would be an awkward wound to inflict while she was alive and was more probably done while Fred was dismembering her body. Again, he decapitated his victim, removed her legs at the hip and kept aside three of her neck vertebrae, her eleventh thoracic vertebrae, the first rib, both her kneecaps, pieces of her hands, toes, and other parts of her feet: more than eighty bones in total. Juanita's butchered remains were then buried three to four feet beneath the cellar floor, between the staircase and the second alcove. The lengths of washing line, and pieces of clothing including a pair of women's briefs, were also thrown into the pit.

There had been no indication that Juanita would run away. She often went into Gloucester for the evening, and had not taken any of her personal possessions with her. Most significantly, she had promised to look after Jennifer Baldwin's children, and it was unlikely that she would deliberately let her down, especially on her wedding day. Yet, despite these suspicious circumstances, Juanita's family failed to report her to the police as a missing person. If they had done so, Juanita's known links with Cromwell Street might have been investigated.

THE police did visit 25 Cromwell Street, and quite frequently, but not to investigate murder. They came to interview Fred about the petty theft and receiving of stolen goods in which he was always involved. They also came to check reports that the Wests' lodgers were in possession of cannabis, and minor 'drug busts' were commonplace at the house. There were at least three unannounced visits from drug squad officers in the early 1970s, one resulting in the arrest of a lodger. Gloucester drug squad detectives Price and Castle became familiar faces at the house, and former lodger Benjamin Stanniland admits that the male lodgers were 'known to police'. This is partly why Fred and Rose began a policy of renting only to young women. Yet the police searches never revealed anything more incriminating than the occasional illegal cigarette (belonging to the lodgers, not Fred and Rose, who had no interest in drugs). The Wests' composure during these visits was remarkable, considering what was concealed beneath their feet.

Fred continued to make regular appearances in the local

courts. On 25 March 1975 he was found guilty of theft and fined £50 by Gloucester magistrates; in November he was convicted of receiving stolen goods and fined £75.

There was little to indicate to his neighbours or to the police that Fred was anything other than a normal, if light-fingered, jobbing builder. He chatted amiably with those he came into contact with and impressed all who met him with his energy and hard work. Fred had recently demolished the garage behind the house and was building a large flat-roofed extension, complete with plumbing for a bathroom, toilet and kitchen. Neighbours noticed that the whole family helped him: digging foundations, mixing cement and carrying building blocks. Fred worked late into the night, long after the children had gone to bed. 'Dad was always building,' says his daughter Anna Marie.

But nothing at 25 Cromwell Street was quite as it seemed, and, unknown to his neighbours and children, part of the reason for building the extension was to cover up the grave of Lynda Gough, the Co-op seamstress whose remains were buried in the inspection pit where the garage had been.

These home improvements cost money, and in the spring of 1976 Fred travelled away from Gloucester to earn some extra cash. He spent seven months in Cumbria, where British Gas were laying a pipeline across the Pennines. Fred was attracted by the high wages of £200 per week, and was taken on first as a general labourer and then as a welder's mate. He was known as 'The Wog' by workmates because they thought he had negroid features.

He lodged at the Belted Will Inn in the village of Hallbankgate on the Tindale Fells, near Carlisle, and at an address in Brampton. Deprived of his regular trips to 'bunny-land' with Rose, Fred had to look elsewhere for sex. One evening he tuned into a radio phone-in programme on which callers offered household items for sale. A lady who had been trying to sell a gas fire on the programme later received a telephone call from Fred.

'I'm not interested in the fire,' he said. 'I'm far more interested in you.' He pestered the woman with telephone calls, often obscene, for several days.

One night Fred disappeared from the Belted Will Inn without settling his £7 bill, leaving a suitcase of clothes behind – and, more significantly, neglecting to collect his pay. He travelled back to Gloucester and was never seen in the area again. It seems he had been picking up women in his usual way when something had gone wrong, forcing him to flee.

BACK in Gloucester, Fred and Rose continued to look for victims, and they devised a sophisticated new method of finding them. A children's home known as Jordan's Brook House was situated in nearby Upton Lane. It cared for delinquent girls, most of whom had already been expelled from other homes. They were vulnerable adolescents, often from deeply troubled families, and easily corrupted by people like the Wests.

Jordan's Brook House had been built in 1970 as an 'Approved School'. Girls were admitted when they were fifteen and a half years old, and part of the institution's function was to introduce them to training and eventually full employment.

It was a strict institution, with an average of twenty-four girls sharing nineteen bedrooms. The girls were graded weekly on their behaviour, and these grades were pinned up for display each Friday tea-time. The amount of freedom the girls were allowed was determined by these grades. There were also curfews, mail was opened, and any boyfriends had to be vetted by the staff. This tough regime often caused the frustrated delinquents to run away. A favourite trick was to set off the fire alarm, as this automatically triggered the opening of secure doors and windows allowing the girls to flee across the fields. The police were immediately contacted, and, usually within a few hours, all were brought back to the home hungry, penniless and tired out.

Fred began to cruise past Jordan's Brook in the Ford Transit van that had now become his main means of transport, offering a lift to girls he saw. The Wests did not snatch these teenagers off the street and rape them; they had thought of a more subtle, less dangerous approach. They tried to forge friendships with the girls, and invited them back to Cromwell Street for orange squash and biscuits. Rose would listen sympathetically to their problems and, at first, nothing happened to frighten or alarm them.

The girls went back to Jordan's Brook and described the fun they had enjoyed at Cromwell Street. They told their friends what nice people the Wests were, that the woman had been in care herself and really understood them. Soon news of the sympathetic couple, and their cosy home, spread throughout Jordan's Brook and other institutions in the area, and many young girls drifted towards the narrow little house by the Seventh-Day Adventist Church. One such girl was a teenager who, to protect her identity, can only be referred to as Miss A.[*]

Like so many of Fred and Rose's victims, Miss A's childhood had not been a happy one. Her parents were divorced and she had been sexually abused by both her father and her brother. At the age of thirteen she was placed in a Gloucester children's home named Russet House, and it was here that she heard about 25 Cromwell Street from an older teenager who gave her cigarettes. One day they visited the house together, absconding from the home – or, as Miss A describes it, 'running away through the windows', as this was literally and spiritually what they did when they left without authority. Rose gave them orange drinks and listened as they narrated their troubles. 'She was nice and pleasant, understanding and caring. She said I could come and cry on her shoulder any time,' said Miss A.

By the summer of 1976, Miss A had moved to Jordan's Brook

---

[*] Miss A's identity is protected by a court order.

House, where she was given a senior 'trustworthiness' grade which meant she could leave the home for extended periods. Also, once every three weeks, usually on a Friday, she was granted a paid visit home to her mother in Tewkesbury. On her way to the bus station Miss A fell into the habit of dropping into Cromwell Street to see Rose.

She could not help but notice that the house was full of children. There were so many children, in fact, that Miss A assumed that some were in care, just like herself. This is odd, because only four children should have been living at the house at this time: Anna Marie, who was twelve in July that year; Heather, five; Mae, who was four in June; and three-year-old Stephen (Fred's other son had gone back to Scotland). But Miss A may be correct in thinking there were more.

There is evidence that the Wests were working as foster parents. It is extraordinary that this could have been allowed to happen, as both Fred and Rose had a serious criminal conviction for assaulting a teenage girl. Yet Rose's younger brother, Graham Letts, remembers his sister looking after at least two foster children. 'She took in a boy and a girl, but she didn't have them very long. I think they were brother and sister. They came together and then they went back to the foster home,' he says.

Miss A ran away from Jordan's Brook House, and went to Cromwell Street because Rose had always been so understanding. She had even received a fifteenth birthday card from the Wests. 'We built up a trust,' she says. When she first called at the house, there was no reply, so she went and waited in The Park, returning at 11 P.M. This time Rose came to the door. She was only wearing underwear, but invited the teenager in. Miss A told Rose about all her problems and Rose put her arm around the child to console her – after all, she had been in care herself when she was fifteen. But now Rose was a hardened 23-year-old woman, and she used her experience to manipulate and betray

Miss A's trust. 'Rose had her arm about me. She started kissing me and my neck and touched my breasts. It was sexual and I pushed her away,' says Miss A. She spent the night at the house and later returned to Jordan's Brook, too embarrassed to tell anybody what had happened.

IT was six weeks before Miss A was trusted to be given another visit home. When she did, she again went to Cromwell Street. Rose was wearing a see-through blouse, and this time they slept together in the lounge. When Miss A got up to go to the toilet, Rose followed and called out to Fred. Miss A heard the Wests talking together outside the bathroom door. When she came out, Rose pushed her into a room where she was startled to see two naked girls, one on the floor and the other on the bed. Fred was also in the room, wearing a pair of shorts and a shirt. One of the naked girls was blonde with brightly painted toenails. She appeared to be aged about fourteen. The other was dark and slightly older. Rose came up to Miss A and said that it was 'all right to touch and feel affection'. Miss A recognised the same manipulative language that had been used to her years before, when she had been molested previously. Rose then undid Miss A's dress, saying they were 'all girls together'. Miss A felt utterly helpless, as if she were pinned to the wall of a fairground ride – terrified but unable to bring it to a stop.

Miss A watched as Rose performed a strip-tease to arouse Fred. Rose then lay on the bed with one of the naked girls, who was struggling to get away. Rose repeated her coaxing line: 'It's natural to touch.' Fred peeled off a piece of brown masking tape and bound the child's wrists, being careful to leave her fingers free. Rose turned the girl on to her stomach as Fred taped her ankles in such a way as to splay her legs apart until she was in pain. Looking around the room, Miss A saw a cat-o'-nine-tails whip (which Fred had made himself) on the wall and strange pictures of animals and people (Fred was fascinated by the idea of sex between women and animals, and it was one of his more outlandish fantasies to watch Rose having intercourse with a bull).

Fred and Rose began to kiss. Rose was holding a vibrator, a white candle six inches long and a tube of ointment. She said to Fred, 'Are you enjoying this now?' and buggered the girl with the vibrator so that she screamed. Rose removed Fred's shirt and underpants as he bent down to kiss the girl's anus. He then penetrated the child while Rose fondled his buttocks – Miss A could see the look of pain on the girl's face. She looked like she was in 'outer space'. When Fred ejaculated, Rose asked him, 'Did you enjoy that?' She then ripped the masking tape from the child, hurting her. 'She had a look of hate on her face,' said Miss A, describing Rose's maniacal expression. The victim of this assault began to suck her hair for comfort.

Miss A found herself naked, with Rose caressing her and saying, 'Enjoy! It's all right.' She was rigid with fear, and Rose said, 'I like stiff ones!' Miss A sat on the bed with her hands covering her breasts, feeling ashamed and knowing that she was next. Rose wound masking tape around Miss A's wrists, binding them together. 'The other girl looked terrified and really sad,' she said. Rose became aggressive and pushed Miss A back on to the bed, where the teenager buried her head in the sheets, counting as Rose wrapped the tape around her ankles five times. She heard a buzzing sound and felt a plastic vibrator moving near her vagina. Rose asked, 'Is that nice, Fred?'

Miss A felt a smooth female hand with long scratchy nails inside her vagina and her nipples being twisted painfully hard. Rose said, 'This is fun! It's great!' Miss A was then buggered either with a candle or a perfume spray; afterwards Fred had intercourse with her. He was telling Rose how close he was to climaxing and Rose encouraged him to ejaculate over Miss A's back. When he was finished, Rose produced a tiny pair of silver scissors which she used to snip away the masking tape, cutting the child's thumb as she did so. Then Miss A went to the bathroom, where she used the bundle of tape to wipe herself. She noticed that she was bleeding. She put her dress back on, but left her shoes and walked barefoot from the house and away from Cromwell Street, crying.

It was now four in the afternoon, and she continued on her journey to her mother's home in Tewkesbury, where she was told off for being late. She felt defiled, but was unable to tell anybody about her ordeal because 'if you were in care, you were bad' – so she hid in her bedroom and rocked back and forth with her knees drawn up under her chin for comfort.

SIX weeks later Miss A was again due for a paid home visit. Before she left Jordan's Brook House, she went to the groundsman's shed and took a Castrol oil can filled with petrol. She carried the can into the centre of Gloucester, and says she fully intended to burn 25 Cromwell Street to the ground. But when she reached the front door of the tall narrow building, the strength of will to carry out the plan deserted her, and she left the oil can behind a shop.

'All this occurred without my consent,' she says of her ordeal at the house. 'They comforted [me] and then they used me. I couldn't trust anybody following this.'

ONE of the little girls that Miss A had seen in the house may well have been Anna Marie, who was twelve but looked older. As Anna Marie had progressed through puberty, she had suffered increasingly severe abuse. She had started to menstruate between the ages of nine and ten, but was denied sanitary towels or tampons by her father. 'Dad said my period blood should flow freely.'

Rose took pornographic photographs of Anna Marie with a Polaroid camera. She also hit her, saying that nobody must ever see the marks that she made. If the bruises were too bad, Anna Marie was kept away from school. The indignities were endless and bizarre: one day Anna Marie was thrust into a bath of almost boiling water, scalding her. Afterwards Rose massaged baby oil into Anna Marie's breasts, scratching with her fingernails until the child bled. On another occasion the West children were instructed to daub Anna Marie's naked body with finger paints. Rose painted the words 'black hole' on her buttocks, with an arrow pointing down. Rose took a photograph and made the child stay in this humiliating position until Fred came home. The woman who instigated these sadistic acts even demanded to be called 'mother'. 'I called her Rose until Dad smacked me,' says Anna Marie.

Rose had become very aggressive, quite different to the doe-eyed teenager Fred had first met. She flew into irrational rages from which nobody, not even Fred, was safe. But she reserved much of her anger for Anna Marie, resenting her because she was not her natural child. Rose beat Anna Marie with a stick, and on one occasion, stabbed her in the arm for being 'a naughty girl'. Anna Marie was locked in the cellar for hours on end and made to do housework until three in the morning, only ever being allowed upstairs to clean.

The ingenuity Fred and Rose employed in their sexual sadism was extraordinary. Fred made a type of chastity belt for his daughter, consisting of a cup with a battery-powered vibrator inside. This was strapped around Anna Marie's waist before she was made to walk around the house wearing it, purely for Rose's amusement. When Fred came home from work, Rose gleefully described the humiliation Anna Marie had endured during the day. At school, Anna Marie became a problem child, a bully, and was eventually expelled. But she knew better than to talk to her teachers about what went on at home.

Anna Marie wanted to attend discos, but her father told her she needed 'a man not a boy'. She was aged about twelve when Rose first made her have sex with her West Indian customers. This happened in the bedroom at the front of the house, known as 'Mum and Dad's Room', which had a plaque on the wall with Rose's name on it. Beneath this plaque was a spy-hole for Fred to look through. A wooden plug was fitted in the door, painted the same green to disguise it, and when it was removed Fred had a clear view of everything Rose was doing (although he had to kneel down to take his pleasure, because the hole was so low). There was a red lightbulb in the living room which was operated from 'Mum and Dad's Room': if it was on, the other children knew not to go in.

Some of the men were workmates of Fred's. At first he stood in the doorway and watched as his daughter had sex with them. Rose was also there in the room. 'Rose said I would be able to please my husband [when she was older]. I was a lucky girl,' she says. Anna Marie was only thankful that she was not being beaten. One day a man brought Anna Marie a gift of chocolates, but Rose took even this little pleasure away from her and ate them all. Rose started taking Anna Marie out to a local night-club called Tracy's, where they would drink Malibu and Coke and pick up men together.

Anna Marie still doted on her father, grateful that he rarely hit her. 'I'm talking about a dad I love,' she says. She even felt love for Rose.

Fred was working as a jobbing builder on house conversions and often took Anna Marie with him when he went out. He had put a piece of carpet down in the back of his van, and whenever he felt aroused, would stop the van and cuddle his daughter. 'He was always ready for sex,' she says. He did not even bother to get undressed, but simply loosened his trousers. Sometimes they had sex in the empty houses where he was working, sometimes in woods. She learned, in her childish way, that if a purple light came up on the dashboard – because Fred had switched the engine off but kept the ignition on to work the heater – then she was about to be raped. When her father forced his tongue into her mouth, she had to struggle to resist a natural urge to bite it off. He later bribed her not to tell Rose, giving her money to buy sweets.

One summer evening, Rose announced that they were taking Anna Marie to a pub. Rose helped her dress and put on make-up, 'like an older sister', but the real purpose was to disguise her youth. She wore a dress because Rose hated her to wear trousers. 'She said she wanted the air to get to me.' When they were ready, Fred took them out into the countryside and dropped them at a small pub.

Rose bought a succession of bottles of barley wine. Anna Marie said she did not want any more, but Rose insisted in a 'nice, but subtly domineering way'. Soon Anna Marie was quite drunk. Rose was flirting with a group of men, but something went wrong and they had to leave in a hurry. It is likely that the men discovered the truth about Anna Marie's age and relationship to Rose, possibly because of something Anna Marie said.

Rose kept looking behind her as they walked away. They were quickly picked up by Fred, who had been waiting in the van. When they were inside Rose turned on Anna Marie 'like an animal', tearing the child's clothes off with such violence that she cut her. Rose said that if Anna Marie thought they could be friends, then she was mistaken; she could not have a joke with her. 'I was held down by Rose as Dad raped me. He'd done it before so I knew what to expect,' she said.

As she lay there, Anna Marie recalled wondering who was looking after her half-brothers and half-sisters.

'I was only a child and I did not understand,' she said.

13

FLESH AND BLOOD

TWENTY-FIVE CROMWELL Street had been divided into two distinct sections by 1977. The upstairs floors had been fully converted into bedsitters, complete with self-contained cooking and bathroom facilities. The West family lived on the ground floor, which had been enlarged by an extension built where the garage had been.

The lodgers were mostly unskilled, single women who worked in local shops and factories. Up to seven of them lived at the house at one time. They became friendly with one another, holding parties in their rooms, going out as a group and inviting boyfriends back to the house. None stayed for long and there was always a new girl around. One of these was a plain young woman named Shirley Robinson.

Shirley had been born in the county of Rutland, the daughter of RAF Corporal Royal Baden Robinson, known as Roy, and his partner, Christa Carling. They lived near RAF Cottesmore in Lincolnshire. Christa left home when Shirley was three, taking the child with her, but it did not work out and Shirley went back to live with her father, then based in Wolverhampton. Shirley soon fell into delinquency, and by the age of thirteen was selling herself as a prostitute. By the age of fifteen she was living in a children's home in Bristol; in 1977, she was transferred into the care of Gloucester social services. Her social worker described her as 'extremely withdrawn and sullen' and noted that Shirley had lesbian girlfriends much older than herself.

She was working as a prostitute in the Gloucester area when she met Rose. Shirley, then aged eighteen, came to live at 25 Cromwell Street, taking a tiny room on the first floor at the back of the house. She found both men and women attractive and was entirely open about being bisexual. Fred and Rose were excited by this, and a *ménage à trois* developed between them.

Fred and Rose were experimenting with the concept of a completely open relationship. Rose went out at nights on her own to pubs, sometimes returning home in the morning with presents of alcohol and boxes of chocolates, sometimes staying away for several days. She even came close to leaving Fred, taking a flat in Stroud Road where she entertained various boyfriends, but Fred found out about this and put a stop to it. 'My father wasn't very pleased,' recalled Anna Marie.

As well as their relationship with Shirley Robinson and others, both Fred and Rose continued to abuse Anna Marie. Rose forced her stepdaughter to bring her to orgasm by performing cunnilingus, while Fred had developed an obsession with trying to breed the 'perfect child'. Tired of simply raping Anna Marie, he attempted to carry out bizarre experiments with her.

One day Anna Marie remembers Rose having intercourse with a coloured man. When the man had ejaculated, the condom he had been using was removed and handed to Fred, who then placed it inside Anna Marie's vagina. She was made to sit for a while before Fred took it out again. Other children were nearby, and Anna Marie watched them as Fred continued with his experiment. She noticed copper piping, a dish and a syringe in the bathroom, and these things also seemed to be involved in what was happening. 'I heard somebody say, "We will see if this works and gets you pregnant,"' she says.

FRED was delighted when Rose became pregnant by one of these coloured men. He said that blacks were 'better breeders' than whites, and more likely to sire the perfect child. He also hoped Rose had a boy, because there were already enough girls in the house. With all this going on it is little wonder that lodgers remember wails of sexual excitement coming from Rose's room, sometimes so loud that lodger Gillian Britt says she had to turn her radio up to drown them out. But these disturbing noises were not only made by Rose. Another lodger, Jane Haymer, remembers children screaming in the night, and the piercing cry 'Stop it, Daddy!' coming from the cellar on one occasion. It was the voice of a young girl, but she did not trouble to report it to any of the authorities.

Shortly afterwards Shirley discovered she was carrying Fred's child. This, too, was quite open. During the hot part of the summer Shirley spent hours sitting out on the wall in front of the house, trying to keep cool and chatting to neighbours about her relationship with Fred, while devouring the red Mr Men ice lollies she reserved specially at the Wellington Stores. One day Rose came outside and cheerfully confirmed the news, pointing at Shirley's stomach and telling neighbour Linda Greening, 'It's Fred's!' She then pointed to her own, more advanced pregnancy and said, 'I wonder what colour it will be?' Rose said they planned to bring up the two children together.

Both Rose's character and appearance became increasingly eccentric as her pregnancy developed. She took to wearing maternity dresses without underwear, and often sat on the back step of the house with her legs open and skirt up. There were other oddities, as one lodger remembers: 'She dressed as a child,

19. Anna McFall came from a poor, unhappy background in Glasgow. She became Fred West's nanny, and then his lover, and was murdered while pregnant with his child in 1967.

20. Mary Bastholm, the fifteen-year-old waitress who went missing in 1968 and has never been seen since. Police, and her brother, believe she too died at the hands of Fred West, but Fred refused to talk to detectives about Mary.

21. Charmaine (left), shortly before she was murdered in April 1971. Her body was concealed in a hole behind the back door of 25 Midland Road. With her are six-month-old Heather and Anna Marie, aged six.

22. Rena Costello, Fred's first wife, murdered by him in 1971. Her background was one of delinquency and prostitution. Fred beat her during their marriage and conducted relationships with numerous other women.

23. Lynda Gough, the Co-op seamstress murdered in April 1973, was a regular visitor to 25 Cromwell Street, where she sometimes looked after the Wests' children.

24. Carol Ann Cooper, known as 'Caz', came from a broken home, and was living in care when she disappeared and was murdered in 1973.

25. Lucy Partington, who went missing in December 1973, was probably murdered in January 1974. She was a university student from a middle-class family.

26. Thérèse Siegenthaler, murdered in April 1974. She was a Swiss citizen, living and studying in London, and had planned to hitch-hike to Ireland for the Easter holidays.

27. Shirley Hubbard, murdered in November 1974, was another teenager with a troubled background. It is not known how she came to 25 Cromwell Street, but her dismembered remains were found there in 1994.

28. Juanita Mott, murdered in 1975. Juanita went missing the night before a friend's wedding. Despite the suspicious circumstances, her disappearance was not reported to police.

30. Alison Chambers, murdered in 1979. Fred and Rose told this impressionable girl that they owned a farm, where she could come to live and spend peaceful days writing poetry.

29. Shirley Robinson, who was pregnant with Fred's child when she was murdered in 1978. Rose had been furiously jealous of Fred's affection for Shirley.

31. Fred and Rose's daughter, Heather. She was raped by her father, and was trying to get a job that would take her away from Cromwell Street when she was murdered by her parents in 1987.

32. Fred and Rose. At Rose's trial for multiple murder in 1995, the court heard that the Wests 'shared a knowledge of each other which bound them together'. They were jointly responsible for the murders of at least nine young women and girls.

33. Twenty-five Cromwell Street, Gloucester, where Fred and Rose West lived for twenty-two years. The remains of nine young women were found here in 1994.

34. Fred, at a children's party in the 1970s, appears happy and carefree. But he was obsessed with sex and was murdering as many as three girls a year.

35. On Christmas Day Fred pauses long enough in his DIY to eat with his family. He is sitting in the breakfast bar area of the downstairs extension to 25 Cromwell Street.

36. Family portrait on Anna Marie's wedding day, January 1985, at 25 Cromwell Street. Rose is on the far left, with Mae in front of her. Anna Marie's new husband, Chris Davis, sits next to Rose holding two children. Next to him is Anna Marie; next to Fred are his son Steve and eldest daughter Heather (far right).

37. Fred West and his brother, John (far left), toast Anna Marie on her wedding day.

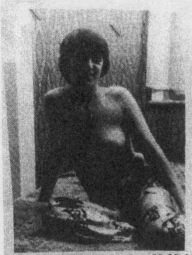

West Indian W.E. male. Age 50-60 for sex with young housewife with view to living in. 417673. See photo. Gloucester.

38. One of the adverts Rose regularly placed in contact magazines to attract new sexual partners.

39. The 'Black Magic' bar, where Rose entertained her clients. It is decorated for the celebration of Mae's twenty-first birthday.

41. Kathryn Halliday conducted a sexual relationship with both Fred and Rose West in the late 1980s. She stopped seeing the couple after becoming frightened by Rose's increasingly violent lovemaking.

40. Caroline Owens worked briefly for Fred and Rose as a nanny in 1972. After leaving Cromwell Street she was abducted by the Wests, beaten and raped. When the case went to court, Fred and Rose were fined £50 each and released.

always wearing white schoolgirl socks. I didn't think she was quite right in the head.'

Rose strode about the house in this unconventional clothing, screaming at the children and giving orders to the lodgers, and even Fred – she had become much more assertive in the relationship. 'Initially my mum was young and impressionable, but as she got older she became more dominant,' says Anna Marie. It was noticed that Fred shied away from Rose when she was angry. 'Out of the two of them, Rose would be expected to lose her temper,' says Liz Brewer, who lodged at the house at this time. Liz also remembers a conversation she had with Rose when Liz had said that a relation of hers was leaving her husband. Rose commented that whatever Fred did, she would never leave him.

Rose had tolerated Shirley's pregnancy at first, but as Fred took his lover into their bed and flaunted the relationship, Rose became jealous. Shirley and Fred were seen kissing outside her room, and boastfully announced their affair to other lodgers. He taunted Rose by patting Shirley's bulging stomach and saying that she would be his next wife. Rose's relationship with Shirley worsened as her rival's pregnancy began to show, and she insisted on walking around the house dressed only in her underwear. Fred revelled in the idea of two women competing for his affection. However, he could also be curiously secretive about Shirley, and was eager to hide the truth from outsiders, including Rose's mother, Daisy, who had become suspicious. When she questioned Fred about his friendship with Shirley, he replied, 'I'm not with that woman. I've got the woman I want – I've got Rosie. I don't want nobody else.' Daisy accepted this assurance, just as she had accepted the disappearance of Charmaine. In the years since the girl had vanished from the West home, Rose's family had done nothing to locate the child other than having one conversation about possibly hiring a private detective to trace her.

In November that year Shirley and Fred devised a bizarre plan to profit by her pregnancy – they decided they could make money by selling their baby to a childless couple. They even had their picture taken for an advertisement. Shirley put on a cream-coloured jacket and a floral dress. Fred brushed his hair and wore a grey three-piece suit with an aquamarine nylon tie. They visited a photographic studio in Gloucester and paid £5.10 for a set of four prints.

Shirley wrote to her father Roy, who was then working as a welder in Germany, enthusing about the relationship and enclosing one of the photographs. The picture showed her and Fred holding hands while looking straight at the camera. 'This is the man I'm going to marry,' she wrote. 'What do you think of him, Dad? I have never been so happy in my life.' Shirley unwisely repeated the marriage boast at 25 Cromwell Street, and it was this that Rose could not tolerate; she became mad with jealousy and Fred realised the affair had gone too far. It had never been his intention to allow Shirley to take Rose's place, and now he began to regret that she was having his child.

ROSE'S father, Bill Letts, had taken voluntary redundancy from Smith's Industries, leaving with a sizeable pay-off. When Bill received the money, he left Rose's mother and travelled around Devon, living the high life, but became unwell after a couple of years and returned to Gloucester to find a business in which to invest his remaining money. Bill had come to accept Rose's marriage, and had developed a grudging respect for Fred, so they agreed to go into partnership together. They first tried to launch a small industrial cleaning business. When that failed, they opened a café, with Bill putting up the money, Fred carrying out the renovation work and Rose's brother-in-law, Jim Tyler, supplying the materials.

By the time the café was finished, Fred had decided to end his relationship with Shirley Robinson. One day over dinner in the café, he told Jim Tyler, 'She wants to get between me and Rose. She wants Rosie out so she can take over and take her place. I'm not having that. She's got to fucking go.'

Rose gave birth to a baby daughter on 9 December 1977: a child of mixed race whom Rose named Tara. Fred was delighted. He thought Tara was a beautiful baby, particularly because of her colouring, and gave her the unusual nickname of 'Moses'. This was meant blasphemously: Fred felt he was God-like because he was overseeing the breeding of 'perfect children'. Both Fred and Rose later told the police about their extreme excitement at the birth of this child, and how they had been 'ecstatically happy' because of it.

The atmosphere of tension and impending violence intensified nevertheless. Rose was more and more antagonistic towards Shirley, intimidating her rival to such an extent that Shirley moved out of her room and began to sleep on fellow-lodger Liz Brewer's sofa, even staying there during the day. Liz believes that Shirley had become frightened of the Wests, and says she 'needed to keep away from them'.

Shirley's baby was due on 11 June 1978. She was nervous and emotional as the date approached. 'She was a lonely person who latched on to people. She didn't have many friends,' says Liz Brewer. On 2 May, Shirley visited a health centre in Cheltenham to see her GP, Dr John Buckley; on 9 May, she posed with Liz for a picture in the Photo-me booth at Woolworths. It was the last picture that was ever taken of her, and the last time she was seen alive.

THE Wests murdered Shirley, probably strangling her to death, because she was a threat to their relationship. Whether it was Fred or Rose who actually throttled her is unknown. If Rose had been in one of her rages, she would have been quite capable of killing her rival. The crime was not motivated by sex, and there is no evidence that Shirley was subjected to torture before she died, like many of the Wests' other victims. Fred and Rose simply wanted to get rid of her.

The cellar was already full of human remains, so Fred dug a hole for Shirley in the back garden, although he probably carried out the dismemberment of the body in the cellar, rather than over the grave. Fred seems to have hacked the corpse into pieces like a man in a rage. Eight distinct marks on Shirley's right thighbone show that a heavy cleaver, or axe, was brought crashing down on her leg. With the ninth blow, Fred managed to chop the bone clean in two. Her kneecaps were removed and her head cut off. He removed two of her ribs, parts of her wrists and ankles – numbering twenty-eight bones – and many of her fingers and toes. It is also possible that Fred scalped his former lover: no hair was ever found in Shirley's grave. This is highly unusual, as human hair can last for decades – even centuries – after death, and hair was found with the remains of all the other victims. This whole extraordinary mutilation of a pregnant young woman would have been a vile undertaking, soaking Fred in blood from head to toe, making his hands sticky where he gripped the cleaver and the floor slippery with human remains.

The foetus in Shirley's womb was eight months advanced, almost full term. It is not possible to know for sure if Fred cut the foetus from her body, but with his expressed interest in abortions, it is not unlikely that he was curious to find out if they would have had a son or a daughter. It has been suggested that Fred removed the foetus after Shirley was dead because he wondered whether it would still be alive. Whatever happened that night, the unborn child's matchstick-like skeleton, also missing several tiny bones, was later found nestled beside the jumbled remains of its mother.

★

THE Wests told the other lodgers that Shirley had gone to Germany to live with her father, and 'probably wasn't coming back'. Fred said she had 'done a bunk', insinuating that she had not paid her rent, and added that he did not care about their baby. Both Fred and Rose seemed very happy. Fred told Liz that she was lucky Shirley had gone, because she had been planning to seduce her roommate and 'rip [her] knickers off'. A month later Rose was seen sorting through Shirley's clothes, putting the ones she did not want into a black rubbish bag.

Nobody bothered to report Shirley to the police as a missing person, and consequently no search was made for her. In a bizarre coda to the murder, a bogus claim was later made in Shirley's name to Gloucester social services, for maternity benefit. Because of existing claims, the request was questioned and letters were sent to Cromwell Street. When the letters went unanswered, a DSS worker called at the house only to find that Shirley was no longer living there. It seems that Rose had been using her dead lover's name to try and make some extra money.

It is surprising that Shirley's disappearance, the non-arrival of her child and the bogus maternity claim did not alarm the midwifery service sufficiently to instigate an investigation. Health visitors, who would have carried out such an investigation, were supposed to keep in contact with this department, and could have contacted the police if they felt something was seriously wrong. But Peter Gregson, the DSS worker who visited the house in 1978, admits he was not authorised to question what he was told and had to accept the information given to him about Shirley going to Germany 'on face value'. As a result, there was no investigation into her welfare that extended to informing the police.

Several weeks later the Wests informed their lodgers that they had heard from Shirley in Germany; she had given birth to a baby boy and named him Barry, they said.

But the dreadful truth was that the dismembered remains of

Shirley, and her unborn child, were buried behind the back door
of the house.

To help out further with the family finances, Rose had begun to
advertise her services as a prostitute in contact magazines. A
typical ad read:

> SEXY HOUSEWIFE NEEDS IT
> DEEP AND HARD FROM V.W.E.*
> MALE WHILE HUSBAND WATCHES.
> COLOUREDS WELCOME

Fred had installed a special doorbell for Rose's customers,
who were known within the family as 'Mum and Dad's good
friends'. The bell was labelled 'Mandy', which was Rose's working name, and when it rang Rose stopped whatever she was
doing and disappeared into her room, often leaving food on the
stove. Everybody in the family, and many of the lodgers, knew
what was going on. 'Fred said prostitution was a good way of
making money. Fred and Rose were very open about sex. Each
knew the other's activities and discussed their exploits,' says Liz
Brewer. Fred had fitted baby-listening intercoms in the house,
and sprawled on the living room sofa with a receiver pressed to
his ear while Rose was entertaining.

Many of Rose's customers were what the family described as
'oddballs'. One had a wooden leg; another, a glass eye. Several
requested unusual sexual services. The money she earned from
prostitution was hidden in a drawer, and later paid in to Rose's
Co-op savings account. It was she who had sole control over the

* Very well-endowed.

family finances, collecting the tenants' rent and even taking Fred's pay packet from him each week. He delivered it to Rose unopened, and she gave him back only enough pocket money for cigarettes. Rose recorded details like this in her diary.

Fred and Rose's relationship stabilised after Shirley's murder. They began to sleep together regularly again, and decided to have another child. In Fred's terminology, he decided to 'pot' Rose (meaning make her pregnant) to stop her 'getting topsy' (meaning bad-tempered). A baby daughter, Louise, was born on 17 November 1978, bringing the total number of children in the family to six. There is, however, some doubt whether Louise is Fred's natural daughter or whether her father was one of Rose's boyfriends.

Fred continued to have full intercourse with Anna Marie, and Rose continued to ill-treat her (the child was admitted to hospital in 1978, with puncture wounds to her feet suspiciously similar to injuries suffered by Charmaine years before). Fred believed that incest was natural, and told his daughters, 'I made you. You are my flesh and blood. I am entitled to touch you.' He said that 'Dads' were better at sex than boys, and it was a father's right to take his daughter's virginity. His incestuous relationship with Anna Marie culminated in 1979, when he made her pregnant. Rose took Anna Marie to a doctor, who said that she was two months advanced, but that the pregnancy had begun in her fallopian tube. A termination was carried out at the Gloucestershire Royal Hospital. It was also during this year that a teacher at Anna Marie's school noticed bruising on the child. Social services were informed and a welfare officer came to Cromwell Street, but somehow Rose talked her way out of the situation, and after the visitor had gone Anna Marie received, as she says, the 'hiding of my life. I then presumed what was happening was right and I shouldn't make a fuss. I was told how ungrateful I was.'

*

ROSE's father Bill Letts had been unwell for some time. He also had financial problems after spending his redundancy money. He was sharing a house with Rose's mother in Lidney, a small town in the Forest of Dean, and, even at this stage in his life, was still capable of cruelty. One day Graham Letts walked in to find his father attacking Daisy. 'He had her pinned up against a wall and had already slapped her. He had his hand raised, and was ready to do it again.'

In the spring of 1979, Bill fell seriously ill with plural mesothelioma, the lung complaint he had contracted working in the Plymouth dockyards. Shortly before he died he told Graham he felt his marriage had been a mistake. 'His last words to me were, "Don't get married to the wrong person."' He died on 24 May 1979, aged sixty. Although Daisy was naturally upset, she felt that Bill had made his own life miserable and did not mourn him for long. 'I always felt my husband was a weak character, really,' she says.

Both Fred and Rose attended the burial at the council cemetery in Cheltenham, and Rose did seem to be moved by the experience – although she scandalised her family by arriving for the burial in 'tarty' clothes and black stiletto heels. But few tears were shed for Bill, and no headstone was erected to mark his grave. It is identifiable only as number 1528, a bare patch of earth in a row of marble tablets, like a gap in a set of neglected teeth.

THE most tragic girl to visit Cromwell Street from Jordan's Brook House was a freckle-faced teenager named Alison Chambers, also known as Ally. Her father, Robert Chambers, had been in the armed services, and Alison was born in Hanover, Germany. She later lived with her mother Joan in Swansea, after her parents divorced. Alison was a headstrong girl who kept running away from home. She was passed into the care of social services in South Wales, and because of her absconding from there, was transferred to Jordan's Brook House. Even here, she managed to run away, once getting as far as London's Paddington Station.

Alison was an unhappy child who frequently withdrew into a fantasy life: she composed romantic poetry and liked to draw pictures of an imaginary farm where she dreamed of living. The other girls at the home could be quite ruthless, and Alison was mocked continually.

Alison was friendly with a teenager named Anne, who already had links with Cromwell Street. One day Alison and her roommate Sharon Compton arranged to play truant from the home and meet Anne outside a Gloucester cinema. Anne then took them to Cromwell Street, where they had orange squash and biscuits with Rose. Two weeks later the girls absconded again and went back to Cromwell Street, where Rose allowed them to stay the night. In the morning, they met a Dutch girl who was arguing with Rose about her rent. The girl wore the distinctive heavy walking boots and thick socks of a hiker, suggesting that the Wests were still meeting young women who were travelling.

Fred and Rose made a point of befriending Alison, even giving her a gold-coloured necklace with her name on it. Rose understood Alison's fantasy life, and told her that she and Fred owned a peaceful farm in the countryside – when Alison reached seventeen and could legally leave Jordan's Brook House, she could come and visit the farm. Rose showed Alison a colour picture, and told her she could lay in the long grass all day and compose her poems. Alison was completely taken in by this, not realising she had been shown a picture from an estate agent's brochure. 'Alison was captivated by it,' says Sharon Compton. When the girls left the house, Rose told them that, if they were picked up by police, they must not say where they had been. Back at Jordan's Brook, Alison lay on her bed and drew ivy around the door of the farmhouse in the picture.

Soon after this, Alison told the other girls at the home that she had met an older man. She said that he was in love with her and gave her gifts, including jewellery. The girls thought this was just another fantasy. 'Alison had a vivid imagination. When she was talking about this older man who loved her and was buying her this and that, nobody believed her,' says another young woman who knew Alison at the home.

On 5 August 1979, four weeks before her seventeenth birthday, Alison packed up her things and absconded from Jordan's Brook House for the eighth time in nine months. She failed to show up for work the next day as an office junior in Gloucester, where she was employed on a Youth Training Scheme. It seems she had decided to move into Cromwell Street, and was no doubt looking forward to being invited to visit the West's farmhouse, where she could lay in the long grass and compose her poetry. She wrote her mother a long letter in which she spoke about living with a 'very homely family . . . I look after their five children and do some of their housework. They have a child the same age as me who accepts me as a big sister and we get on great . . . The family own flats and I share with the oldest sister.' Other girls at Jordan's Brook had noticed that Alison had a key to 25 Cromwell Street.

SHE had probably already begun a sexual relationship with both Fred and Rose, but the sex soon became frightening. One day the Wests gagged her with a purple fashion belt, three-quarters of an inch wide. Unable to scream, she was raped, tortured and finally killed, just like Lynda Gough, Carol Ann Cooper, Lucy Partington, Thérèse Siegenthaler, Shirley Hubbard and Juanita Mott.

Alison was almost certainly dismembered, although her bones were not marked by knives as the remains of several of the other victims had been. Fred buried her remains in a hole dug in the garden next to the wall of the recently-built bathroom extension.

He kept a number of her body parts aside: sections of her wrists, fingers, ankles and toes, two ribs, both kneecaps, the second thoracic vertebrae and part of her breastbone.

When Alison's friends asked what had happened to her, the Wests gave them the impression that she was living on their farm. Sharon Compton asked if she could visit Alison there, and Rose nervously replied that she would have to wait. Then she changed her story, saying that Alison was not at the farm, but was staying with relatives. 'It was obviously a sore point,' says Sharon.

Alison was reported to the police as missing on 5 August, but because of the letter received by her mother she was later officially discharged from care and police no longer considered her a vulnerable person.

It seemed that Fred and Rose's latest secret was safe.

14

HEATHER

DURING HER LAST years at Linden Road Secondary School, Anna Marie West was given the nickname 'Tank' by the other pupils because of her size and her aggressive, bullying personality. She used the aggression to camouflage her miserable life as a child prostitute, a secret she was too frightened ever to speak about with friends or teachers. Fred and Rose were so worried she might talk that they allowed Anna Marie just ten minutes in which to return home from school each day. She could only complete the journey in time by leaving as soon as lessons ended and running virtually the whole way, and was viciously strapped if even one minute late.

The future held an even greater terror than the present for this unhappy schoolgirl: Anna Marie believed something dreadful would happen to her when she reached her sixteenth birthday. She was not certain exactly what this was, but instinctively knew it would not be wise to wait and see. After all, she had already suffered a lifetime of sadistic abuse – and had even been made pregnant by her own father. In the past Fred had rarely struck her, but eventually this changed. Anna Marie had been viciously kicked in the face by Fred, who was wearing steel toe-capped boots at the time, when she tried to intervene in an argument between him and Rose. When her stepmother saw blood on the child's face, she laughed and told her that this would teach her not to be so 'cocky' with them. It was largely because of this increasing violence, and the vague but pervasive fear of even greater terrors, that Anna Marie left home at the age of fifteen, when she went to live with friends.

THE children at 25 Cromwell Street in 1980 fell into two groups: the older ones, all of whom Fred had fathered, and the younger children, some of whom were Rose's by other lovers, including coloured men.

The first of the younger children was three-year-old Tara, who was of mixed race. (Because Fred was not her natural father, he had little to do with the girl.) Then there was two-year-old Louise, whose paternity was also in doubt, and in June 1980 Rose gave birth to Barry, a white child, who appears to have been fathered by Fred.

The eldest of the senior group was Heather Ann, who turned ten in the autumn of 1980. Heather was a slim, serious girl, with prominent front teeth, dark eyes and thick black hair, looking much like her mother had at the same age. Heather was an intelligent and able pupil at St Paul's Infants and Junior School, and she also did well when she moved to Hucclecote Secondary. Fred had an antipathy towards Heather; lodgers and visitors noticed how he called her names, said she was ugly and was generally cruel to her. After Heather came eight-year-old May, or Mae as she preferred to spell her name, who took after her father's side of the family in looks. She was Rose's favourite, and shared a room with Heather on the first floor of the house. Rose liked to dress the girls in rather boyish clothes, and had their hair cut very short. Stephen, seven, known as Steve, had the same startling blue eyes as his father. He was Fred's favourite and slept on the second floor.

Fred and Rose needed complete control over their children to ensure that what went on in the house remained secret. Every effort was made to keep the children away from other adults, or from situations where they might arouse suspicion. They were not allowed to go out and play on their own in the street, no matter what the weather, being confined instead to the back garden and cellar play room, and they visited the homes of relations only when Fred and Rose were there too. School friends were not allowed back to 25 Cromwell Street and the West children were forbidden from visiting the homes of these friends.

The children's free time was mostly occupied with household chores, in exactly the same way that Bill Letts had made Rose's brothers and sisters work. When the elder West children reached the age of seven, Rose demonstrated washing and ironing for them – from then on, they would be expected to do their own laundry. Heather, Mae and Steve were despatched to the shops to buy their own provisions, and from the age of ten, they cooked a number of their own meals in the kitchenette Fred had built as part of the extension. 'We had a job every single day when we came home from school, in the living room, kitchen or bathroom. We used to come home and do it straight away without talking. If you spoke or if it wasn't done properly, Mum would go mad,' says Steve.

Care of the children was Rose's sole responsibility, and it was her that they were afraid of. Her disciplining of the older children was outright sadism; her rages frightening and unpredictable. Even years later, most of the West children – including Anna Marie – retained affection for Fred simply because he did not beat them with Rose's insane violence. 'Mum hit us for no real reason,' says Steve. 'It could be anything. She made reasons up, like if the dishcloth went missing. She would stand there and keep screaming, "Where is the dishcloth?" You used to be running around trying to find it and she beat us until we found it.'

The older children were fully aware that their mother was a prostitute – there was even a photograph album containing provocative pictures of Rose with her boyfriends. The children knew that these things went on in 'Mum and Dad's Room', which was now on the first floor of the house, and that they must not go in there. (The bedroom had a plaque on the door which read 'Rose's Room', and its interior was decorated in garish fashion, with a painting of a naked woman on a horse, the silhouette of Rose in the nude that Fred had made in Leyhill in 1971, a candelabra hanging from the ceiling and special knick-knacks on the window ledge.) One day, however, Steve broke the rule and barged in to find his mother in bed with a man. Steve turned and ran back down the short flight of steps, across the passageway into the living room, lifted the trap door and disappeared down into the cellar, which at this time was divided into a play room for the children and a workshop for Fred. 'My dad ran down after me and I got the beating of my life,' he recalls.

Fred was usually more concerned with work than with the children, and this was a rare example of his hitting them. After coming home from the Wingate factory, where he was a general labourer, Fred ate a quick meal before going out on his 'cobbles'. This was the Gloucestershire phrase he used for work that was not declared to the Inland Revenue – usually general maintenance for neighbours. Fred often did not return home until the rest of the household was getting ready for bed. Fred also continued to dabble in petty crime, and on 2 October 1980 he was convicted at Gloucester Crown Court of receiving stolen goods. He was given a nine-month prison sentence, suspended for two years, and was fined £50.

The children seldom received presents at Christmas, being told by their mother that they 'did not deserve any'. One winter night, Heather, Steve and Mae were sent to bed with the familiar order to go straight to sleep. Fred had fitted a baby intercom in the upstairs rooms where the children slept, so Rose could hear what they were saying. Suddenly she came out of her bedroom on the ground floor and pounded upstairs to their landing, appearing at the foot of their beds naked. She had Fred's leather belt in her hand and beat all three of them, making sure to catch them with the buckle. Then she ordered the children downstairs and pushed them out the front door.

A foot of snow lay in Cromwell Street that night. The children huddled up together for warmth by the door as midnight came and went. Occasionally a drunk stumbled past the house, heading for one of the seedy bedsitters in the street. Three hours passed before they were let back in and sent to bed with another beating. Small wonder the children remained silent when asked at school if they had enjoyed a happy Christmas.

HEATHER was receiving even more beatings than the other children. One of the few friends she had at school was Denise Harrison, the daughter of Fred's Jamaican-born friend Ronalzo Harrison. Denise liked Fred, as most people did, but was struck by the odd way in which Heather lived. 'It was like they were in a prison camp,' she says.

Heather was self-conscious about her body, wearing long-sleeved cardigans and shirts even at the height of summer. During PE lessons she was more concerned about keeping her socks up than taking part in the games, and afterwards, when the other girls carelessly dropped their sports kit and ran for the showers, Heather refused to join in despite the strict rule that girls had to shower after sports. She was frequently sent to the Headmistress's office because of her refusal to comply with this rule, yet nobody appears to have investigated why this normally studious girl was repeatedly being so disobedient. Denise Harrison discovered the reason one day when her friend was forced to take a shower: Heather had red weal marks and bruises all over her legs and arms where she had been beaten.

Heather was in a desperate situation at home, but was too terrified to tell anybody what was happening to her. Now that Anna Marie had left 25 Cromwell Street, Fred transferred his demands for sex to Heather, telling her it was a father's right to touch his daughters, that he had 'made her' and could do what he wanted with her. Fred commented on the development of her breasts and ordered her to show him her body after she had a bath.

Her younger sister Mae has since claimed that she was also pestered by their father. She has said that he threw a vacuum cleaner at her, splintering her bedroom door, when she rejected his advances. Mae says that she and Heather used to stand watch for each other when they took a shower, and became used to Fred bursting in on them early in the morning when they were getting dressed, or pulling the sheets from their beds. He touched and fondled Heather, even wrestling her to the floor and beating her when she refused to succumb to him. Fred and Rose were always careful not to touch her face, so the marks would not show.

ANNA Marie, who was working as a cleaner in a café, met a window cleaner named Erwin Marschall, and began a relationship with him. They spent one night together at Cromwell Street, but Erwin could not sleep. In the middle of the night he heard a protracted scream, lasting between ten and twenty minutes. It was the voice of a young girl, and he could make out the words 'No, no, please!' In the morning Rose told him it was only Heather, having one of her nightmares.

Shortly afterwards Anna Marie went to live with a boy named Chris Davis, lodging with him at a public house in Gloucester. She was using tranquilliser drugs to help dull the memory of her childhood, and had been to see a psychiatrist when she felt unable to have sex with Chris. (Some years later, Anna Marie would undergo a hysterectomy. Doctors told her that her tilted womb was a result of the two daughters she eventually bore, but it seems possible the abuse she suffered as a child also contributed to the condition.) In 1982 Anna Marie and Chris had to leave the pub, and, with nowhere else to go, reluctantly moved into a bedroom on the first floor of 25 Cromwell Street. Anna Marie told her boyfriend all about what had happened to her as a child. She made him promise not to say anything to Fred and Rose, and never to leave her on her own with them. A month after they moved in, Rose gave birth to Rosemary Junior, another mixed race child whom Anna Marie and Chris helped look after.

Chris noticed how withdrawn Heather was. She bit her fingernails, day-dreamed about leaving home, and had developed a habit of watching Fred warily from a corner, or doorway, of whichever room he was in. Her reproachful gaze disturbed Fred. He demanded to know what was wrong with her, and complained that she was always 'miserable'.

Heather took up smoking and began to drink alcohol. She also went shoplifting, and in August 1982 was caught stealing from WHSmith in the city centre. Heather, who was then coming up for twelve, was charged and signed a note admitting three other offences, but because of her age the case did not go to court.

She was uneasy in the company of males. When one of her uncles began talking to her about boys, and what they might want to do with her, Heather replied that if any boy touched her she would 'put a brick over his head'. She also absconded from a school camping trip because she did not like the male teachers. Fred and Rose convinced themselves that she was a lesbian, and were furious about it, even though Rose herself was actively bisexual.

THE family increased in size again in July 1983, when Rose went into hospital to give birth to another mixed race daughter, whom she named Lucyanna. Fred did not appear upset by this. In fact, he seemed to think more of these children than he did of his own; they were 'perfect'.

After Lucyanna's birth, Rose flew into increasingly violent rages, lashing out with her hands or with whatever she was holding. She punched her older children in the face and stabbed them with kitchen knives, jabbing at them in a frenzy until they were covered in cuts. When she caught Steve sitting on one of her new kitchen units, she picked him up by the neck and throttled him, actually lifting his body off the floor. Afterwards his face was blotchy, and there were livid marks on his neck where her hands had been. 'I had to take a note to school to say I was messing around with a rope in a tree, and fell out with the rope round my neck,' he says.

Her anger was often irrational. One day Heather broke the rule about going into 'Mum and Dad's Room'. She found her mother's pornographic magazines and decided to take a selection to school. When Rose discovered that part of her collection was missing, she assumed that Steve had taken them and telephoned for him to be sent home. Steve ran all the way, thinking something was wrong, and when he got back he found Rose alone in the house. She ordered him to go into the bathroom and take off his clothes. (The bathroom was also known within the family as Fred and Rose's 'office', because they would ensconce themselves in there with the door closed when they wanted to talk privately.) As he undressed, Steve saw two pieces of wire and a belt hanging on the towel rack. When he was naked, Rose came in and tied one of the wires around the boy's hands, and then, ordering him to lie on the floor, tied him to the toilet bowl with the other wire. Then she beat him, screaming, 'What have you done? You took my magazines from upstairs!' When Steve denied it, she lashed him until he was bloody, then told him to get dressed and go back to school. Later that day Heather was found to have the magazines and was sent home, but Rose laughed at her mistake, telling Heather not to worry because Steve had already received her punishment.

Fred lost his temper on occasion, although not nearly as often as Rose. One night he came in late, and Heather, who was ironing in the living room, told him in a lighthearted way that his dinner would be spoiled yet again. Fred's blue eyes opened wide in anger and he jerked out a quick, hard punch which connected with Heather's shoulder, knocking her several feet sideways. With his anger vented, Fred returned to his normal self and sat down to eat.

If the violent anger which Fred and Rose regularly exhibited took the form of murder during this period of their lives, there is no direct evidence of such crimes. It is highly probable that the Wests, having killed at such an intensive rate just a few years previously, would not suddenly have ceased murdering young girls – they were, almost certainly, still abducting unfortunate victims like Shirley Hubbard and Lucy Partington, and killing them after their lust had been satisfied. But the graves of these other, unknown victims have never been discovered.

THE abuse and misery suffered by the older children were so intense that Heather ran away from home; but she soon returned, finding the outside world even more hostile than Number 25. Steve was the next to try and escape. For three weeks he slept rough, sometimes staying with friends, until it dawned on him that his parents were not at all concerned that he had gone and would not be coming to look for him. He slunk home like a whipped dog, and was welcomed with another beating. 'I got used to the beatings after a while. It was the fact that she laughed afterwards. She just laughed at me. It is the worst thing anybody could do,' he says.

More degradation was in store for the boy. Fred told Steve that he would soon have to have sex with his mother. Fred said to Rose, 'When he's seventeen he'll be ready to sleep with you.' Then he turned to his son, winked, and said, 'You'll be all right then!' Steve looked in amazement at his parents, and saw that they were laughing.

Heather was then studying for eight Certificate of Secondary Education (CSE) examinations, and was expected to pass them all. She was such a good student that Denise Harrison would copy Heather's homework on the bus to school in the morning. It was guaranteed that Heather would have completed her assignments; Heather knew she had to work hard because she had to find a good enough job to leave home by her sixteenth birthday.

As her birthday approached, Fred's attempts to rape her became more frequent and more insistent. Heather began to fear for her safety, believing that 'something terrible' was about to happen to her – just as Anna Marie had. Her sleep was broken by nightmares.

At the same time, gossip about Rose's eccentric sex life reached the pupils of Hucclecote Secondary School. The West children had been virtually brainwashed into keeping silent about what went on at home, but when Heather's classmates asked her whether the stories about black babies were true, she unwisely confirmed that her mother did have coloured lovers. She let a few other details slip as well. Fred and Rose soon found out about the indiscretions and were not pleased, wondering what else Heather might now say. Fred was so concerned that he began to escort her to and from school.

Anna Marie married Chris Davis in 1985, and they moved into a house on the White City estate in Gloucester. Heather confided in Chris one day, smoking nervously as she spoke. She did not explicitly say what was wrong, but talked about her home life in such a way that it was obvious there was a serious problem. She said she was thinking of running away, and had considered living rough in the Forest of Dean. She said she never wanted to see any other people. Chris told Anna Marie he was going to talk with Fred and Rose. 'I said I'd had enough and was going to do something. She said, "For Christ's sake don't, because they'll kill us both!"' Heather also begged her half-sister to let her stay with them, but Anna Marie said it was pointless because Fred and Rose would only come and take her back.

HEATHER sat her CSE examinations in the summer of 1986. In the last week of exams, a little less than a month before the official end of school, she finally broke her silence about what was happening to her at home. Her friend Denise Harrison was walking home through the Eastgate Shopping Centre one day, and as she approached Cromwell Street she saw Heather standing on the pavement, and noticed she was upset. When Denise asked what was wrong, Heather started crying. Denise assumed it was because Heather had spoken at school about Rose's lovers, but Heather sobbed that it was worse than that: she said that her father came into her room at night. 'She said he was having sex with her. I said, "Haven't you told your mum?" and she said her mum didn't believe her.' Denise encouraged Heather to go back to school and tell the teachers; she had seen the marks on Heather's body during PE. Heather confirmed that Fred had done it, adding that Rose thought she was a 'little bitch' and deserved her beatings.

'I asked her whether she had told anyone, and she said she was too frightened,' remembers Denise, who decided to tell her parents. But Ronalzo and Gloria Harrison were friends of the Wests, and Mrs Harrison told Denise that Fred would not do such a thing. Denise did not consider it her business to repeat at school what she had been told in confidence, so she let the matter drop. 'We left school about three weeks after this, so I never saw her again,' she says.

*

HEATHER was in a very dangerous position when she left school: Fred and Rose were extremely concerned that she was on the verge of talking about what they had been doing to her. Heather knew she had to leave home as soon as possible, and began looking for a job that would take her away from Cromwell Street. But finding a good job was no easy matter, and Heather became even more dejected and withdrawn. Years later, Rose described her daughter during this time in these words: 'When she left school she just sat in the chair. She didn't want to know me anymore . . . She was a stubborn girl. She didn't want to do her own washing, didn't want to clear up muck.'

Heather's sixteenth birthday came and went that October, and still she had not found a job to escape to. Months went by, so she registered for unemployment benefit, and was seen at Gloucester's Department of Social Security on 29 May 1987. She continued to write off for jobs, and by early summer was pinning her hopes on an application she had made to work at a holiday camp in Devon.

One June evening Heather received a telephone call. A lady from the camp said that she was sorry, but her application had been unsuccessful. It was a crushing disappointment, reducing Heather to tears and making her cry all night, so loudly that she kept her brothers and sisters awake.

IT was raining hard the next morning when the West children trooped off to school. Heather had nowhere to go, so she stayed in bed; Fred could not work because of the weather so he also stayed indoors. When Heather came downstairs, wearing culottes and a blouse tied in the middle, she found she was alone in the house with Fred and Rose.

An argument developed between them as they spent the day cooped up in that little house with the rain pelting down. It may have started with Fred trying to rape Heather, although it is just as likely that Rose turned on her 'miserable' daughter, upset after losing the holiday camp job, and picked a fight with her: she was no good; she should do what her father wanted. Rose later told a neighbour that there had been a 'hell of a row'. It should also be remembered that Heather had grown up in the West home as a number of women had been murdered, one after another; if she had discovered any of her parents' terrible secrets – and logic dictates that she must have learned something of them over a lifetime in close proximity with Fred and Rose – she would have been a particular threat to their well-being, and this may be another reason for what happened to her.

It is also likely that Fred and Rose accused Heather of being a lesbian, which had become almost an obsession with them. They may have attempted to force her into having sex with them both, tying her hands with two lengths of rope, 22½ and 15½ inches long, which were later found by police. Orange, brown and green nylon fibres from a tufted carpet were later found to be trapped in the rope, suggesting that Heather had been held down on the floor as she was being tied up. Interestingly, there was no gag found: Heather's terror alone was probably enough to keep her quiet. The fact that her remains were found without any clothing also suggests that she had been stripped naked before death, and that some sex act had been forced upon her.

Whatever started 'the row', or assault on Heather, it soon spun madly out of control. Somebody put their hands around Heather's throat. Fred later claimed that he did it, but it was an action more typical of Mrs West; it was always Rose who lost her temper. Father, mother and daughter were in the hallway. When the hands came away, Heather was dead.

WHICHEVER of the two actually strangled their first-born child, it was Fred's job to dispose of her corpse. He cut her body into pieces with the same passion he had used to dismember Shirley Robinson, hacking at her with a cleaver, or, more likely, with a heavy serrated knife which had come with the Wests' fridge/freezer, for the cutting up of frozen meat, until he chopped her left thigh clean in two. He then held the corpse of his daughter face down, and cut through the back of her neck while her chin was pushed on to her chest, decapitating her. He removed her kneecaps and parts of her hands and feet, and may have tortured his child by ripping out her fingernails. (Fingernails – but not corresponding fingers – were later found in her grave.) Covered in her blood, Fred put the remains into black bin bags. He may have stored them overnight in a dustbin under the stairs on the ground floor of the house. He told the children when they came home from school that the dustbin was full of old plaster.

Then the children noticed that Heather was gone. 'Where's Heather?' asked Steve.

'She's left home,' said Fred.

'What do you mean?' asked Steve and Mae together.

'A girl picked her up in a Mini, and she's gone to work at the holiday camp,' their father replied, explaining that the lady from the camp had telephoned again while the children were out, and had given Heather the job after all. Fred said that he and Rose had given her some money to help her on her way. He seemed perfectly calm as he told this cold-blooded lie, just a couple of hours after he had finished hacking at her body. Fred was so calm, in fact, that he asked his son to help dig a hole in the garden: he said he was thinking of installing a fish pond.

A couple of days later Steve noticed that the hole he had dug had been filled in – his father had apparently changed his mind. Steve believes he unwittingly helped bury his own sister.

OVER the following weeks several people asked where Heather had gone, and Fred and Rose gave a variety of conflicting reasons for her disappearance. Rose told one friend, Anne Knight, who had an office in Cromwell Street, that 'There was a hell of a row here a couple of nights ago. We found out that she was going with a lesbian from Wales, and has gone to Wales with her.' She told a neighbour named Margaretta Dix that she 'didn't care if Heather was alive or dead or if she ever saw her again'. Fred, on the other hand, told his friend Ronalzo Harrison that Heather had been assaulting the younger children, which had resulted in Rose giving her a good hiding, a few days after which she had left home. When Ronalzo said how concerned he was about Heather, Fred replied that they knew she was living somewhere in the nearby village of Brockworth, and that she would telephone them. He also seems to have forgotten the lesbian story, because he told Denise Harrison that Heather had run off with a boyfriend. The Wests were asked again and again about Heather over the following years; at one stage they even claimed to have reported her to police as a missing person, but this was yet another lie.

Fred decided to pave the back garden. He acquired several dozen square slabs, half coloured a ruddy pink and the other half vanilla yellow. The slabs were molded so that the surface had the texture of slate. Fred called upon Rose, Mae and Steve to help with the work; when they were finished, a cheerful patio in nursery colours was laid out over the pit where Heather's remains lay buried two feet deep near the fir trees.

Flushed with the success of concealing another crime, Fred and Rose gathered the unsuspecting children together to celebrate their work with a barbecue supper.

15

BEHIND THE MASK

IN THE SUMMER of 1987, shortly after the death of Heather West, Fred decided to convert the cellar of 25 Cromwell Street into bedrooms for Rose's younger children. The project gave him an excuse to properly entomb the five young women whose remains were buried there. He was concerned about the crimes being discovered. The first stage in the renovation was to re-surface the floor, where the five graves dug between 1973 and 1975 formed a circle of scars clockwise around the edges of the cellar in order of the victims' burial. Fred asked his son Steve and brother-in-law Graham Letts to help with the work, giving no clue as to his secret purpose.

Rose's younger brother, Graham, whom she had masturbated as a child in Bishop's Cleeve, had grown into a slightly-built man who wore a moustache. He was a painter and decorator by trade, but had several minor criminal convictions to his name and had served more than one prison sentence. Graham, his wife Barbara and their two children were among the few relations with whom the Wests kept in contact.

Before Graham and Steve set to work at Cromwell Street, Fred had ballasted the cellar with sand and gravel. Then a truck-load of ready-mixed concrete arrived and the three men

laboured all day to spread the grey sludge before it set. Barbara
Letts kept Rose company while they worked, and the children
of the two families played together in the back garden, where
Fred had recently built a large Wendy house. By late afternoon
the cement had been levelled and was turning a pale grey as it
hardened into an impervious slab.

While the decoration of the cellar was carried out, Rose's
younger children were moved into the attic, where they slept in
bunk-beds 'like battery chickens', as one visitor describes it.
Fred put a felt underlay down in the cellar and then covered the
floor with linoleum. He clad the walls with imitation pine
boarding, the fluorescent strip lighting was improved and a set of
permanent wooden steps were built leading up to the trap door.
The front area was also filled in and the window blocked. There
was a fluffy white carpet in the room above, so he covered the
hatch with a piece of the carpet. 'You could walk on it and not
know it was there,' said Ronalzo Harrison. Wallpaper was hung
and pine beds were moved in. When the renovation was completed, Fred happily showed off the new bedrooms to visitors,
who complimented his 'beautiful work'.

The rear section of the ground floor of the house was also
turned over to the children, with its kitchen, lounge area, toilet
and bathroom all clad in the same yellow pine boarding and lit
with fluorescent strip lighting. The children had their own television, shower and easy chairs, and a snack bar with a speckled
Formica surface. School drawings were pinned on the walls, and
coloured felt pens, cartoon annuals and other toys were carelessly
jumbled about.

But appearances were deceptive at 25 Cromwell Street. Fred
and Rose's real purpose in improving the children's area was to
cordon off the bizarre adult world upstairs. The first- and sec-
ond-floor rooms could only be accessed through a doorway at
the bottom of the main stairs, which was kept locked after the
renovations were finished. Rose wore the key around her neck

on a string, and the children had strict instructions not to go upstairs even if the door was open. A set of wrought-iron gates had been installed outside the front door, which were also locked, to prevent the children straying from the property.

Fred had made alterations to other bedrooms in the house so he could spy on whoever was in the room. One had a hole cut in the door, concealed behind a lucky horseshoe. A letterbox, of the type found in front doors, was fitted into the wall of another room.

The first floor of the house was converted into a self-contained flat, where Rose entertained her customers. The room overlooking Cromwell Street became a garish lounge with a fully stocked bar. Bottles of gin, vodka and Malibu hung upside down, fitted with optical measures. A 'Flowers Fine Ales' ashtray, bar-mat and glasses were set out, just like in a public house.

The lounge had one central window hung with net curtains; beside this was a large display cabinet filled with a library of up to two hundred video cassettes. These were all pornographic films; either home-made or bought. The former were filmed by Fred and Rose using their video camera – some were taken in the back of Fred's work van while Rose had sex with other men; others were made by Rose on her own after setting the camera up on a tripod; and one showed Fred lying on a table while Rose urinated on him. Many were extended close-ups of Rose masturbating herself and being penetrated by real and artificial penises.

The illegally-bought films featured most types of extreme sexual behaviour, including the abuse of children and animals, but the majority of the videos, home-made and commercial, were concerned with bondage: showing women being sexually abused while tied up, gagged or smothered. Some of these may well have featured the girls who had been murdered. In the commercial films, models were dressed in outlandish rubber suits which left only their eyes, mouths, breasts and genitalia visible.

Some wore gas-masks and others could breathe only through pipes or tubes like vacuum-cleaner hoses. One film showed an obviously distressed and naked girl being forced down into a cellar, where she was suspended from a ceiling beam and whipped by two men. Virtually all the bought films were poor-quality copies smuggled in from continental Europe.

The decorations in the bar were designed to appeal to Rose's predominantly West Indian customers: one wall was papered from floor to ceiling with a mural of a tropical island, and ornaments on the bar included African figurines. A sofa was pushed up under the window facing the television and video player, and an embroidered cushion on the sofa was incongruously decorated with a childish picture and the words MUM and DAD.

Across the hall overlooking the back garden were Rose's self-contained kitchen and bathroom, the former decorated in rose-patterned wallpaper. School photos of her children, still in their cardboard frames, were propped up on shelves. Fred had taken great care to tile the bathroom and finish it with pine fittings – including a toothbrush holder and shelf for shampoo bottles – as neatly conservative as any suburban home. But there were odd touches even here: Rose had stuck a number of nude photographs of herself around the mirror.

Their video camera was an expensive model bought from a high street store on hire purchase, and was usually set up in the bedroom Rose used to entertain her clients, on the second floor of the house at the front, overlooking the street. A lace canopy hung from the four-poster bed, and spotlights fitted to the bed posts were angled down at the mattress.

FRED and Rose were always looking for new sexual partners, and they corresponded with many couples who answered their personal advertisements in 'contact' sex magazines. Many of these ostensibly conventional couples had mailed nude photographs of themselves before visiting Cromwell Street. The Wests took part in many 'wife-swaps' and kept every letter and photograph they were ever sent, storing them in boxes in the attic.

They also continued to look for women who would live in the house and work with Rose as prostitutes. One of the women they tried to involve in this lifestyle was Kathryn Mary Halliday, a thirty-year-old brunette.

Kathryn was lodging with another woman in a bed-and-breakfast flat at 11 Cromwell Street, having recently left an unhappy marriage. One of Fred's 'cobbles' was to carry out maintenance work on flats in the street owned by West Indian friends. In the late autumn of 1988 he was called to repair a leak in the bathroom above the room which Kathryn rented at Number 11. He chatted as he worked, and when he discovered Kathryn was bisexual, cheerfully invited her back to Number 25, saying, 'If you're interested in that sort of thing you should come round to my missus. She'll sort you out.'

Kathryn was lonely, and accepted the invitation. At Number 25 she was shown into the first-floor lounge, where Fred poured her a large drink. Kathryn noticed that Fred had an odd twitch in one of his pale blue eyes. He asked if she wanted to watch a film from his collection, and Kathryn requested a 'normal blue movie'. The most conventional film Fred could find was a highly explicit pornographic video which still involved some bondage scenes. The door opened and Mrs West came into the room. Rose wore her customary large spectacles with dark rims, a blouse and a mini-skirt which rode up around her plump thighs as she wiggled down on the sofa next to their guest. Kathryn saw that she was not wearing any underwear. Within minutes Rose had taken off all her clothes and had started to remove Kathryn's. Then she led her out of the lounge and upstairs to a bedroom on the second floor.

She fondled Kathryn, and was soon initiating aggressive sex in a persistent, almost violent way. 'It wasn't really human contact that Rose wanted. She liked pain. I wouldn't call it making love.'

Fred was filming with his video camera. After a while he became aroused, and had intercourse with Kathryn from behind while Rose fondled her. Later he did the same to Rose, but gave neither much pleasure, ejaculating within seconds on both occasions. 'You needn't have bothered,' Rose told him, and Fred meekly went to get the women another drink.

Kathryn became a frequent visitor to the house, although she was not welcome on Thursdays as Rose had a regular male customer on that day. Most other mornings Rose called for Kathryn on her way back from taking the children to St Paul's Primary School in New Street, on the opposite side of The Park.

The Wests had found out what Kathryn liked to drink and what brand of cigarettes she smoked, and stocked the bar with these items. Kathryn took full advantage of their hospitality. 'I'm afraid I used them for it. I was on the dole. I didn't have any money. Why not?'

Invariably she and Rose ended up in bed, and they were often still there when Fred came home in the early evening. Kathryn helped settle the children down for the night in the cellar, and then the adults would retire upstairs to watch pornographic films. Some of these were extremely unsettling, showing women being abused in what Kathryn recognised as Fred and Rose's bedroom. One woman was tied hand and foot to the bed while a very large phallus was forced into her. The woman was clearly in pain. Kathryn asked Fred if he had any normal sex films. He replied, 'What do you mean "normal"?'

The films rarely failed to excite Rose, who was seemingly insatiable. Sex could last for hours without her tiring or becoming uncomfortable. 'She wanted orgasms all the time, like a machine.' There was no affection shown. Rose did not kiss or hold her lover tenderly, and neither did she confide in Kathryn, limiting her conversation to banalities such as her latest shopping trip. It was only bestial sex that interested Rose, and Kathryn decided that her lover was 'thick – a bit short of a load'.

Rose talked openly about prostitution, giving the impression that she enjoyed her work and was emotionally attached to some of her clients. There were photographs in the house of these men, and some were recognisable to Kathryn as respected and prominent members of the local community.

As for Fred, he would normally be content to be a voyeur, and in all the dozens of times that Kathryn had sex at 25 Cromwell Street, he was only actively involved on four or five occasions and hardly ever penetrated his wife. Kathryn decided he was a pathetic figure, and completely dominated by Rose: 'a wally, always clowning around'. His conversation consisted of leering sexual observations, but he himself was neither virile nor physically appealing. Fred's naked body was plump and hairy, 'like a monkey', and several of his lovers have remarked on his small penis.

As the relationship progressed, the sex became more violent. Kathryn was spanked, slapped, and eventually beaten by Fred with a belt. Fred and Rose enjoyed tying Kathryn up. She was bound with nylon cord by the hands and feet so tightly and skilfully that she complained, asking for the ties to be loosened. Rose seemed to relish Kathryn's discomfort, and asked how she would feel 'if we left you all day and just came back up and tormented you every so often?' When Kathryn was finally untied, there were livid red welts on her wrists.

One night, when all three were naked, Kathryn was led across the hall to a room she had not been in before. A cupboard door was open, and she was shown a collection of black bondage suits and face-masks arrayed on hangers like corpses. The masks were particularly frightening. 'You couldn't breathe very well if you put them on. There were no nose holes in some of them, just black masks with zips.' Kathryn estimated that the suits were too small to fit Rose, and yet they were creased and soiled and had obviously been used often. More suits were stored in a suitcase at the bottom of the wardrobe, together with catalogues of bondage clothing and equipment. The bed itself was nothing less than an instrument of torture, with a wooden beam over the headboard fitted with what appeared to be butcher's meat hooks. Fred showed Kathryn chains and two whips: a bull whip and a cat-o'-nine-tails. She realised it was a test, to see how she reacted, but Kathryn had seen women wearing the suits in Fred and Rose's home videos and was justifiably frightened. She talked her way out of the situation and all three went back to the other bedroom, where Kathryn was tied up by her hands and feet. Fred was excited, and, unusually, joined in the sex.

In the days after Kathryn had been shown the secret room, their sex sessions became progressively more extreme. Rose tried to force increasingly large phalluses into Kathryn. 'They were trying to take me beyond my limits.' Rose had always been dominant, but now she ordered and pushed her lover about, spanking and blindfolding her, until one evening when Kathryn was tied up and Rose held a pillow over her head. Unable to move or see, Kathryn must have been in a similar situation to that of Lucy Partington, Lynda Gough and several of the Wests' other victims shortly before they died. It was a nightmarish experience. Kathryn explained what went through her mind:

'When you are tied up with a pillow over your head you don't know what is happening. All you think about is yourself and trying to get free. You don't think of what they are doing to you. Your mind and everything goes and you don't know where you are. It's a horrible, horrible feeling.'

Rose put her mouth next to Kathryn's ear and whispered, 'What does it feel like not being able to see?'

Then more pressure was exerted, so the pillow folded over Kathryn's eyes and ears, muffling her hearing. 'The next thing is she's having a go at me . . . he is . . . somebody is holding the pillow. She was talking to me and the next thing somebody, or something, is inside me.'

One of the sex toys Rose used was a monstrous flesh-coloured phallus studded with latex nodules. Rose called it her 'Exocet', after the missile used during the Falklands War. Rose delighted in using the phallus on herself. It made her scream. She also had a box of black phalluses of various sizes which she liked to use on Kathryn.

Fred and Rose then had sex with Kathryn, who tried to get the pillow away from her face. Rose bent down and mocked, 'Can't you breathe? Aren't you woman enough to take it?' Rose said that, if she could not take it, she would be punished, and Kathryn felt something sharp and cold pressing against her stomach. When she was finally released she saw a half-inch cut near her navel. 'She [Rose] would cause as much physical pain as she possibly could. She had no limit to what she would do,' says Kathryn. 'Even then I knew they were dicing with death. They played with me and the idea that I was frightened. They got their thing from seeing other people frightened.'

The Wests wanted Kathryn to move into 25 Cromwell Street, but she decided it was wiser to end the relationship there, and stopped coming to the house. Fred and Rose tolerated this, but ignored her pointedly when they saw her in the street.

Kathryn believes she was only allowed to escape with her life because Fred and Rose knew she had family who would be suspicious if she disappeared.

BY the autumn of 1988, Fred had not spoken to his daughter, Mae, for almost two months. He was furious that she continued to reject his sexual advances. Fred bitterly accused Mae of being a lesbian, just as he had accused Heather before her. Partly because of these taunts, Mae started to see a young man named Rob Williams, whom she met in Gloucester's Pint Pot pub on 14 October 1988, Rob's eighteenth birthday. Mae was sixteen. Within four months Rob had moved into 25 Cromwell Street, where, to his surprise, he was encouraged to share Mae's bedroom.

Fred and Rose warmly welcomed Mae's boyfriend into the house, pleased that their daughter was having a sex life, and Fred stopped making advances to her. He became fond of Rob, who delighted the Wests by making a wooden plaque for the upstairs lounge bar. It was inscribed with the words *Black Magic* and decorated with palm trees, another gesture towards Rose's West Indian customers.

It was clear to Rob that Mae's parents were obsessed with sex. Fred and Rose talked constantly about their sex life, no matter who was present, and happily allowed Rob to borrow their pornographic films, even those which featured Rose. In the mornings Fred would often ask Rob what he had done in bed with Mae during the night, and Fred was known to put his hand under Rose's skirts and then hold his fingers up, saying, 'Smell her!'

Rob noticed that the curtains were always closed, and that the house was lit, day and night, by electric light. In fact, the house was full of all types of electrical equipment: fires, televisions and stereo music systems, washing machines and tumble dryers, most of which had been bought new on hire purchase from the Midlands Electricity Board (MEB) showroom in the city centre. Fred was not concerned about the amount of power the family were using because he had bypassed the meter and connected the house directly to the main supply, a piece of electrical do-it-yourself that could easily have killed him. A month before the MEB man called to read the meter, Fred switched from his illicit supply to the conventional system, so that it appeared he was using some electricity. In a similar way, Fred had also tapped into the main gas supply.

Mae was allowed to continue living at home because of her sexual relationship with Rob. But Steve was told that he had to leave, because he was approaching sixteen and was therefore 'coming of age'. Steve had been his father's favourite, but Fred now turned on the boy. One day Steve tried to mend one of the

children's bicycles and Fred hit him, shouting that it was his
house and he would 'do what had to be done'. He then beat
Steve, sending him scuttling for cover. Rose put Steve's belongings outside the front door, and told him that he could come
back on Sundays for one hour to visit his brothers and sisters.

The same urge to be rid of their children by the time they
were sixteen had contributed towards Heather's murder. Now
Fred and Rose were showing signs that they were haunted by
this crime. Every photograph of Heather was removed from the
house, and Rose was never heard to mention her name, becoming very quiet if anyone else did. The other children rarely spoke
of their sister, telling each other they would not know what to
say to her if they saw her now. Only Fred behaved differently,
bringing Heather back to life with sporadic reports that he had
seen her in the street and that she had waved cheerfully. Rose
watched her husband silently when he made these statements.

As the years went by, Fred and Rose became more concerned
with maintaining the façade of a respectable life, particularly
after two unannounced visits by social workers acting on information that children were being left on their own in the house
(neither visit uncovered any evidence of this). They even decided
to celebrate Christmas in the traditional way, with decorations
and gifts – quite different to earlier years. School drawings of
baby Jesus in the manger were brought home and displayed on
the walls; the downstairs lounge was decorated with gold tinsel,
and a poster of Snoopy dressed as Santa Claus.

On Christmas morning Rose put on her faded pink towelling
dressing gown and came downstairs to watch the children excitedly unwrap their gifts. There was an electric car for Barry,
slippers for Rosemary and crayons for Tara. Afterwards Rose
cooked a turkey dinner, complete with mushrooms, potatoes,
peas and gravy. A bottle of sherry was put on the checked

tablecloth, and Fred stopped work long enough to join the family at the table.

OTHER parents at St Paul's Primary School were impressed that either Mr or Mrs West was there every day to collect their children from school. Fred was often the only man standing outside the school at going-home time, invariably wearing his dark-blue donkey jacket and chatting to one of the young mothers. If it was raining he would have his white Ford Transit van ready, and was quick to offer them a lift. Fred talked about all the comforts he had provided for his family, and charmed many of the mothers.

Once a year the school held a dressing-up day, when the pupils paid fifty pence to charity for the privilege of dressing in whatever clothes they liked. There was a competition for the most inventive costume and Rose enthusiastically took part, helping to turn nine-year-old Barry into a pirate, complete with eye patch, hooked hand and parrot; six-year-old Lucyanna into a rabbit; ten-year-old Louise into a sad clown and Rosemary Junior, seven, into a cat with whiskers and pointy black ears.

The children posed obediently for a photograph before leaving for school. But despite the jolly eye patch and red bandana, the pirate looked forlorn; the big, cut-out smile of Louise's clown face left her own blank expression clearly visible; and the unhappiness of the children was plain to see behind the masks.

16

DETECTIVE SAVAGE

Walter West's last years were mostly spent in bed in his room at Moorcourt Cottage, Much Marcle. He could look out over the farm land of Herefordshire, seeing as far as May Hill, while surrounded by the bric-à-brac of his life. Walter had been a formidable man in his prime, but he had not really been well since the tractor accident which left him with only one good lung. The rugged farm labourer who had done so much to shape Fred's mind was now a feeble invalid, too unsteady to collect his own pension or visit the Wallwyn Arms for a pint of beer.

In the spring of 1992 the old man's health worsened, and he was taken into hospital. Doug and his brother John, who was working as a dustman, told Fred that he should see his father before it was too late, but Fred did not come. Walter died on 28 March, aged seventy-seven. The funeral was held at St Bartholomew's, where the Wests had been christened, married and buried for generations. Walter was laid to rest next to Daisy on the shale side of the graveyard, a patch of stony ground near the fence that he had reserved after Daisy's funeral in 1968.

There was bad feeling between the brothers that Fred had not visited his father in hospital, and also squabbles over who would keep Walter's few valuables. Partly because of these problems, the family did not immediately pay for a headstone, as they had for Daisy. The grave would only be identified by a metal marker.

Walter's death was a milestone in Fred's life. It was thirty years since he had left home; he had murdered at least twelve young women in that time and still his freedom was not threatened. Yet, strangely, it was at this point – while he engaged in a petty disagreement with his family over Walter's belongings, and years after the majority of his and Rose's crimes had been committed – that their secret life began to unravel.

It started simply enough. One of the many young girls who had found themselves in the clutches of Fred and Rose decided to tell a friend about what was going on at Cromwell Street. The girl was thirteen years old.* She told her best friend at school that she had been abused by the Wests, claiming that Fred had raped her while Rose encouraged him. She was terribly upset by what had happened and shared this secret with her friend because she had nowhere else to turn. Her confidante, another thirteen-year-old girl, went home and thought about what she had been told. She did not want to go to the police, but there seemed to be no alternative.

There was a beat police constable in the area where the girl lived, and she told this officer what she believed the Wests had done to her friend. A police investigation was launched, in tandem with Gloucestershire social services. Unfortunately for the Wests, one of the most tenacious female police officers in Gloucester was assigned to the case.

Hazel Norma Savage is a talented and industrious police officer who has enjoyed a distinguished career. She first entered the Criminal Investigation Department (CID) in 1968. It was rare in the 1960s to find a woman officer in plain clothes, and for Hazel to become a Detective Constable was a considerable

---

* The child involved in these allegations cannot be named for legal reasons.

achievement. Because of her energy, and obvious ability, it was thought that she might be promoted further, but she stayed as a Detective Constable and still held that rank twenty-four years later, when the West case began in 1992. By then, Hazel was a veteran of several major inquiries, particularly those involving women and children. She had become a trusted old hand, well liked within the constabulary for her robust sense of humour and her professionalism.

Hazel's hair is cut short, and she normally wears a pair of large, tortoiseshell-framed spectacles. She does not smoke and hardly drinks alcohol. Hazel has been divorced for some years, and colleagues say that the job is her life. But, after twenty-eight years in the force, she would soon be due for retirement. This is normal in the police service, even though Hazel was not yet fifty.

When she opened the file, she remembered: it had been a few weeks before Christmas 1966 when she first heard the name Fred West. Hazel was then a WPC, and had been sent to Glasgow to collect and bring back to Gloucester a young woman named Rena West, who was due to stand trial for a number of burglaries.

As they flew south, Rena had confided in Hazel about her life. She spoke about her violent, feckless husband, Fred, with whom she had a child. Fred was sexually depraved, she said, probably quite mad, and had moved another girl into the caravan where he lived. Rena was worried about her children, who were with her husband. She said that she had committed the burglaries to spite him and the other woman, who had been her friend.

Hazel first saw Mr West in the flesh two weeks later, when he appeared as a witness at Rena's trial. He was a rather strange-looking young labourer, shabbily dressed, with bushy dark hair, blue eyes and unusually simian features. It was not a face that one quickly forgot.

Twenty-six years later, the file in Hazel's hands showed that Fred was living in Gloucester, not far from headquarters. He had a large number of children and was married to a woman named Rosemary. The allegations against them were extremely serious. As she read the notes, Hazel must have wondered what had ever happened to Rena.

A routine check was made to see if Fred and Rose had any criminal history, and it was discovered that, most notably, they had been jointly convicted of assaulting a young woman in 1973. Fred had numerous other convictions, but they were minor matters. He appeared to be a persistent thief who handled stolen goods and did not bother to keep his car taxed. His record showed that he had been sent to prison when these offences had accumulated, and when he had offended whilst on parole. Mrs West, on the other hand, appeared to have led a blameless life for the past nineteen years: apart from the 1973 assault, she did not have a single conviction against her name.

ON the morning of Thursday 6 August 1992, police arrived at 25 Cromwell Street with a warrant to search for evidence of child abuse, including pornography. Fred and Rose, together with Rose's youngest children – Tara, Louise, Barry, Rosemary Junior and Lucyanna – were all in the house at the time. Fred decided to go to work as police conducted their search. While he was out, they seized an extraordinary array of pornographic material and devices, including five dildos, a box of dildo heads, rubber underwear, a rice flail, a whip, various buckles and straps, and ninety-nine pornographic videos (both home-made and commercial).

At 9:05 A.M. Rose was arrested for aiding and abetting the rape of a young girl and for obstructing the police.

Fred was working full-time for a small building company named Carson Contractors. One of the company's contracts was to carry out general repairs at a home for autistic people, the Stroud Court Community Trust, near the village of Nailsworth. Fred was on-call to perform routine maintenance there, retained his own set of keys and often worked unsupervised late into the night.

At 2:15 P.M. on 6 August, Fred was back at Carson's yard near Stroud. He was arrested and taken into custody, where he was questioned about sex abuse at Cromwell Street, pornography, and the rape and buggery of the thirteen-year-old girl.

The next day Hazel Savage began to interview friends and family of the Wests. One of the first addresses she went to was a council house on Gloucester's White City estate. This was the home of Anna Marie, who was separated from her husband, Chris Davis, and living with her two daughters. When Hazel asked if Anna Marie knew of anything improper happening at 25 Cromwell Street, Anna Marie's horrific story emerged.

IN what became the first of a series of long and emotional interviews, Anna Marie told Hazel of the 'physical, mental and sexual abuse' she had suffered at the hands of Fred and Rose from a young age. She described how her father had raped her and how Fred and Rose had forced her into having intercourse with other men. They had tied her up and subjected her to all types of sadistic treatment. It was an astonishing interview, made even more poignant when Anna Marie said she still loved her father and Rose, as a surrogate mother, and had never understood why they had treated her in this way.

Anna Marie also talked about her half-sister, Charmaine, and her natural mother, Rena, whom Hazel remembered from 1966. 'I have been trying to trace her for years,' said Anna Marie.

Hazel then went to see Chris Davis, who suggested that she find and interview Heather. She would know more than anybody, he said, but she had disappeared. He and Anna Marie had tried to track her down, but to no avail. Other members of the family were questioned, but most of the older children were too frightened to talk candidly to Hazel. 'We were threatened [and told] to keep our mouth shut about anything we saw,' explains Steve West. 'They said, "Don't you dare say anything about anything you see in this house." We knew what the consequences were. We knew we would get the worst beating of our lives.'

Not only had Hazel found strong evidence of child abuse in the home, but it now seemed that at least three members of the family were missing.

FRED was kept in custody, but Rose was allowed to go home. All five of her youngest children were being taken into care by social services, and 25 Cromwell Street was eerily quiet. Her sister-in-law, Barbara Letts, arrived to comfort Rose, and the women put together clothes for the children to take. As they sorted through the bedrooms, putting tops and trousers into a bag, Rose broke down and cried.

The following day Fred appeared briefly in court. He was charged and remanded to Gloucester Prison, where he had been held in 1969.

After talking to members of the family, Hazel Savage had begun to appreciate the importance of interviewing Heather. But nobody knew where she was, so Hazel attempted to trace Heather using her National Insurance number and the official records of both the Department of Social Security and the Inland Revenue. If Heather had worked, paid income tax, claimed state benefit or used any branch of the National Health Service since leaving school, it would be on file somewhere.

She had also gathered enough evidence to arrest Rose for the indecent assault of the young girl, which she duly did at 8:30 A.M. on Tuesday 11 August. Rose telephoned her solicitor, a heavy-set local man named Leo Goatley, and prepared herself for the gruelling interviews that followed.

The questions put by Hazel Savage were mainly concerned with the child abuse allegations, but she also asked repeatedly where Heather was. Rose replied that Heather had finished school when she was aged sixteen and had then left home; she had not seen her since. Beyond that, her answers were vague and unhelpful. For example:

POLICE: *Where is she [Heather] now?*
ROSE WEST: *Don't know.*
POLICE: *Have you had any contact?*
ROSE WEST: *None.*
POLICE: *In what circumstances did she leave?*
ROSE WEST: *I went out shopping and [when I got back] she had gone.*
POLICE: *You obviously reported her as a missing person?*
ROSE WEST: *I'm not sure of that one.*

And later on:

POLICE: *Would Fred have reported Heather missing?*
ROSE WEST: *I don't know.*

Hazel suggested that losing contact with her first-born child must have been distressing, to which Rose glibly replied, 'It's been awful.' Then Hazel revealed the results of her checks using Heather's National Insurance number and the records of the DSS and tax office. She said there had been no trace of Heather whatsoever for four years, which meant that she had not taken a regular job, claimed any sort of state benefit or even visited a doctor in that time. This was almost impossible unless Heather had completely changed her identity, left the country, or was dead.

Rose replied that the police must 'believe what they want'.
Heather had apparently told her mother that she intended to
leave home, and Rose claimed she had said to her daughter:
'Please don't do so — we've got more to talk over.' Rose maintained that she had then gone out shopping for approximately
two hours 'as per usual', and that when she came back, Heather
was gone.

POLICE: *Did she [Heather] have any money when she left?*
ROSE WEST: *I don't know.*

Hazel then told Rose that her attitude made the situation an
alarming and frightening one, but Rose just said that she hoped
Heather was 'happy in her life' wherever she was.

After lunch the police tried again. This time Rose said she
believed Heather had left home in a Mini driven by another
woman. This had apparently happened while Rose was out
shopping. It was suggested to Rose that she did not know
whether her daughter was alive or dead. 'Is there any reason
why she shouldn't be alive, apart from having accidents and
stuff?' she retorted. 'If my child don't want to know, what can I
do about it?'

She volunteered a bizarre explanation for why she had not
bothered to look for her. This was the exchange that took place
at 5:22 P.M.:

ROSE WEST: *I can remember now why I didn't pursue Heather —*
          because things pointed to Heather being a lesbian.
POLICE: *A what?*
ROSE WEST: *Lesbian, and wanted left on her own.*
POLICE: *Are you a lesbian?*

ROSE WEST: *No.*
POLICE: *Have you ever been a lesbian?*
ROSE WEST: *No.*

Rose added that she did not want her other children being exposed to Heather's sexuality, and had given her £600 to help her on her way, completely contradicting what she had earlier told police about not knowing if Heather had had any money when she left. Rose then said that Heather telephoned occasionally to say that she was well, indicating that this was a secret between mother and daughter, because Fred and Heather did not get on and she did not want the rest of the family to find out that they were in touch.

At another point in the interviews, Charmaine's whereabouts were discussed. Rose explained the child's disappearance in this way: 'She went with her mother and stayed with her mum . . . because it's what she requested.' Hazel appeared to accept this explanation, for now at least, and said that she could not understand why Rose had simply not told them that before. The police then returned to the main charges concerning the thirteen-year-old girl, but as they continued to talk, Rose must have realised she had told two fundamental lies about Heather and Charmaine. If their remains were ever found, those lies could incriminate her.

Rose was kept in police custody overnight, and appeared before Gloucester magistrates in the morning. She was charged with child abuse and granted bail on condition that she did not communicate with her younger children, her stepdaughter, Anna Marie, or Fred.

It was bad enough going back to an empty house, but life without Fred seemed impossible. Rose was depressed, and started drinking. She found some pills and swallowed them in a fumbling attempt to end her life. Steve found his mother collapsed on the floor. At 1:50 A.M. on Thursday 13 August, Rose was taken to Gloucestershire Royal Hospital where her stomach was successfully pumped.

Fred was kept on remand in Gloucester gaol, where he was a 'Rule 43' prisoner (the system whereby sex offenders are kept apart from the general prison population, who often try to harm them). He was frightened of the other inmates, and it seemed to his visitors that he had shrunk in stature and confidence. Fred cried when his older children came to see him, and, speaking in a timid voice, made this cryptic confession to his son, Steve: 'I have done something really bad. I have done it at night when you were asleep.' No further explanation was offered, for the time being.

AT Cromwell Street, Rose had to face up to the practical problems of surviving on her own. The Wests had always been careful with money, but although Fred worked hard, he had never been well paid. There was a mortgage on the house and the little they had saved over the years had largely been spent on recent home improvements. Because of this, Rose was forced to take a cleaning job at the Gloucestershire College of Art and Technology, and relied more heavily on the small amount of money she earned from prostitution.

She missed Fred, and was unusually affectionate when he telephoned from prison. Rose called him 'sweetheart' and 'darling', words she had seldom been heard to use aloud before. Rose also wrote to her husband, including a letter which assured him that, if they were caught, they would go together. Fred treasured the letter.

Rose bought a tank of tropical fish and obtained two mongrel dogs from a local rescue centre for company. One dog was a small wire-haired terrier type which she named Benji, the other a white-haired animal she named Oscar. Rose attempted to train the dogs, disciplining them in a typically brutal way: if one barked, she grabbed the animal by the collar and beat it until it howled. Benji and Oscar did learn to fear their mistress, but they were never house-trained and frequently snatched food from the kitchen table.

Rose comforted herself with eating. Using a pram as her shopping trolley, and wearing white schoolgirl socks, she was a familiar eccentric customer at Marks & Spencer in the city centre. When she came back home, Rose took off all her clothes and sat in front of the television, gorging on M&S chocolate eclairs whilst watching children's videos like *Hook* and Walt Disney's *Snow White and the Seven Dwarfs*. She particularly enjoyed the cartoon short *Road Runner*, shrieking with delight each time Wile E. Coyote was battered.

In September, after spending one month in Gloucester Prison on remand, Fred was moved to the Carpenter House Bail Hostel in Birmingham. He was visited there by Steve, Mae, and Mae's boyfriend, Rob. Fred was depressed. He cried with self-pity, and gave his visitors the impression that the child abuse allegations were a prelude to greater horrors. 'I've been a bad boy,' he said. 'It's about time you went to the papers and made yourselves some money.' He also spoke about Heather in a dream-like way, telling his visitors she had been to see him there in Birmingham. He said she was a prostitute now, making lots of money from selling her body and dealing drugs. He spoke about this lifestyle as if Heather had become a successful and important person. Fred also said she had told him she would intervene in the case and help effect his release. When Rose discovered what Fred had been saying about the children going to the newspapers, she told them to pay no attention.

Both Fred and Rose were interviewed by a psychologist at this time, because of the impending court case, and a detailed profile of their relationship was drawn up. It shows them to be a loving couple who had no secrets from each other, with a marriage

described as 'close and caring . . . they are well able to communicate and rarely argue . . . they discuss everything together
[and] all decisions regarding their marriage and relationship are
jointly made'. A love letter from Rose to Fred at this time bears
this out:

> *To my darling,*
> *Well, you really tired me out on Saturday, but it was a won-*
> *derful day . . . Remember I will love you always and everything*
> *will be alright.*
> *Goodnight sweetheart*
> *Lots of love,*
>
> > *Rose*

The letter was decorated with a large heart with an arrow
through it, and in the middle of the heart were the words 'Fred
and Rose'.

In the autumn of 1992, one of the West children in care told
a social worker that Fred had threatened them with violence if
they ever talked about what went on in the house – Fred said
they would be killed and buried under the patio, just like their
sister, Heather. This extraordinary story about Heather being
under the patio was not a new one, and several of the Wests
seemed to have already heard it, although no one seemed to
know where it had started. It had also been blurted out during
a family row between Steve, Mae and Anna Marie. The social
worker who heard this rumour did not pass it on to the police at
this time, however, and it is unclear whether the police (who sat
in on interviews with the children) were aware of the story.

The suggestion that Heather was lying under the patio slabs
became a macabre joke at Cromwell Street. Rob Williams
remembers asking Steve which stone he thought his sister was

under. 'I used to say, "It's three up and nine across."' But it was no joke to Rose, who looked out on that patio every evening as she washed up at the sink and every morning as she got up, knowing full well that her daughter's remains were indeed buried under those candy-coloured slabs.

IN March 1993 Fred was transferred to another bail hostel in Birmingham, Welford House, and from there to an unsupervised hostel in Holly Road, where there was an 11 P.M. to 6 A.M. curfew. Although Rose was forbidden to see Fred under the conditions of her bail, she started to travel up from Gloucester by train, taking sandwiches and a two-man tent carried in a rucksack. Fred and Rose pitched the tent near the hostel and had intense, sexually-charged reunions. At first Rose's illicit visits were only at weekends, but they became as frequent as every other day, and Fred even managed to sneak back to the house in Cromwell Street. As long as he was at the hostel for the morning head count, nobody appeared to know that he was missing.

FRED later claimed that he murdered a woman in Birmingham during this period of his life. There is no evidence to support this, but it is clear that he had an urgent need for violent sexual satisfaction and it is highly unlikely that he simply stopped killing after Heather's death in 1987. The pressures of life in Birmingham, away from Rose, and the freedom he was allowed there may well have led him to claim another life.

EACH time they met, Fred presented Rose with 'gifts' – which were, in fact, no more than pieces of rubbish he found in the street. They included a child's dummy, crisp packets, an old photograph frame, spent phone cards, Kinder egg toys, half a twenty-pound note and pieces of small change. But Rose cherished all these items, displaying them in a glass cabinet at Cromwell Street as if they were priceless china.

On Sunday 6 June 1993, Fred left Birmingham for his trial. He was so agitated that he forgot to take his personal belongings with him. Fred and Rose met the next day in the dock of Gloucester Crown Court, where he was charged with three counts of rape, and one count of buggery and cruelty to a child. Rose was charged with encouraging and inciting him to have sex with the same thirteen-year-old girl, and with cruelty. Video-link monitors had been set up in the court, so that child witnesses could give evidence for the prosecution from a separate room.

But before the jury were sworn in, the prosecution counsel informed the judge that two important witnesses were not prepared to testify against the Wests. One of these was the young girl.

'Without that evidence there is no case,' said Peter Thomas for the prosecution. 'We take the view that we cannot proceed, and accordingly we offer no evidence against these defendants.' Judge Gabriel Hutton entered formal not guilty verdicts in respect of all the charges, and Fred and Rose hugged each other in the dock. They left the court and went home to Cromwell Street, where they sat together on the sofa holding hands. A few days later, on 28 June, Rose signed an authorisation for the police to destroy the ninety-nine pornographic videos, and other materials, seized from her home. (Because of this action, it will never be known whether the torture or murder of any of the Wests' victims was recorded on film.)

The case may have collapsed, but it had at least brought to light the mystery of Heather West's disappearance – and there was one determined police officer who was not ready to close the file on the West family just yet.

17

UNDER THE PATIO

IN AUGUST 1993, Gloucester social services contacted the police to emphasise their concern over the whereabouts of Heather West. They could find no trace of the girl, and were concerned for her safety because of the repeated family 'joke' about her body being under the patio. As a result of this, Detective Constable Hazel Savage was officially appointed to investigate Heather's disappearance further.

Hazel could still find no record of Heather, despite renewed checking with the Inland Revenue, the Department of Social Security and other official sources. She began to fear that Fred and Rose's eldest daughter was dead, and that she was most probably buried under the patio of 25 Cromwell Street – as one of their younger children had said. Everything Hazel had learned about the couple during the recent child abuse investigation told her that the Wests were quite capable of this, the most heinous of crimes. Although only months remained until Hazel was due to retire, she tried to convince her senior officers at Gloucester police headquarters to apply for a warrant to look under the patio.

Her enthusiasm was not immediately encouraged. The word of a child did not necessarily constitute enough evidence upon which to launch an inquiry. The Wests had already beaten one set of charges, and were adept at claiming to be victims of harassment. There were also financial considerations: the cost of excavating the back garden would be enormous, and if Hazel was wrong, and there was no body, the Wests might be able to claim considerable compensation.

As months passed without any further action being taken against them, Fred and Rose had reason to hope they were in the clear. Both heartily disliked Hazel, but did not appear afraid of her now that they thought she was making no progress. The Wests told everybody that the charges against them had been a pack of lies, and that Hazel Savage was pursuing a vendetta. 'Fred was never frightened of Hazel. He used to laugh and shrug her off,' says Rob Williams. 'Rose would call her a bitch and an arsehole and say she was going out of her way to make trouble.'

But this was bravado. In reality Fred and Rose were worried and chastened people.

Fear had the effect of bringing man and wife closer. They behaved like young lovers, holding hands and sitting together in the evening, watching television or playing cards. As they were curled up on the sofa, Fred sometimes tickled Rose's feet. On summer evenings they walked the dogs in The Park. Fred bought a heart-shaped glass ornament decorated with doves for Rose's birthday, which she treasured; when it was accidentally broken, Rose was anxious that Fred did not find out, 'because it would hurt his affections'.

Rose's five younger children did not return to Cromwell Street, although the social services had no power to keep them after the child abuse case collapsed. It seemed to Rose that Tara, Louise, Barry, Rosemary Junior and Lucyanna were happier in an institutional home than with their own mother, and this had a devastating effect on her morale. Rose broke down and wept when she was told they were not coming home – it was yet another rejection that convinced her she could rely only on Fred. When the younger children did eventually try and make contact with Rose, she turned them away.

Most of the Wests' relations had long since stopped talking to them. Rose had not seen her mother since 1988, when she and Fred had visited Daisy's flat in Berkshire. She had told her mother at the time that she was happy with Fred and that they were hoping to have more children, but Rose's prostitution, together with the fact that she had several children by other men, had put an intolerable strain on her relationship with Daisy and they did not see each other again. Neither was Rose in contact with her sisters, one of whom had become a devout Christian and was scandalised by Rose's lifestyle. Rose did not even know that her eldest sister, Patricia, had Alzheimer's disease and was dying.

Fred too was now estranged from virtually all his brothers and sisters. Since Walter's funeral he had not even spoken to John West, whom he had always been closest to.

Rejected by their own families, Fred and Rose decided to start a new life and have more children. This was a problem, because Rose had been sterilised after the birth of her daughter Lucyanna in 1983. She would not be dissuaded, however, and attended the Gloucestershire Royal Hospital in the summer of 1993 to undergo an operation to reverse the sterilisation. Rose succeeded in becoming pregnant just a few months before her fortieth birthday, but her happiness was not to last. She miscarried during the winter of 1993, and later visited her doctor complaining of depression.

The Wests became increasingly paranoid about who they could trust, and who was talking about them to the police. They knew that Anna Marie, for one, was helping Hazel, so Fred and Rose decided it would be wise to sever all remaining links with their families. Even Graham Letts found himself turned away at the door. The last to be rejected was Graham's wife, Barbara, who had been Rose's closest friend in recent years and had stood by her throughout the child abuse case. Shortly after Christmas 1993, Barbara and her two children were visiting 25 Cromwell

Street when Rose suddenly ordered them to get their coats and leave. Barbara believes it was Fred's idea. 'He didn't like her having any friends. She had told Fred that she wanted to keep me as a friend. She had no others that I know of. Then she told me that Fred didn't like me and didn't want me around. She started being funny, telling us to go.'

AT the beginning of 1994, one of the five West children who were living in care again said that they were scared to talk about what went on at Cromwell Street. Their father had threatened that, if they betrayed his secrets, they would be murdered and buried under the patio like Heather. When Hazel was told about this, she knew there could be no further delay.

She went back to her senior officers and argued strongly for a warrant to dig up the garden. Hazel detailed the checks she had made that showed no trace of Heather, explaining precisely what the children had said, and this time she succeeded in persuading her bosses to apply for a warrant. Colleagues later said that if Hazel had not been held in such high esteem within the force, and had not been so persistent, nothing would ever have been done.

The police appeared before Gloucester magistrates on Wednesday 23 February 1994 to apply for a Section Eight search warrant. The warrant was granted, allowing them to search the house and garden of 25 Cromwell Street for the remains of Heather West. This was officially recorded as Day One of the investigation. It came over a year after social workers had first heard that Heather might be buried there, and six months after the police had officially been asked to investigate the case.

The practical problems of searching Cromwell Street were considerable. The garden was approximately sixty feet long by fifteen feet wide. Most of the area was covered by concrete slabs, and the police did not know where under the patio Heather was supposed to be buried. There were more complications: an extension to the main house had been built (without planning permission) covering another portion of the garden. This might have to be demolished. There was a large Wendy house-cum-toolshed obscuring another section, and the boundaries of the property had also changed over the years. The only course of action would be to start digging at the bottom and work up to the house; a task which would involve a large team of police officers and the hire of mechanical equipment. The whole enterprise would be extremely expensive, and could not fail to attract the attention of the local press.

The investigation would be based at Gloucester's police head-quarters, a large modern office block known as Bearland situated next to the law courts near the River Severn, a short walk from Cromwell Street. A thoroughly reliable man was sought to lead this problematic inquiry, an officer who would conduct the investigation strictly according to the rules. The man chosen was Detective Superintendent John Bennett.

Tall, slim, with fine, sandy-coloured hair that lies flat across his head, John Bennett has blue eyes with brows so pale they are almost invisible. He has rather prominent teeth, fleshy lips and an open expression. As a detective, he does not wear a uniform to work, but a blue business suit, discreetly patterned shirt and tie and shiny black shoes.

Born and brought up in the nearby Cotswold town of Stroud, John Bennett speaks with an unaffected Gloucestershire accent, not dissimilar to Fred's, and is a little sensitive to being thought unsophisticated. After leaving grammar school he joined the police cadets and went on to serve as a beat Constable and then Detective Constable in Cheltenham and Stroud. For fourteen years he was a police scuba diver. He was promoted through the ranks, becoming a Detective Sergeant and eventually, in 1991, a Detective Superintendent. He was approaching his forty-ninth birthday when the inquiry began.

*

DAY Two of the investigation, Thursday 24 February, was damp and bitterly cold. The sky above Gloucester was malevolently grey, threatening rain. Fred had left the house early, to treat wood timbers in the loft of a building near Stroud. Rose and their eldest son, Steve, were at home when a police van with four officers pulled up outside. It was not unusual to see police in Cromwell Street; a patrol car had been at Number 25 only a few days before, and hardly a week went by without the police being called to a disturbance at one of the houses in the street.

'Get Fred!' yelled Rose to her son when, at 1:25 P.M., the police told her they had a warrant to dig up the garden. She was hysterical. Steve attempted to reach his father on his mobile phone, but could not get through. With Rose still screaming for her husband, Steve telephoned Fred's employer, Derek Thompson of Carson Contractors. It was he who reached Fred, on a land line. 'I told him to ring Rose straight away. I didn't tell him what it was about,' says Thompson. It was the last time he would ever speak to his employee.

Fred telephoned Cromwell Street and was told by Steve that the police were about to dig up the garden. Steve said he would try to delay them until Fred returned.

Fred could have driven back to Cromwell Street within thirty minutes, but there was still no sign of him a full hour later, by which time a small team of police officers, wearing blue protective overalls, had already started lifting the patio slabs at the bottom of the garden. Steve again dialled his father's mobile phone. When Fred answered, he sweetly asked 'Who's that?' as if nothing were wrong, and then reassured his excited son that he was on his way. Fred said he was in the nearby council estate of White City, where Anna Marie lived, and would be home soon.

The wooden fence at the bottom of the Wests' garden was pulled down and thrown on to a patch of wasteland behind the house. Police were trying to manoeuvre in a small mechanical digger, via a strip of land behind Cromwell Street where the Wests' neighbours parked their cars. Several vehicles had been double-parked by college students who rented flats near to the house, and the police went to the GLOSCAT campus to find the owners. Neighbours assumed that the men in blue overalls were preparing to work on the street's drains, which were notoriously troublesome.

Lamps were set up to illuminate the garden. At about 4 P.M., as the daylight was fading to gloom, the search team started to dig a hole at the farthest point from the house, while Rose and the older children watched from an upstairs window. When the police found a bone that turned out to be from a chicken, Steve clowned about making clucking noises. Work was stopped for the day after about an hour.

Fred finally arrived home just before six, by which time the detectives had left the house. Almost four hours had passed since he had been alerted to what the police were doing, yet he gave no explanation of where he had been or what he had been up to. 'Thinking time, perhaps,' suggests Superintendent Bennett.

Fred made his own way to the police station, where he spoke to Hazel Savage. Fred was angry and excited. The police were harassing him, he said. He complained that they wanted to put him back in prison on another false charge. The detectives explained, in the dry language of police work, that they were executing a search warrant for evidence concerning the disappearance of Heather West. At no point did they accuse Fred of killing his daughter, or even suggest that she had been murdered. Yet Fred decided to announce, unprompted, that he had not murdered his daughter, repeating this to a local newspaper reporter who later called at the house to ask what was going on. 'Basically they are accusing me of killing my daughter, but I wouldn't do that,' he said.

Steve and Mae went to the station to offer statements, and detectives returned to the house to speak to Rose. At 7:55 that evening she grudgingly invited two officers, Detective Sergeant Terry Onions and WPC Debbie Willetts, upstairs to the Black Magic bar. Rose was nervous, and spoke to the detectives in a jittery, excited way. During the interview that followed she was aggressive, often shouting and swearing, and even storming out of the room at one stage.

The questions all concerned Heather: how the child had left home and where she was now. The police asked what Rose thought of her:

POLICE: *What's your feelings towards your first-born?*
ROSE WEST: *Well, I'm her mother. What do you think? . . . But I'm afraid we didn't hit it off that well . . . she didn't seem to want to know me that much, she was all her father, not me.*

This was the exact opposite of what Rose had said when she was interviewed in 1992 by Hazel Savage: at that time Rose claimed that Heather telephoned *her* because the teenager did not get on with her father. Rose said there had been a family row the night before her daughter left, and that she had given her £600 to help her start a new life. Rose again said that Heather was a lesbian. When she was asked for details of the bank account from which the money had been drawn, so her story could be corroborated, she shrieked indignantly, 'No, I was upset at the time, I cannot fucking remember! . . . It's a bloody long time ago . . . What do you think I am, a bloody computer? . . . If you had any brains, you could find her . . . It can't be that bloody difficult.'

Rose gave an unflattering assessment of her daughter's char-

acter, saying she was a stubborn, negative child. 'You imagine the
flipping work I put [in], and then they turn around and just
turn their back on you and say I don't want to talk to you any
more,' she complained in a shrill voice. 'She has always been an
obstinate child. She wanted to do the opposite to what everybody else was doing.' Asked again why she had not troubled to
at least report Heather as missing, Rose sneered: 'So I have to
snitch on my own daughter now, do I?' DS Onions enquired
what Rose had done to discipline her children if they had been
unruly. 'Just sent them to bed,' answered Rose.

Rose went on to say that she had nothing to worry about.
The interview continued:

POLICE: *They are going to dig up the patio. The whole patio . . .*
and everything . . .
ROSE WEST: *Sick!*
POLICE: *It might sound stupid . . .*
ROSE WEST: *There's nothing you'll stop at is there, hey?*

WPC Willetts suggested that surely Rose wanted to see her
daughter again. Rose was enraged by this, and replied angrily
that it was not only Heather who did not want to see her, but
her other children too. 'They don't want to see me!' she said, and
then stormed out of the room.

When she came back, Terry Onions asked if Rose thought
that Heather was dead, and received this reply: 'Not unless
something horrible has happened to her.'

POLICE: *Well, she's disappeared for . . .*
ROSE WEST: *But come on, there's hundreds and thousands of*
kids go flipping missing.

Ever mindful of the financial cost of the inquiry, the detectives said they were spending expensive resources. Rose retorted that nobody had asked them to. Terry Onions rounded up the interview by telling Rose that he simply did not believe her; he felt that Heather had been dead for a long time, and was buried either under the floorboards or in the garden. He said that Rose knew this but had shut her mind to it, and now Heather was 'dust or bones'. Even the use of this vivid phrase failed to move Rose, who sneered sarcastically, 'Oh, you're lovely, aren't you?'

The police had found no evidence to hold Fred, so he was allowed home later that evening. A uniformed officer was guarding the excavation at the bottom of the garden. Fred and Rose could see the hole from the kitchen window, and whispered together conspiratorially as Rose washed up. They then discussed the events of the day with Mae and Steve: Fred was concerned about the damage done to his patio and said that the police had better put it back the way they had found it; Rose and the children discussed the possibility that they might all be on the television news. Towards midnight Fred and Rose switched off the lights and climbed the stairs to their room. The pact they had made many years before, to keep the terrible secret of murder between them, must have exercised their minds that night as seldom before.

THE team of diggers returned shortly after dawn, resuming their work with a methodical purpose that impressed Fred, who was watching from an upstairs window. This was the sort of manual labour he had done all his life, and he calculated that it would not be long before they found what they were looking for. He realised that the patio would be destroyed in the process, and that they might well stumble upon other graves – those of Shirley Robinson and Alison Chambers, whose remains were also buried out there.

Fred pulled on a patterned blue sweater and quilted nylon body-warmer. When he was dressed, he hunted around the house for items last used in the hostel in Birmingham, including his 'prison lighter', a stripped-down wick and flint that gave a tiny, economical glow. He looked up and saw that Steve was watching him curiously from the doorway. As they regarded one another, father and son could hear shovels biting the earth outside.

'Son, I will be going away for a while,' said Fred. 'Look after Mum and sell the house . . . I've done something really bad. I want you to go to the papers and make as much money as you can and start a new life.' He went to the bathroom window to take another look at the diggers. Steve stood in the hall and watched him, confused by what his father had said. When Fred turned away from the window, his face was contorted with malevolence. 'He looked at me so evil and so cold. That look went right through me,' remembers Steve.

At around eleven o'clock that morning Hazel Savage arrived back at the house. Rose became angry when Hazel asked for details of Rose's mother, so she could interview her as well. Fred mediated between the women, telling the police he would 'go and have a word with Rose quietly'; he took her aside and told her to go upstairs and keep out of the way. Then he came back into the corridor, where Hazel was waiting, and told the police to take him with them. Shouting and bawling his innocence, Fred was led out of the house to the police car waiting outside. He caused a commotion in the street, bringing many of the neighbours out to watch, yelling 'I didn't kill her!' But when he got in the CID car, Fred said for the first time that he had killed Heather, but the police were looking for her in the wrong place.

Fred was arrested and taken to the Bearland police headquarters, where Hazel urged him to tell the truth. It was explained to him that the police were prepared to dig up the whole garden.

Fred was in an impossible situation. All he could do now was try and protect Rose by taking the blame for Heather, and hope they did not find the others. At about 5 P.M. that afternoon Fred decided to offer a full confession about the killing of his daughter. He said he had buried her remains under the patio near the back door, and wearily agreed to go back to the house and show them exactly where. He made a number of lewd comments about Heather's sexual conduct, claiming that she did not use underwear and often wore revealing tops to show off her breasts. In fact, once he had decided to talk about his crime he seemed unable to stop, and confessed not only to Hazel Savage and the other interviewing detectives, but to his solicitor and even his cell guard as well.

He said he had strangled her and then chopped her up with a special knife used for cutting ice and frozen meat. Hazel asked what he had done with Heather's clothes and belongings; Fred replied that he had stuffed all her things into a black bin bag, and left it with other rubbish outside a vet's surgery in St Michael's Square because it was 'bin day'. He added that he had not killed Heather 'intentionally' – it was not murder, he had just lost his temper with her.

FRED WEST: *I just wanted to shake her, or wanted to take that smirk off her face.*
HAZEL SAVAGE: *But as a result of what you did . . . she died.*
FRED WEST: *Yeah, and that's the bad part of it.*

When he was told that his son Steve had come to the police station to see what was going on, Fred became extremely excited and told the police to keep the boy away from him. 'Be careful with him,' he ranted. 'I mean, I don't want to fight with him . . . I'm not going to stand there and let nobody knock me about. I mean, so what if I injure one of them badly?' A few minutes later he was talking about giving the house to Rose, Mae and Steve, so they would have something to sell and make money.

Before the police could bring Fred back to Cromwell Street, they wanted to get Rose away. Detective Sergeant Onions and other officers arrested Rose and took her into custody. So that there could be no chance of her communicating with Fred, Rose would be interviewed in Cheltenham, within the office block that was the county headquarters of the Gloucestershire Constabulary.

Fred returned home with a group of officers. He was shocked to discover that the police were no longer just digging at the back of the garden – they had extended the search area, and he noticed to his dismay that they had almost stumbled upon the grave of Alison Chambers, the teenager from Jordan's Brook House whose remains he had buried near the bathroom wall. Fred told the detectives that they were digging in completely the wrong place. He pointed to a general area behind the back door of the kitchen, several feet away, and said that this was where they would find his daughter. He told them to dig down about four feet, and not to waste their time looking anywhere else.

There was relief, particularly for Hazel Savage, that progress was being made, but there was not great excitement within the police team. 'What we had was a domestic murder. We'd had two in Gloucestershire already that year,' says John Bennett.

Fred was taken back to Bearland and asked if he wanted legal advice. He chose Howard Ogden, a well-known duty solicitor who had represented him during the 1992 child abuse investigation. Ogden is an overweight, bespectacled man who runs a small private practice in Cheltenham High Street. He makes a modest living by being on-call twenty-four hours a day to represent the burglars, car thieves and drunks who are brought into local police stations and ask for a solicitor on legal aid. It often means he is called out of bed in the middle of the night. In an attempt to drum up new business, he had recently advertised his services on local radio with the catch phrase: 'If you've been nicked, call Oggie.' He had never represented a man facing a murder charge before.

The police were concerned about Fred's sanity. Because of this, John Bennett's team were obliged to call in an 'appropriate adult' who would attend Fred's interviews; that is, an independent observer whose presence is required under the terms of the Mental Health Act when the sanity of the prisoner is an issue. The observer would monitor Fred's state of mind and look out for his mental well-being.

Rose was interviewed at Cheltenham police headquarters that afternoon. Although she did not know that Fred had confessed, Rose was well aware that she had been arrested in connection with a murder investigation, and the seriousness of her situation had subdued her. She answered questions almost timidly, and sobbed whenever she was put under any pressure.

She spoke in a pathetic way about how she felt rejected by her family. She said she had not seen her younger children for eighteen months, and had lost contact with Anna Marie. When she was questioned about Heather's disappearance, Rose replied, 'Past experience told me . . . that once a child does cut you off, there's not a lot you're going to do about getting them back.'

Asked again about when Heather had last been in contact with the family, Rose said that she believed Heather had visited Fred in the bail hostel in Birmingham within the past eighteen months, and that Fred had said she looked 'rough'. Rose said that she hoped Heather was alive somewhere in the 'big bad world'.

The detectives then solemnly informed Rose that there had been a major development in the case. They told her that Fred had confessed to murdering Heather. Rose, who had been speaking almost in a whisper, gasped aloud, '*What?*'

'So you know where she is?' she added.

'He's told us where she is,' replied Terry Onions.

In a high-pitched, almost hysterical voice, Rose asked, 'So she's dead? Is that right?'

Rose was told she was involved.

'Why does it automatically implicate me?'

'Our suspicions are aroused that you are implicated in it, that you are involved in it.'

Rose screamed, 'It's a lie!'

Sobbing loudly, she would answer no more questions for the time being and was allowed to take a break.

The interview started again approximately three and a half hours later. It was suggested to her that, if she really did not know that Heather had been murdered, she was either blind, extremely naïve, or a liar. But Rose had another explanation. 'Or I was sent out,' she suggested, adding that Fred had often made her spend the night with other men. 'I was more or less given a certain time to come back in.' This would be Rose's alibi: she had been completely oblivious to her husband's murderous activities because she had not been there when they happened. The police wondered aloud what this said about their marriage. 'Well, put it this way,' said Rose. 'I feel like a bit of a cunt, to be blunt with it.'

POLICE: *What's your feelings towards Fred now then, now that you know he's slain your eldest daughter?*

ROSE WEST: *Put it this way, he's a dead man if I ever get my hands on him.*

18

THE HOUSE OF HORRORS

ON THE MORNING of Saturday 26 February 1994, the police search team began to excavate a hole in the back garden of 25 Cromwell Street – the place where Fred had said they would find Heather.

The garden was a claustrophobic place in which to work. The red brick wall of the Seventh-Day Adventist Church hemmed it in on one side, and there was a row of tall evergreen fir trees on the other. The narrow strip of earth between was crowded by the search team and their equipment, and there was barely enough room left to operate the small mechanical digger that had been brought in. Conditions became even more uncomfortable when it started to rain and the trampled garden turned to mud.

John Bennett had called upon one of the Home Office's most eminent scientists to help identify the human remains he expected to find. Professor Bernard Knight was aged sixty-two when the murder investigation began. Knight, who trained as a barrister and writes crime novels in his spare time, is a professor of forensic pathology. From examining human remains, he attempts to describe the victim in life, and, where possible, to give an opinion on how and when they died. The professor estimates that he has performed over twenty-five thousand autopsies on men, women and children who have met every type of violent death. He is an atheist who claims to prefer the company of animals to people. In a revealing interview for the radio programme *In the Psychiatrist's Chair*, he said, 'I think the human race is pretty rotten. The more I see of it, the more rotten it becomes . . . We are a malignancy on the face of the earth.' The task before him could only reinforce those beliefs.

The professor and John Bennett were obliged to wait at the police station while the search team, now wearing bright yellow coveralls with the hoods up, laboured under the pouring rain. It had been hoped that digging the pit would be straightforward, but as the hole deepened, its water-logged sides crumbled and caved in. The bottom was also obscured by a dirty brown puddle, making it hard to see what progress was being made.

Despite Fred's advice that they should not bother looking elsewhere in the garden, the police persisted in searching the general area. This seemed to be a sensible approach, particularly as – several hours after the main team had started digging – they still had not found Heather's remains. It was while the police were probing an area by the back door of the house, near the church wall, that just after 4 P.M. they stumbled upon what they thought might be a piece of human bone. Because it was found on its own, some distance from where Fred had said to look, the discovery was not deemed important enough to move the focus of the dig. 'Gloucester is built on a number of Roman burial grounds, and it is not unusual to find human remains,' says John Bennett. Nevertheless, the bone was sent back to the station for Professor Knight's investigation.

But because Heather's grave remained elusive, the search area was widened. Later that afternoon, when a secondary hole on the left-hand side of the patio by the fir trees had reached a depth of two feet, a member of the team spotted a large dark-brown object. It was carefully removed by Professor

Knight and washed clean of mud. The professor identified it as a human thighbone, discoloured after years in the ground. The hole was filled with glutinous black matter — decomposed human flesh and bodily organs mixed with earth. The smell was appalling. Professor Knight (who, luckily for him, has no sense of smell) reached down and began cautiously probing the 'quagmire', as he describes it, where the femur had been found, and uncovered a mass of human bones all jumbled together in a tiny hole just a foot across. Fragments of a black bin bag were under the ribs; large teeth and clumps of hair lay near a skull. Professor Knight also recovered fingernails and two short lengths of rope.

The bones were washed and taken in dustbins to Gloucester police headquarters for closer examination. Professor Knight told John Bennett that, from examining the size of the skull and the pelvis, he suspected that these were the remains of a young woman, and the early signs were that she had been dismembered and decapitated before burial. It was almost a complete skeleton when put together, but the professor noticed that curious body parts, notably the kneecaps, several bones from one foot and some from the hands, were missing.

It was then confirmed that the other bone found earlier in the day was also a human remain, but not a part of the main skeleton. Neither was it an ancient artefact of Roman Glevum. John Bennett now realised there might be a second victim buried in the garden.

THAT evening Rose was told that the police had found Heather's grave, but she did not appear to be shocked by this news. She was then told that the search team had come across evidence of another murder victim, which did excite her: she exclaimed, 'Oh, this is all getting too much!'

★

At the Bearland police headquarters, Fred told detectives he had strangled Heather in the hallway of the house after the other children had gone to school. He said he had stored her body in a dustbin while he waited for an opportunity to dig her grave. Fred seemed fairly relaxed as he spoke about this, although he frequently stopped to smoke cigarettes. He would not give an explanation for the missing parts of Heather's skeleton.

It was put to him that Heather was not the only murder victim in the garden. The detectives told Fred that they had found another human remain.

It is difficult to know what motivated Fred to go further in his confession. Possibly it was a relief to unburden himself, or maybe he was just caught off-balance by this piece of news. Whatever went through Fred's mind, he decided to admit that there were two more victims in the garden. It emerged that one was a former tenant at the house, a young woman named Shirley Robinson. Fred admitted that she had been pregnant with his baby, and also said she was a lesbian. The third victim was another young woman, but Fred was unable to provide her name and referred to her only as 'Shirley's mate'. He said he had buried her near the bathroom wall.

Fred was asked about his criminal history, particularly the attack on Caroline Owens in 1972. (The police had actually found a faded local newspaper clipping about the case when they searched the house, as well as Fred and Rose's rather incriminating love letters in a box in the attic.) The detectives were curious to know about Rose's involvement in the attack. Fred agreed that Rose had been an accomplice, and that the kidnap of Caroline Owens had been a test to see if he could make the women have lesbian sex together. He had hoped that this would develop into bondage sex and that the outcome would be Caroline's murder, because Fred admitted he would almost certainly have gone 'too far again'.

By this time it was obvious that the scope of the murder

inquiry had changed dramatically. 'We knew we weren't looking for one any more, for certain,' says John Bennett.

Following Fred's interview, Rose was also put under arrest for the murders of Shirley Robinson and the second, unknown female. At lunchtime on Sunday she was questioned about these murders and told that Fred had 'seen sense and told the police all'. It was suggested that she did the same. Rose was obviously unsettled by this, and in a quavering voice, remarked that there was 'something wrong with the bloke altogether'.

Fred was officially charged with Heather's murder on Sunday night. He appeared before Gloucester magistrates the next morning, still dressed in his patterned jumper and blue body-warmer. He had been in custody for almost seventy-two hours, and his beard had grown dark. His solicitor, Howard Ogden, told the court that Fred had admitted to killing his daughter, was being 'utterly co-operative', and was also helping police with two other murder inquiries. Fred was formally remanded into custody and taken back to the cells.

Rose was released on police bail and returned home, where she watched the dig from behind net curtains. She had been interviewed for a total of just four hours; this short period of time was partly because her answers were so terse and unhelpful. She had refused food throughout her time in custody, and had consequently been given a medical examination before leaving the station. Mae and Steve stayed at the house with her. Steve had already spoken to the local newspaper, saying that he and Mae supported their parents and did not think it was possible that they had killed anybody.

It had continued to rain hard, and large puddles of muddy water had formed in the back garden and the alley behind Cromwell Street. The police brought in pumping equipment to drain the site and erected a large yellow tarpaulin. Screens had also been set up to hide the work from curious passers-by.

Fred had been brought back to Cromwell Street and was

asked to point out the graves in the garden. He was mortified by the damage done to his patio and complained bitterly, telling the bemused detectives that he expected everything to be put back the way they had found it when they finished. Then he indicated that the third, unknown victim was buried near the bathroom wall. Under the watch of Professor Knight, the search team excavated the grave Fred had identified, and at 5:20 P.M. on Monday, as the daylight was fading, they uncovered a set of bones in the pool of liquid mud at the bottom of the pit. The bones were jumbled, and it seemed that the body had been dis-membered, like Heather's. Numerous foot and hand bones, and some other body parts, were missing. The remains of the head were separate, and a belt was fastened around the skull from under the chin to the top of the head.

Fred had also given instructions about where in the back garden the search team would find his former lodger, Shirley Robinson, yet there was nothing to be found where Fred had said they should dig. It was only after the search area had been widened that, at 9 P.M. that evening, the team uncovered a third set of bones, buried just behind the back door of the house, partly under the wall of the church next door. The grave was left for Professor Knight to excavate fully in the morning.

All this activity drew attention to the case, and national news-paper journalists began to drift into Gloucester. They spoke with Fred's neighbours, and were told that he worked very hard and was always willing to help out with any odd job. It was clear that Cromwell Street was an unprepossessing address: it was shabby, and many of the houses had been split into low-rent flats used by a transient population of college students, the unemployed and psychiatric patients who had been released from the decommis-sioned Coney Hill mental hospital. There was also a criminal element – one former resident was serving a prison sentence for attempted murder, and another young man was a well-known drug dealer.

Some of the neighbours claimed they had always suspected something was wrong at Number 25. They spoke of banging noises and screaming late at night. A terrible smell was said to have come from the house, and one neighbour remembered a plague of flies emanating from the cellar.

Members of Fred's family were traced, and gave their reaction to the discovery of Heather's body. 'I can't believe the news. Fred was always such a gentle guy,' said his youngest brother, Doug. The developments had such a dramatic effect on John West that he feared he was experiencing a heart attack. The next day Fred made the daily newspapers in a story headlined: GARDEN OF EVIL.

PROFESSOR Knight returned to the house in the morning, and carefully excavated the remains of the body Fred had named as Shirley Robinson. This was the only grave where the distinct remnants of any human organs were preserved: there were scraps of brain tissue inside her skull. It appeared from cut marks on her bones that the young woman had been hacked to pieces: her head had been cut from her spine, and again, many foot and hand bones were missing. Beside her remains, Professor Knight found the skeleton of a foetus, almost at full term.

John Bennett decided he had to widen the investigation. 'With three bodies in the garden, we were searching the house properly,' he said. Rose was moved out to a police safe-house in the market town of Dursley, thirteen miles south-west of Gloucester, and police moved into 25 Cromwell Street. Every single item of furniture was removed and put into storage: fitted cabinets, baths, sinks and major appliances were all taken out; carpets and linoleum were rolled up. When this was done, the police began to inspect the floorboards and the concrete floor of the cellar.

*

ON Thursday morning Fred again appeared at Gloucester Magistrates Court. This time he was charged not only with Heather's murder, but with that of Shirley Robinson* and the unknown young woman found near the bathroom wall. The hours of questioning had clearly taken their toll, and Fred was pale and tired. When he heard that he was being charged with the murder of Shirley Robinson, his arms shot up into the air, his legs buckled and he slumped down on to a chair.

FRED was made aware that his painstaking home improvements were being ripped apart. At the same time, the police began to ask him in detail about what had happened to his first wife, Rena, and also Charmaine, whom they assumed to be Fred and Rena's daughter. They had discovered that Rena and the child had not been seen for twenty years. It was put to Fred that he had killed them, too.

The interviews went on for up to sixteen hours each day. They were conducted by two shifts of detectives, each made up of one man and one woman. Hazel Savage was part of one of these teams. There was a major breakthrough shortly after Hazel had impressed upon Fred that police now intended to search the entire house. A handwritten note was passed to John Bennett. It read: 'I Frederick West authorise my solicitor Howard Ogden to advise Supt. Bennett that I wish to admit to a further (approx) 9 killings, expressly, Charmaine, Rena . . . and others to be identified.'

Fred was asked whether there were any more bodies in the house. Fred already knew that the police were searching the cellar, so there seemed little point in lying; also, he was anxious to

---

* There were never any charges brought for the killing of either Shirley Robinson's unborn child or Anna McFall's, as there is no such crime under British law.

take the blame and protect Rose. On Friday evening Fred decided to tell the police about the other girls buried in his home. He said they were mostly hitch-hikers and runaways. He did not know all their names. Most were under the cellar floor; another was under the bathroom floor. He could not remember exactly how many there were.

Fred had prepared a plan of the cellar, and, in a genial mood, sat down with detectives to show them where to look. It was an extraordinary moment. When Hazel Savage asked 'How many bodies are there in Cromwell Street, Fred?', he was unable to answer, and after a moment of thought, agreed with his solicitor Howard Ogden that they were only 'talking an approximation'. Apart from 'Shirley's mate', he said there was 'the girl from Newent' and a girl named Lynda.

> HAZEL SAVAGE: *Lynda who?*
> FRED WEST: *Um, Gough, is it?*

It was obvious that either Fred's memory for these tragic events was not good, or that he was trying not to say anything that would incriminate Rose: in his own words, he was 'not one hundred per cent sure on some of these'. He talked about the killings in a shockingly matter-of-fact way, without any passion or distress. The only time he became agitated was when he learned that the police were planning to demolish parts of the house. 'What, they're gonna actually knock the building down?' he cried in dismay.

The detectives were dumbfounded by this torrent of information, but they believed him – even though they were beginning to recognise that Fred lived in a fantasy world at times. 'We got an impression when he was telling the truth,' says John Bennett.

Fred repeatedly told detectives that Rose had never been present when he had strangled his victims. It seems that he was trying to cover up for her. Fred said he had picked up the girls at various places, and had relationships with them, but had strangled them when they had threatened to tell Rose or had demanded money. He said he had taken the girls back to Cromwell Street to abuse, kill, cut them up and bury their remains.

He spoke about the sexual aspect of the crimes, but did not agree that he had raped anybody – Fred thought that all the victims had *wanted* to have sex with him. In fact, Fred considered himself to be a perfectly normal, rather nice man.

When he was in the interview room with other men, Fred spoke at great length about sex and his sexual fetishes, but he became reticent when Hazel Savage or another woman came in. He also refused to explain why there were bones missing from the victims and why a belt was tied around the skull of the unknown girl.

Asked about the condition in which the remains had been found, Fred said that he had cut up the bodies to make them easier to bury, and that he had decapitated them to 'make sure they were dead'. The fact that there were no clothes found in the graves suggested that the girls had been naked when they were killed, pointing to a sexual motive.

John Bennett decided that he was dealing with a psychopath – a man who could butcher young women, bury them under his garden and house and yet carry on as if nothing were wrong – but felt there would be no harm in obtaining an expert opinion on Fred's mind. The police called in the criminal psychologist Paul Britton to compile a professional 'profile' of Fred's mentality. This was done by studying Fred's interviews and noting not only what he said, but the way in which he said it.

The inquiry team were struck by Fred's remarkably relaxed attitude towards his crimes. When Fred spoke about what he had done, it was without passion or anguish. From what the detectives were now learning about Fred's psychology from Paul Britton, it was felt that Fred's blasé manner might indicate that he had been killing for such a long time that he was now quite used to murder. Fred was fifty-two years old. It was not lost on the detectives that, if he had been killing since he was a young man, then he had almost certainly murdered many more than those dozen or so girls he had already talked about.

IDENTIFYING the remains was proving difficult. Heather was not such a problem, but there was hardly any information about the other two victims. Fred had identified the third set of remains as those of a lesbian named Shirley Robinson. Yet there was no police report of such a person having gone missing, and Rose claimed to have only the vaguest memory of her, despite the fact that they must have been pregnant and living in the house at the same time. The other young woman was an even greater mystery.

The scale of the inquiry was growing by the hour, and a large incident room was set up on the ground floor of the Bearland headquarters to handle the incoming information. John Bennett decided to use the relatively new computer system HOLMES (Home Office Large Major Enquiry System) to bank the mass of data, and computer-imaging software (named 'Watson') to help his detectives save time in analysing the data for evidence. 'Watson' produced easily-understood charts and diagrams.

An early priority was to compile an accurate list of all the Wests' children. Until police knew how large the family was, they could not work out who was missing. Interviews with Anna Marie and others suggested that Fred had fathered children all over the country – Fred himself claimed as many as forty-two – and that they came and went from Cromwell Street with bewildering frequency. Another piece of computer software, known as the 'Analyst's Notebook', was used to create the complex West family tree.

Work in the incident room was controlled by the 'action allocators' who handed out the assignments to the inquiry teams. These detectives were sent away to interview potential witnesses. Information they brought back to the incident room was then given to the 'home teams' who programmed the data into the HOLMES computer. Statement readers went through transcripts of interviews that had been completed, marking passages that needed further investigation. Together with the four officers who were interviewing Fred full-time, the search team at Cromwell Street, the uniformed officers who were guarding the site and John Bennett and his senior staff, it was already a major inquiry involving over thirty men and women.

At his laboratory in Cardiff Royal Infirmary, Professor Knight was carrying out examinations of the remains that had already been found. He measured the dimensions of the bones and conducted chemical tests to establish the sex, approximate age and height of the victims. He was also able to describe how they had been dismembered and work out approximately how long they had been underground. Proving cause of death would be more difficult, because all the flesh had long since rotted into a kind of black mulch, and there were no wounds to study – just old bones.

A new electronic device was hired to probe 25 Cromwell Street for the bodies Fred had pointed out. The ground-probing radar machine (GPR), also known as Surface Penetrating Radar, had been developed by a company named ERA Technology to locate land mines on the Falkland Islands. The company had been trying to convince the Home Office of its other possible applications in criminal investigations, and tests had been carried out using the buried carcasses of pigs. Costing £50,000, and looking rather like a sophisticated lawnmower, the GPR was not able to find actual bones, but emitted an electronic pulse that could detect cavities in the ground, including air pockets, where flesh and other material had rotted away. The GPR was attached to a computer monitor which displayed a colour image of whatever it found.

The machine was brought into the house late on the afternoon of Friday 4 March. It was first tried in the ground floor bathroom, where Fred had said a body was buried in an old inspection pit under the floor. Just after 4 P.M. a positive red image appeared on the computer screen, and John Bennett was called to the house. The machine was then moved into the cellar, where it was used late into the night. Fred was brought back to the house that same evening, and was aghast to discover it had been stripped by police of every stick of furniture. Fred was led down into the cellar. Using an aerosol can of paint, he then sprayed 3' × 3' square markers on the concrete floor where he recalled burying bodies. Afterwards he was taken back to Bearland.

By Saturday morning, the GPR had located what appeared to be five more sets of remains – Fred had evidently lost count when marking them the previous evening, as he had indicated six.

Pneumatic drills were brought in to start breaking up the cellar's concrete floor. Just before lunch on Saturday, the police found human remains buried in front of a false chimney breast. In the pit with the bones was a knotted loop of cloth: this was found to be a scarf square, folded, or rolled, and tied so as to form a loop approximately 13½ inches in circumference. It had been tied in a bow, and fragments of hair were trapped inside the knotted part of the cloth. Again the head appeared to have been decapitated and body parts were missing. The soil around the bones had been stained by the decomposition of human flesh.

Another set of bones was found a little before 3 P.M., also in the cellar. This grave was directly opposite the previous one, against the other wall adjacent to a fireplace decorated with Marilyn Monroe wallpaper. The victim had been decapitated, her legs had been severed, and bones, especially from the hands and feet, were missing. The surrounding clay had been stained dark brown. A mask of adhesive tape was wrapped around the skull eleven or twelve times, and a narrow plastic tube was protruding from the nose. A second length of tube, bent in a U-shape, was also in the grave.

Later that evening John Bennett addressed a press conference in Gloucester, admitting, in his cautious way, that his team had found 'suspected evidence' of at least two more bodies. But he warned that the GPR machine could not distinguish between hollows caused by bones and those of general debris. The full story of what the police had been told by Fred, and what they had found, appeared on the front page of the next morning's *Sunday Mirror* newspaper, under the headline HOUSE OF HORRORS, the name that became synonymous with the case.

On Sunday morning the sixth set of bones was discovered, buried in what detectives described as the 'nursery alcove' of the cellar on the same side as the fourth victim. The bones were between two and a half and three and a half feet beneath the floor, and had been dismembered and jumbled on top of each other just like the others. This time the decapitated skull had a length of cloth wrapped around it, and a large, well-worn knife with a wooden handle was found with the bones, some of which again were missing. The knife was still sharp. There was also a piece of rope and an oval of adhesive tape approximately sixteen inches in circumference; two hair-grips and hair fragments were caught in the adhesive. From what Fred had said about the girl buried there, it appeared that these were probably the remains of Lucy Partington, who went missing in late 1973. John Bennett,

in particular, remembered the case, as he had been one of the
young police divers who had dragged local rivers and ponds in
the search for her body twenty years before.

Just before lunch on Sunday, the team discovered another
grave on the opposite side of the cellar in an alcove by the wall,
where a staircase had once been. The grave was about three and
a half feet deep, and again the soil had been stained. With the
decapitated, dismembered remains was a plastic-covered rope,
like a clothes line, still wrapped around the upper arm bone, the
right leg at knee level and the thighbone. Another length near
the elbow went under the spine, with two small wrist- or ankle-
sized knotted loops. A band of fabric, made of two nylon socks,
a brassière and two pairs of tights one within the other, was
wrapped around the jaw of the skull.

The next evening – while Bernard Knight excavated the
remains in the basement – the police broke up the concrete in
the downstairs bathroom, uncovering more remains in what had
been the inspection pit. The grave also contained a loop of adhesive tape that had almost certainly been used as a gag. The victim
had been dismembered and decapitated; many bones were missing and the skull was embedded in the wall of the excavation
near the gag. There were also two pieces of tape, a length of
string and pieces of knotted fabric, but nothing that could have
clothed the girl. Like all the others, she must have been naked
when she died.

On Tuesday, at 7:10 P.M., the ninth set of remains was found,
buried three feet beneath the cellar floor, away from the wall
and adjacent to a wash-basin. The skull was face down, with an
elasticated cloth band covering the jaw. Other pieces of fabric
and a length of clothes line were nearby. The victim had clearly
been cut up and decapitated. The earth and clay beneath the
cellar were sodden from the high water table and mixed with
sewage from a nearby drain. (There had been an ancient moat
beneath Cromwell Street and the footings under the houses

were generally damp.) This complicated Professor Knight's work, because he felt the bones could have moved around over the years in the semi-liquid medium in which they were buried.

BY Day Fourteen of the investigation, the bones of nine young women had been discovered at 25 Cromwell Street. Some had clearly been buried for many years, and apart from three, the police had absolutely no idea of the victims' identities.

19

THE TOOTH FAIRY

'THE MAIN PART of the investigation was the identification. We had no idea who they were,' admits John Bennett.

The remains of Fred and Rose's victims amounted to no more than piles of broken and decaying bones. They were not even complete skeletons. The remains were numbered in order of their discovery and passed into the care of Professor Bernard Knight, who was able to say what gender they were, give an idea of their physical build and approximate age at death. But to put names to these young women was quite another matter.

Fred could help to a certain extent: he said that the remains known as Number One were those of Heather, and there was little reason to doubt him. He said that Number Three was Shirley Robinson. But as to the other seven found at Cromwell Street, Fred could give only the vaguest clues. Several were hitch-hikers or girls he had picked up at bus stops. He had called one hitch-hiker 'Tulip' because she had a foreign accent and another girl 'Truck' because she wore a badge in the shape of a lorry. But, like many of the others, he had never known her real name.

The inquiry team consulted Gloucestershire's missing persons files and came up with several names, including those of the university student Lucy Partington and the waitress Mary

Bastholm. The Gloucestershire force had been involved in large-scale searches for both girls. When their names were put to Fred, he indicated that one of his victims might be Lucy Partington, but was unhelpful in the case of Mary Bastholm.

Then Fred said that at least two of the victims were from the Worcester area, but he also invented bizarre stories about them, telling police at one point: 'What all these girls apparently was doing, as I said, [was] prostituting.' He got their names and descriptions mixed up, confusing 'the Dutch girl' with a German girl, and told police that he had rarely seen their faces in daylight.

When asked if he had cut his victims up before burial, Fred became oddly coy and said he could not remember for certain. For example, this is how Fred replied to one particular question about dismemberment:

POLICE: *Was she [one of the as-yet-unidentified victims] all in one piece or did you cut her up?*
FRED WEST: *I ain't sure.*
POLICE: *Do you remember what you did?*
FRED WEST: *I ain't sure, no . . . I don't think any of them were cut up . . . I wouldn't be one hundred per cent on that one, mind.*

John Bennett contacted West Mercia Police to see what missing persons they had on their files. West Mercia came back with several names, including Carol Ann Cooper, who had been living in the Pines Children's Home, and Shirley Hubbard, who had been on the work experience course at Debenhams in Worcester.

Now that it was clear that not all the victims were local to Gloucester, John Bennett decided to contact all the neighbouring police forces and the Missing Persons Bureau in London. He asked for details of any young girls who had gone missing since the late 1960s and who might have been to the Gloucester area. The response was almost overwhelming – hundreds of names came back.

These were fed into the HOLMES computer at the incident room in Bearland. Then the inquiry team began to work through the mass of information, trying to compile a shortlist of names which were then put to Fred. He continued to be co-operative, looked at photographs he was shown and even helped draw portraits of his victims from memory. In fact, Fred was so genial that the officers who watched his cell were told to stop chatting with him. But he simply did not know the names of most of the girls he had killed.

THE murder squad was faced with the problematic fact that thousands of young people go missing every year. Many more disappear but are never officially reported, as their families either care little about them or assume they do not wish to be troubled. John Bennett's team feared they would never succeed in identifying all the victims.

When it became known that 25 Cromwell Street was a charnel-house of missing girls, dozens of telephone calls came in from families who had lost their daughters. Many were confused by press reports of 'bodies' being found, and begged to come in to the station just in case they could recognise their loved ones. They did not understand that the police were dealing with piles of bones rather than corpses with faces.

It was a scientist based at the University of Wales College of Medicine who was to solve the problem. Oral biologist Dr David Whittaker was fifty-four when the investigation began, a slim man who speaks with a distinct Lancashire accent. He divides his work at the university between teaching, research and forensic science.

Dr Whittaker explains: 'It so happens that the teeth and surrounding structures actually contain more information about the lifestyle of the individual than any other part of the body.' This is because teeth grow sequentially over a period of years, starting before birth and ending in the twenties, and once mature do not renew themselves, as human bones do. Therefore everything that happens to the body during life is permanently encoded in the teeth.

Dr Whittaker had already received the skulls and lower mandibles of the Cromwell Street victims from Professor Knight. He began to study these in his office within the Dental School at the University of Wales.

The gender of the victim is recorded in chromosomes preserved in tooth pulp. The precise age of the victim at death can be discovered by extracting amino-acids from the teeth, and then working out the ratio of molecules (which change in a standard way as the body matures).

Dr Whittaker was even able to discover what illnesses the victims had suffered as children, as the drugs they had been prescribed leave traces in the teeth. It is possible to say exactly when the illness occurred, from the position of these traces. 'One removes all this information scientifically, and builds up a dossier on the individual. This enables the police to narrow down on, let's say, half a dozen putative missing people of the right age and sex,' explains Dr Whittaker.

'What we do then is get the police to produce as many photographic records of those individuals as possible, and as close to the time of death as possible.' This is so the doctor can carry out the process of Facial Superimposition. It is this which brought about the positive identification of the victims of Fred and Rose West.

Dr Whittaker's team of technical experts analysed the photographs given to them by police. In each case, they worked out the focal length of the cameras used to take the pictures. This is essential because, contrary to the aphorism, the camera *does* lie. All classical photography distorts the image, and cameras lie in different ways depending on the focal length of the lens used. Once the technicians had worked out which type of lens had taken the picture they had been given, an electronic camera was set up, programmed with exactly the same degree of distortion. This would be used to photograph the skull.

Each skull was fixed to a goniometer. This is a complex stand, with calibrations, that allows the skull to be positioned at any angle through 360 degrees. This is necessary because the skull had to be photographed in exactly the same position as in the picture the police had provided of the victim in life: if the girl's head was slightly bowed forward in the snapshot, for example, then the skull must be bowed forward. When the angle was exactly right, the electronic camera took its picture.

The camera then took a second picture of the original snapshot. When this had been done, Dr Whittaker had an image of both the skull and the original photograph taken with a camera set at precisely the same focal length and at exactly the same angle. If the skull did belong to the girl in the picture, then they should match up.

The image of the skull was printed on to blue transparency film, like the type used for overhead projectors. The girl's face in life was printed on another transparency film and coloured sepia. 'Then we merge the two together to see if they fit. We check about fifteen or sixteen separate points around the face: eye sockets, the bridge of the nose, the sides of the jaws and so on,' says Dr Whittaker.

To see the blue death's-head grinning through the sepia-coloured face of a smiling girl was a shocking experience for the detectives working on the case.

By the middle of March, Dr Whittaker with his remarkable computer technology was able to identify positively the skull of victim Number Nine as that of Carol Ann Cooper. The grateful

detectives awarded the biologist the affectionate nickname of
'The Tooth Fairy'.

Carol's stepmother, Barbara Cooper, had already been warned
to expect the news, but it was still disturbing. She said, 'I never
believed she was killed. I always thought she was living somewhere else. She was a rebellious girl and used to say I wasn't her
real mum, but I did my best for her. I'm glad that it's all over
now.'

FROM interviews the police had conducted with witnesses and
members of the West family, it was clear that Rose was both violent and sexually perverse. It was in her character, even more
than Fred's, to lose her temper, beat and strangle somebody. She
had done just that many times. The statements of Caroline
Owens were particularly telling: she firmly believed the attack
had been Rose's idea. But, after retracting his earlier comments,
Fred steadfastly refused to implicate his wife. Whenever he spoke
about his crimes, he went out of his way to say that Rose had
not been there, even inventing elaborate excuses for her absence.

But Rose had betrayed Fred. She had turned against him in an
attempt to save herself. She told police that she 'didn't know
nothing' about what had been going on at 25 Cromwell Street
and said that Fred was insane. Rose assumed the role of a victim,
a woman who had lost a daughter and a stepdaughter to a
maniac.

She was not in custody, but living under close observation in
the safe-house provided for her in Dursley. Rose was accompanied by her children, Mae and Steve, and her pet dogs, Benji and
Oscar. Mother and children soon fell out. When Steve said he
wanted to see his father, Rose was furious and told him to leave
the house, yelling, 'You're as nuts as he is!' Steve spent several
days sleeping rough before he decided to grant an interview to
the *News of the World* newspaper about his parents' sex life.

Shortly afterwards he had acquired a smart suit, mobile phone and an expensive four-wheel drive.

Rose was irritated by the damage that was being done to 25 Cromwell Street. She had been told that the floorboards had been pulled up, wallpaper was being stripped and that internal walls were being demolished. There were also plans to dismantle the extension and send divers down a well beneath the property. The house was in such a weakened state that concrete had to be poured into the basement to stop it falling down. Via her solicitor, Rose suggested that she might seek compensation for the damage.

Public feeling against Rose was running high: John Bennett was regularly stopped in the streets of Gloucester and asked why he had not 'locked that bitch up yet'. Because of fears for her safety, Rose was moved from Dursley to another police safe-house in Cheltenham. It was sparsely furnished and not particularly comfortable, but once inside Rose was too frightened to leave. She rarely changed out of her dressing gown and wiled away the time smoking, watching cartoons on television and playing her own version of Scrabble, whereby only words to do with sex could be used. Her sister-in-law, Barbara Letts, was asked to visit, and the two women spent several hours together. 'She didn't want to know anything about Fred. She hates Fred now,' said Barbara afterwards. Rose was unaware that the house she had been living in had been bugged by police, with the special authority of the Chief Constable himself, and that every word she uttered in the living room was being tape-recorded.

JUANITA Mott's name had been suggested as one of the victims. She had never been reported to the police as a missing person, but her sister Belinda Moore told the inquiry team that she had been searching for Juanita for years. In a bizarre coincidence, Belinda had actually visited Cromwell Street because one of her friends lodged there. The family gave the police good quality photographs of Juanita, and Dr Whittaker superimposed these over the skull of Number Seven. They matched.

By the end of March the inquiry team were able to announce that they believed Lucy Partington, Juanita Mott, Lynda Gough and Alison Chambers were among the dead of Cromwell Street. For the families it was the end they had long expected, but there was still pain. 'I didn't want to believe she could be one of the bodies, but now the police have said they are sure she is, I feel numb,' said Juanita's sister. Alison Chambers' mother, Joan Owen, said, 'It's going to take a long time to sink in, even after all these years. Alison will always be with me.' Lucy Partington's father, Roger, said, 'The grief is still there, but uncertainty is worse.' Lynda Gough's parents, John and June Gough, issued a joint statement, which read: 'We have lived in the hope that she would come home. Now we know she will not.'

FRED was taken out to Much Marcle to show the police where he had buried Rena Costello and where he believed Anna McFall's grave was (although he insisted he had not killed her). He helped detectives mark out parts of Letterbox and Finger Post fields, but had difficulty saying exactly where they should look because the topography of the area had changed since he had dug the graves.

Fred had also been taken on a tour of other places in Herefordshire and Gloucestershire where he had lived and worked. It was hoped that, if there were more graves, then he would show them where. But what little Fred did say was too vague to warrant digging.

It had been noticed that the information Fred was giving was becoming less reliable, if not bizarre. Fred broke off from interviews to talk about the weather, or wonder about his garden and the welfare of his tropical fish. At one stage he told the detectives of his 'friendship' with the singer Lulu – in his fantasy, Fred believed they had travelled around the world together. He had also started to contradict his earlier confessions about the murders, and talked about the deaths of Rena, Anna McFall and Charmaine as if he were a bereaved victim, rather than their killer.

Despite these problems with believing what Fred said, John Bennett decided to lead a second search team to the windswept fields between Much Marcle and neighbouring hamlet of Kempley. They set up camp in Letterbox Field on Monday 28 March. The police referred to this site as Kempley A, because it is just inside the Gloucestershire border and Kempley is the nearest Gloucestershire village. The 'A' is because the police also planned to excavate a second site nearby.

A large blue and white tent was erected over an area near a hedgerow where Fred had said they should find Rena's remains. Three officers started to dig a trench three feet wide and four feet deep. The earth was shovelled on to conveyor belts, where two more officers inspected the sticky clods with their fingers. The earth would later be sieved, literally, so that tiny bones – and the all-important teeth – were not overlooked.

FRED was reunited with his son Steve after another remand court appearance on 8 April. 'Sorry was the first thing I expected him to say, and he didn't,' said his son afterwards. Fred was emotional, and instructed Steve to pass on his love to Rose.

A chance telephone call had solved the mystery of the victim known as 'Tulip'. A police detective from London called the incident room at Bearland and suggested that Tulip might be Thérèse Siegenthaler, a missing Swiss student whose case he had worked on in 1974. John Bennett contacted the Swiss bureau of Interpol and applied for a *commission rogotoire*, a letter of introduction, to enlist the help of the Swiss police. It was they who contacted Therese's brother, Jürg, who had been to Britain several times over the years to search for his sister. Thérèse's father, Fritz, had died four years earlier, apparently of a broken heart. 'Thérèse was my husband's *liebling*,' said his widow. The inquiry team were also able to name the Worcester Debenhams girl, Shirley Hubbard, as a victim.

On Sunday 10 April, after digging a trench 135 feet long and 6 feet deep, the search team at Letterbox Field found human remains. The police were confident that they were the bones of Rena Costello. The discovery of a child's boomerang within her bones provided police with a macabre and inexplicable mystery. The team then moved a couple of hundred yards across the fields and started digging at Yewtree Coppice in Finger Post Field. Fred had said that they would find the remains of his nanny and former lover Anna McFall here. The site was named Kempley B.

ALTHOUGH Rose continued to live at the Cheltenham safe-house on bail, John Bennett's detectives had been busy collecting evidence about her part in the crimes. They had found ample testimony to Rose's sexual sadism, and it was this that initially put her behind bars.

Rose was brought before magistrates in Gloucester on 21 April. She was jointly charged, alongside a 67-year-old coloured man, of raping an eleven-year-old girl at Cromwell Street in the 1970s. She was also charged with assaulting a small boy at the house in 1974. The charges were enough to deprive Rose of her liberty: she was refused bail and later transferred to Pucklechurch Prison near Bristol – the first time she had ever been inside a gaol. Three days later another man appeared in court charged with raping the same girl.

Rose was now questioned more closely about the murders,

particularly those of Heather West and Lynda Gough. She was asked about the day when Lynda's mother had come to Cromwell Street and found Rose wearing the girl's slippers. Rose could not explain this; nor could she explain why Lynda's clothes had been hanging on her washing line. Her only reply was to say, 'I'm innocent' – and apart from this she said nothing at all. The next day she was charged with Lynda's murder.

ON 25 April John Bennett's men began to search the ground-floor flat and basement of 25 Midland Road. The address was as plain and unlovely as it had been when Fred and Rose had lived there, more than twenty years before. If anything, it had become even less salubrious, due to the increased traffic on nearby Trier Way. Fred had been back to 25 Midland Road with detectives to look at an extension at the rear of the property. He said that he had originally buried Charmaine behind the back door, but that the extension, which he had helped to build in 1976, now covered the area.

While these operations continued, the case against Rose was growing in strength. A number of women who had been sexually abused at Cromwell Street had come forward, and their statements helped make John Bennett feel confident enough to charge her additionally with the murders of Carol Ann Cooper and Lucy Partington. Again Rose said 'I'm innocent,' but added not a word more.

CHARMAINE'S remains were found on 5 May under the extension at the back of 25 Midland Road, when the top of a child's skull was uncovered. Despite what Fred had said about not dismembering her body, the skeleton was in pieces (although it is possible that this could have been caused accidentally when the extension was built). There were no clothes with the remains, suggesting that Charmaine was probably naked when she was killed and may have been sexually abused. Her remains were ceremoniously carried from the house in a box covered by a black cloth. Members of the search team left flowers on the doorstep.

POLICE had questioned several members of the extended West family, including Graham Letts, Barbara Letts and Fred's dustman brother, John. All three of them had been close to Fred and Rose and had frequently visited Cromwell Street. Like his brother, who was one year older, John West was a powerfully built man, but his shock of hair had turned completely white. Police searched his home in the Abbeydale area of Gloucester, and towards the end of the month, charged him with raping two under-age girls in the 1970s. Rose was already charged with raping one of these children.

THE dig at Finger Post Field dragged on without success. At one stage the search team were flooded out by storms; by June, they were sweating under a blazing sun. An enormous amount of earth had been moved, and the field looked like the site of an archaeological dig, partly because the farmer who owned the land had raised the level of the field in the years since Fred had buried his lover. John Bennett was criticised by the press for using police officers for manual work – it was suggested that the search had gone on too long and was costing too much money. After all, they had already found the remains of eleven bodies.

Everybody connected with the case knew that there were more, possibly very many more victims. Even the cautious John Bennett says that he believes the police never found them all. 'I have never made a secret of the fact that I think there are more,' he says. As Fred was being led down to the cells one day after a court appearance, he told a guard: 'They think they know it all, but they don't know the half of it.' He had even tantalised the murder squad by saying that he had 'done one' in Birmingham when he was in the hostel there, and hinted at other bodies in Scotland, as well as more in Herefordshire. He told prison visitors that he had killed Mary Bastholm, and many others, and that he would tell the police about these only when he was good and ready.

THE police noticed that several of the known victims had been murdered within a short space of time. There were suspiciously long periods between the other crimes.

Assuming that Anna McFall was the first woman Fred killed, then the murders started in 1967. Mary Bastholm disappeared in 1968. There then followed a three-year gap until 1971, when Charmaine and Rena both disappeared. Caroline Owens was attacked in late 1972. Two girls died in 1973, three died in 1974 alone, and a further one in 1975. This made a total of eight girls murdered by Fred and Rose within four years. Then came another long gap until 1978, when Shirley Robinson was killed. Alison Chambers went missing the following year, and after her murder, there was an eight-year gap until Heather West was killed in 1987.

An examination of these dates shows that Fred and Rose killed a great many people within apparently isolated, short periods of time. It seems highly unlikely that such a craving for murder could then be left unsatisfied for periods of up to eight years.

Then there is the *rate* of killing to be considered. Fred and Rose killed as many as three women in one year, and Fred's first known murder was committed in 1967. If he, and later he and Rose, had killed once a year on average until 1994, they might be responsible for as many as twenty or thirty murders, and were quite capable of killing twice or three times a year. It is anybody's guess how many of the hundreds of missing girls on file at Bearland Fred and Rose really accounted for.

42. In the second week of the investigation, the police search team continue to dig up the back garden of 25 Cromwell Street. They had already discovered the remains of Heather West and Shirley Robinson in this strip of muddy ground, and would soon find the remains of Alison Chambers. The earth was literally sieved (see bottom right of picture) so the team did not miss any bones.

43. The House of Horrors. On the day this picture was taken, 5 March 1994, two sets of human remains were found in the cellar. The remains, and any other discoveries, were removed in black plastic bins.

44. Home Office pathologist Professor Bernard Knight (left) discusses the excavation of 25 Cromwell Street with police, 7 March 1994. Seven sets of remains had already been found.

45. Bernard Knight (carrying suitcase) is watched by hundreds of onlookers and press as he arrives at Cromwell Street, 10 March 1994. The case attracted extraordinary media attention as the house surrendered its secrets.

46. The 'GPR' surface penetrating radar machine is used to scan the garden of 25 Cromwell Street for more human remains. The machine was developed to find land mines on the Falkland Islands.

47. The fields just outside Much Marcle where Fred buried the remains of his lover, Anna McFall, and his first wife, Rena. Finger Post Field is to the left of the tractor; Letterbox Field to the right. The piles of earth are the result of the police excavations.

48. Letterbox Field, where the remains of Rena Costello were found on 10 April 1994. The excavations were so extensive because the police could not, at first, find what they were looking for. The site came to look like an archaeological dig, and eventually raised questions about the cost of the inquiry.

49. A police diver emerges from the well in the rear garden of 25 Cromwell Street, 22 April 1994. Detective Superintendent John Bennett, a former police diver himself, is on the right of the picture.

50. A policeman carries the remains of Charmaine West from 25 Midland Road, 5 May 1994.

51. The interior of the extension at 25 Midland Road. Charmaine was found underneath where the table stands.

53. Detective Superintendent John Bennett, who masterminded the investigation into the activities of Fred and Rose West. He found the massive media interest in the case difficult to deal with.

52. Detective Constable Hazel Savage, whose persistence led to the initial search at 25 Cromwell Street. Her first involvement with the West family had been in 1966.

54. Mae West says she stood guard while her sister, Heather, was in the bathroom at 25 Cromwell Street. Both girls were terrified of their father's sexual advances. Mae is pictured here (centre) at her brother Steve's wedding in July 1994.

55. Fred's son, Steve West, visited his father several times in prison. Fred indicated to Steve that he had killed the waitress Mary Bastholm, and many more young women. Steve is pictured here with his wife, Andrea.

56. Fred's brother, Doug, with his wife Christine. They still live in Much Marcle, where Fred and Doug grew up.

57. Fred West being led from Gloucester Magistrates Court, 28 July 1994, where he and Rose were charged with the murders of nine young women.

58. Rose leaves a brief remand appearance at Gloucester Magistrates Court on 13 December 1994, where she saw Fred for the last time. She had blanked her husband as they stood in the dock together. This rejection devastated Fred: he fell into a deep depression and killed himself in prison days later, on 1 January 1995.

59. The funeral of Fred West. His cheap wooden casket bore a plaque inscribed simply 'F.W. West'.

60. The police van carrying Rose West arrives at Winchester Crown Court on 3 October 1995, the first day of her trial.

Detectives from Gloucestershire looked at several sites around the country where Fred may have buried these unknown victims. They visited Glasgow, where the M8 motorway had been built over Fred's allotment. The detectives also looked at the caravan sites where Fred had lived, the café where Mary Bastholm had worked and the Stroud Court Community Trust where Fred had worked as an odd-job man. But the truth was that unless Fred himself confessed and led them to the precise spot where he had buried these other victims, there was nothing that could realistically be done. The cynical view within the murder squad was that there had only ever been one person in charge of the investigation – and that person's name was Fred.

FINALLY there was success at Finger Post Field. A member of the search team came across human remains at 6:15 in the evening on Tuesday 7 June. These would later be identified as the bones of Anna McFall. Bindings, similar to those found at Cromwell Street, were in the grave, and the skeleton of a near full-term foetus was by her side.

All digging work officially ceased on 17 June – one hundred and fifteen days after John Bennett had been granted a search warrant for 25 Cromwell Street. The past months had been a unique police investigation. Never before had so many officers dug up so much of the countryside looking for bodies. Police forces from all over Britain and abroad had helped identify the remains. The inquiry team at Gloucester had comprised a core of between thirty and forty officers, rising to approximately eighty when the investigation was at its height – even more had been employed carrying out clerical work. The scars of the investigation were plain to see: 25 Cromwell Street was a shell of a building; the extension had been demolished and taken away; the garden was a rutted building site strewn with rubble; the windows had been blocked in and the front gate chained. The distinctive wrought-iron address sign had been taken down from the front of the building, to foil souvenir hunters who had already stolen street signs. In the fields outside Much Marcle, mounds of red earth were piled up like the work of giant moles.

There were disappointments, not least for Peter Bastholm, whose sister, Mary, had not been found despite high hopes. The reasons were explained to him in patient telephone calls by John Bennett, and he accepted that – although the police strongly suspected that Fred had murdered Mary – Fred had chosen not to co-operate, and they simply did not know where to look.

FRED and Rose were reunited when they made a joint appearance at Gloucester Magistrates Court on 30 June; the first time they had seen each other since February.

There was a fascinated silence as Fred was led up from the cells into court Number Two. His mouth hung slightly open as he glanced around at the journalists, police officers, officials and curious onlookers – a crowd of at least eighty people. It was as though he were an animal in a zoo looking out at the visitors. Rose was led up next: a plump, dowdy woman wearing large spectacles with purple frames. Husband and wife had to stand together in the same tiny dock. As Rose squeezed past, Fred laid his right hand gently on her shoulder. Rose shrank from his touch.

The Wests were told that they stood jointly charged with nine murders, and that Fred was charged with the additional murders of his first wife, Rena Costello, and Rena's daughter, Charmaine.* Rose sat down for the few minutes it took to discuss the remand arrangements. Fred stood behind her, swaying slightly. His son, Steve, was in the crowd and tried to catch his

---

* Fred had not yet been charged with Anna McFall's murder because Dr Whittaker had not finished identifying her remains.

eye, but Fred was only concerned with Rose. They were told to stand again for the magistrate to formally remand them into custody. The hearing was finished.

As a police officer tried to lead Fred away, he resisted, and moved towards Rose. Again she shrank from him, and when he raised a hand to touch her, it was pushed away by an officer. Rose later said that being next to Fred had made her feel sick.

20

ALONE

ON A BLAZING July afternoon in 1994, Steve West married his girlfriend, Andrea Davis, at St George's Church in the village of Brockworth. It was a pretty service on a perfect summer's day, and both Fred and Rose sent their best wishes from their respective prison cells. Fred signed his good-luck card 'Dad', as was his habit. Rose gave the couple a cushion she had made.

There was a flurry of excitement in August when Fred parted company with his solicitor, Howard Ogden. It emerged that Mr Ogden was planning to sell his account of the case: an agent had prepared a three-page synopsis listing what was on offer. The material included tape recordings of Fred's prison interviews, his confession statement, details of the 1992 child abuse case, psychological reports of Fred and Rose, and footage from their home-made pornographic videos. Howard Ogden said that he had written permission to do this, but Fred was granted a High Court injunction stopping him. The matter was brought before the Law Society and Howard Ogden later returned all the tapes.

In September a Gloucestershire police report revealed that the murder inquiry had cost £1.3 million, and was still running at the rate of approximately £2,000 per week as John Bennett's team prepared for the trial, a date for which had still not been scheduled. Overtime alone had accounted for £309,000; a further £78,000 had been spent on demolition and excavation work. It was an enormous financial burden for the force, and the Home Office was asked for a contribution. The request was turned down.

FRED spent his fifty-third birthday, 29 September 1994, behind bars in Birmingham's Winson Green prison, where he had been since April. With the bulk of the police investigation over, and the long wait for the trial ahead, he seldom found himself troubled by visits from detectives, who had tape-recorded 108 hours of interviews with Fred. He had never spoken to them about the sexual torture of the victims, or the masks, or why so many body parts were missing. It had also been realised that the video tapes seized from Cromwell Street in 1992, some of which may have featured evidence of this torture, had been destroyed because the Wests had not wanted them back. (Only four videos were taken in 1994, including graphic film of Rose pleasuring herself intimately, but none were of any use to the police.)

Some of Fred's time was occupied with drawing, for which he had a fair aptitude, and with making an attempt to improve his literacy – Fred hoped he would be able to understand his legal papers. His children Steve and Mae were almost his only visitors. Steve remembers his father's low spirits: 'He said he loved Rose and missed her. He wished she felt the same, but she didn't.'

Fred confided that he had begun to write his autobiography. Each chapter would be dedicated to one of the women in his life. Chapter One had already been written, and was all about Anna McFall. Fred had entitled it 'I Was Loved By An Angel'.

If Steve missed a prison visit, his father became agitated and angry that he had been embarrassed in front of the guards. Fred was allowed telephone cards, and used them regularly, chatting with Steve about his marriage and the impending birth of twins to Steve's new wife. He also wrote crudely-spelled letters offering advice for the future, some of which were reprinted in the *News of the World* newspaper, which made corrections to the excerpts for the sake of clarity. 'Always know what's going on in your home please son,' he wrote. 'Always spend as much time with your wife and children as you can and love your wife and children.' In another, Fred wrote that he now regretted working so hard day and night and cautioned his son not to do the same, in case he, too, came to a bad end. He also advised him not to have too many children because 'babies cost money, lots of money'. Expressing himself curiously in the past tense, Fred wrote 'I loved you all' and said he was sorry for what had happened. He urged the family to sell 25 Cromwell Street and start a new life together. Seemingly in despair, he wrote in another letter that 'my case is a mess', and accused Rose of trying to break up the family.

But he could easily snap out of this gloom. One day Fred asked the prison warders for his clothes, convinced that he was about to go home.

FRED and Rose met again at another remand appearance at Gloucester Magistrates Court in December. By now they were jointly charged with nine murders, and Fred faced a further three murder charges, making a total of twelve. He appeared tired, and looked all of his fifty-three years. His hair, which had always been bushy, was cropped short, and a hearing-aid had recently been fitted because he was complaining of deafness. Two police women stood between Fred and Rose. He had been warned beforehand that Rose did not wish to talk to him. Rose glanced at her husband just once, giving no sign of the affection he craved.

When the New Year's honours list was published on 31 December, Hazel Savage was at last recognised for her tenacity.

She was made a Member of the Order of the British Empire, and her Chief Constable, Tony Butler, paid tribute to 'an exceptional police career'.

ON New Year's morning, 1995, Fred rose as usual in his cell on the third floor of D-wing at Her Majesty's Prison Winson Green. His was an old cell, painted cream, with a sink, toilet, and table and chair. The solid door had a spy-hole with a cover that flipped up so the warders could see in. As a remand prisoner, as yet convicted of no crime, Fred was allowed some home comforts. He had his own bed quilt, pillowcase and stereo music system. He had even put curtains up over the tiny, barred window that looked out on to the prison wall. Fred did not share the cell.

Prisoner WN 3617 dressed in issue clothing of brown jeans and a blue and white shirt. It was a cold day, with flurries of snow, so Fred also pulled on a warm sweatshirt and a brown prison-issue jacket. He had lost weight recently, and the clothes hung on him a little. After a breakfast of cereal and eggs, Fred went into the exercise area, where he was told he could choose a special New Year lunch. When he had made his decision, Fred went back to his cell to listen to compact discs on his portable stereo and write a note to Rose. It read:

To Rose West,
Happy new year darling. All my love, Fred West. All my love for ever and ever.

Despite the modest comforts he enjoyed, which are not unusual for remand prisoners, Fred was a desperately unhappy man, heartbroken that Rose had rejected him. Each time one of his children visited, Fred entreated them to tell Rose that he loved her, yet Rose sent no message back. He had not received one encouraging word from her since the day he was arrested – Rose had turned against Fred completely. At the end of their long relationship, it was she who had proved to be the stronger of the two, she who was fighting her case while Fred had given in and co-operated with police. (She had said nothing to them during a total of forty-six interviews between 23 April and 1 June, apart from asserting her innocence. In Fred's case, on the other hand, the police had 6,189 pages of transcribed interviews – enough evidence to put him behind bars for life.) Because of this he was overwhelmed with depression, and often wept.

Fred was also worried that other prisoners wanted to harm him. The inmates in Winson Green had an ambivalent attitude towards Fred. On one hand they found him amusing, awarding him the macabre nickname 'Digger' and yelling out 'Build us a patio, Fred!' when he went by. But as a child-abuser and child-killer, he was detested in the same way as the sex offenders on the landing directly beneath him. He was relatively safe as long as he was segregated, but there were still times when Fred came into contact with other prisoners, and on these occasions he appeared to be aggressive, fixing a demented grin and warning anybody who came near to go away. This was only an act: in reality Fred was terrified. His fear had increased since November, when the American mass murderer Jeffrey Dahmer had been battered to death by a fellow inmate in his Wisconsin gaol.

When Fred arrived at Winson Green there had been concern that he might take his own life. He was categorised as a 'vulnerable prisoner' because of his unstable mind, and was placed on suicide watch where a warder checked his cell every fifteen minutes. There were also random searches for implements he might use to try and kill himself. Fred gave the warders good reason to think he might attempt suicide, yelling out 'I'm going to do it!' when he was first brought in.

But Fred settled down after a few weeks. He even made the warders laugh by calling out cheery greetings to them in his rustic accent. 'He would say, "Good morning, guv'nor," like he was Farmer Giles leaning over a gate back in Gloucestershire,' said one fellow inmate. Fred became so amenable, and cheerful, that he was soon put on a more relaxed regime.

At 11:30 on New Year's morning Fred was allowed to collect his chosen meal of soup and pork chops, returning to his cell at twelve noon. When the door was locked behind him, Fred knew he would be left alone for one hour to eat. He listened to the warder walk away, and then turned from his food and pulled a sheet from his bed.

He tore the cotton sheet into strips and plaited these strips together until he had formed a strong ligature. Standing on a chair, Fred reached up and threaded one end of the ligature through the barred opening of the ventilation shaft above the door of his cell, tying it securely. He fashioned the other end into a noose, which he slipped over his head. Fred then kicked the chair from beneath him.

His neck did not break, so he did not die straight away. Instead he slowly strangled himself, suffering considerable pain.

Fifty-five minutes later, a prison officer returned to let Fred out to wash his plate, but the warder could not open the cell door. Fred's body was holding it shut. Another officer quickly arrived on the landing and together they forced the heavy door open. They took Fred down and laid him on the bed. His body was still warm and they made strenuous attempts to revive him, trying both mouth-to-mouth resuscitation and heart massage. A nurse also rushed to help, but it was too late. By the time the doctor arrived, all that was left to do was to confirm that Fred West was dead.

★

WORD of the suicide spread quickly through the echoing halls of
the Victorian prison to the door of the deputy Governor. John
Bennett was one of the first people he called.

The Detective Superintendent was spending the day at home
with his family. He was feeling content with himself, having
managed to catch up on his reading work, and was looking forward to a relaxing afternoon. The telephone call was a
considerable surprise. John Bennett had feared that Fred might
meet a violent end in prison, but not this. 'We didn't think he
would top himself, but people thought it would be better if he
was bumped off,' he said. Ever mindful of the victims, John
Bennett ordered his staff to get to Bearland and telephone all
Fred's relations and the families of all the victims. He said this had
to be done before the press told them.

Rose received the news in Pucklechurch Prison in an official
telephone call from the Home Office. Her solicitor, Leo Goatley,
left a family party and drove straight to see his client. When he
arrived, Rose was smoking heavily, but was composed and had
not shed any tears. She had made no secret of her expressed
hatred for Fred in recent months, and had assumed the air of a
victim, crocheting baby clothes for her new grandchildren and
making toy teddy bears in the prison workshop. She had also
struck up a friendship with a 73-year-old nun named Sister
Mary Paul, who visited Rose regularly to hear how Mrs West
had been betrayed by her 'rascal husband'. On this fateful day,
Sister Mary was at her station and came to Rose's cell. She
suggested that they pray together.

Whatever Fred's crimes, he was still a brother and father, and
most of his relations were sorry for his death. Anna Marie said,
'He was my dad and I loved him. No matter what people do you
cannot turn away from your own parents.' Hours later she was
taken to hospital, where she was treated for an apparent overdose.
Mae was driving to Oxford when she heard the news on the car
radio; she turned onto a lay-by and cried. Steve, spending the

day at the home of his parents-in-law, was so befuddled by tears that he could not make his fingers dial the correct number of the prison. Out at Much Marcle, Doug West shook his head in bewilderment, and said he could not believe Freddie had killed himself. He had gathered his thoughts by the morning, when he offered a considered apology to the families of Fred's victims. 'I would like to say how sorry I am to all those who have suffered as a result of what my brother did,' he said.

There was little sympathy from the families of the victims. Alison Chambers' mother, Joan Owen, said that, although she thought of herself as a Christian and would have liked to have seen Fred stand trial, she was glad that he was dead.

Fred's death was front-page news in every national newspaper and led the television and radio bulletins. There was criticism in the press and from politicians of the prison service, and, ultimately, of the Home Secretary Michael Howard, for allowing Britain's most notorious remand prisoner to take his own life and deprive the public, and the families of his victims, of a trial. Fred's solicitors, Bobbetts Mackan, issued a statement describing their extreme surprise that such an event could have happened. Inquiries were launched by both West Midlands Police and the prison service. But the truth remains that if a prisoner is determined to take his own life, then there is little anybody can do to stop them.

A week after Fred's death it was revealed that Hazel Savage had been speaking with a literary agent about writing her memoirs, including her account of the murder case. The *Sunday Express* newspaper suggested that a figure of £1 million was being asked. The news came after similar stories about Fred's former solicitor, Howard Ogden, and one of Mr Ogden's clerks. An inquiry was launched by the Police Complaints Authority, and Hazel was moved off the case to other duties – a humiliation for the woman who had done so much to bring the whole affair into the open.

*

ROSE had been put on suicide watch in case she tried to follow Fred's example, although she showed no signs of doing so. She was transferred to a special suite of rooms within the hospital wing of Pucklechurch Prison, where warders sat at her door watching her twenty-four hours a day. There was also concern that she was a target for other inmates, and additional security precautions were taken after threats were made. Rose's meals were individually prepared and brought to her in sealed containers to prevent razor blades or ground glass being slipped into her food.

Her solicitor, Leo Goatley, suggested that Rose could not stand trial after Fred's death. He said the case had always been flimsy and press reports had now made a fair trial impossible. He also claimed that Fred had exonerated his wife in interviews with detectives. The Crown Prosecution Service considered these points and decided that a pre-trial committal hearing would be held to test the prosecution's evidence. At the same time it was announced that Rose was additionally charged with the murder of her stepdaughter, Charmaine, bringing the total of murder charges against her to ten.

THE first of the funerals of Fred and Rose's victims was held on 24 January, when Juanita Mott was buried. Family and friends gathered at St Oswald's Church in Coney Hill, Gloucester, to sing 'All Things Bright and Beautiful', and remember a girl nobody had seen in nearly twenty years.

THE committal hearing began the following Monday. A disused court-house at Dursley had been opened and decorated especially; over one hundred journalists arrived to cover the event. There were far too many reporters to fit into the courtroom, and most had to be content to sit in an annexe, where the proceedings were relayed through speakers. A few local people, mainly school children, lined up outside behind crowd barriers to jeer Rose's arrival.

The case would be heard by the country's most senior magistrate, 63-year-old former naval officer Peter Badge, a distinguished white-haired gentleman who peered at Rose through half-moon spectacles. Rose stood alone in the dock, wearing her customary large-framed spectacles and a voluminous white blouse. Ten charges of murder and two of rape were read out (the only murders she was not charged with were those of Rena Costello and Anna McFall, crimes for which there was not enough evidence to prove she had been involved). She pleaded not guilty to all charges. It was announced that the Crown would not continue with the charge of assault against an eight-year-old boy. Rose murmured that she understood and smiled as she was given leave to sit.

Rose's defence team was represented by a petite junior barrister named Sasha Wass. (The leading defence counsel, Richard Ferguson QC, would only appear at any eventual trial.) Her case was that Rose 'knew nothing of the victims, how they were killed and the bodies concealed'. The defence strategy was to try and have the proceedings stopped on the grounds of adverse publicity, an unreasonable delay in bringing the case to court, and insufficient evidence. Her legal argument continued for the rest of the day. As Rose's van left the court at around 5 P.M., it was pelted with eggs; school children, grinning at their naughtiness, shouted: 'Burn her!'

At the start of the second day, Peter Badge announced that he was not prepared to stay the proceedings. He did not agree with the defence's claims and signalled for the Crown's evidence to be heard.

The evidence against Rose was contained in over twenty-five lever-arch files and boxes of papers that were stacked chest-high in the gangways of the courtroom. The Crown's prosecutor,

Neil Butterfield QC, began by outlining the case against Rose, describing 25 Cromwell Street as 'a charnel-house, a graveyard' and the victims to have been the sexual playthings of Fred and Rose. He readily admitted that the prosecution had to rely upon circumstantial evidence, but said he was confident that it could prove that Rose had a strong, aberrant sexual appetite, and, with her husband, took pleasure from tying up and abusing young girls – and that this abuse ended in murder, either because of what they had done, or because they could not allow their victims to walk free.

Mr Butterfield then handed over to his junior, Andrew Chubb, who set about reading out the dozens of witness statements that would form the committal evidence against Rose. This process took up the next few days. Rose dabbed at her eyes during the most powerful passages of evidence, as if she were crying, but her demure performance was undermined when, on the fifth day of the hearing, tape recordings of Rose's police interviews were played to the court. In marked contrast to the homely, unprepossessing woman in the dock, the court listened to a belligerent, foul-mouthed creature who spoke about Charmaine, Heather and Anna Marie in crude language entirely without love. When Rose was taken down to her cell, she ranted and raved about the evidence against her, cursing everybody in sight for the mess she considered herself to be in.

A rainstorm pounded the court-house roof on Monday morning as Neil Butterfield summed up for the prosecution. Sasha Wass for the defence said there was no evidence that Rose had murdered anybody. She said that Rose's unusual sex life did not mean she was a killer: 'The lesbian activities of Mrs West, and the hideous and yet unknown activities of Mr West, when the girls were killed and chopped up, are separate. There is no evidence at all that Mrs West was involved in that.'

On Tuesday morning Peter Badge informed Rose that there was enough evidence for the case to go to court, and that he was committing her for trial. In a surprise move, she was also charged with two new rape offences on two young girls in the 1970s. These offences were committed jointly with Fred, it was alleged. She was also charged with two counts of indecent assault.* At the same time, joint charges of rape against her and two other Gloucester men were dropped.

Rose left the dock, her face betraying no emotion.

SHORTLY after the hearing, Rose was transferred from Pucklechurch to a maximum-security wing at Durham Prison, where it was felt she would be more secure. She became one of forty-eight prisoners of the gaol's refurbished maximum-security H-block, and found herself alongside convicted terrorists and other hardened criminals. Soon after her arrival she was joined by Britain's other most infamous female prisoner, the Moors murderess Myra Hindley, who had been moved to Durham after serving many years at Cookham Wood in Kent, where she had recently been refused parole. The women could not help meeting each other and struck up something of a friendship when they did, cooking together and watching television. They were particularly amused by the Australian series *Prisoner: Cell Block H.*

FRED'S corpse remained refrigerated in the Birmingham city morgue, although the coroner was ready to release it. Fred had apparently held very particular ideas about his final resting place. He had told Anna Marie that, in the event of his death, he wanted to be buried in the family plot at St Bartholomew's, Much Marcle; he hoped that she, too, would be buried next to him when her time came. Steve claimed that his father had asked for an arched marble headstone, inscribed 'Dad'. Fred stressed

---

* The girls involved in these charges cannot be named for legal reasons.

that he wanted to be buried because he was terrified of the idea
of cremation.

In the end, Fred's funeral was as wretched as his whole life
had been. Anna Marie and Doug West were furious when they
learned that undertakers employed by Steve and Mae had
secretly removed Fred's body from the morgue. The funeral
took place two days later on Wednesday 29 March 1995, at
Canley Crematorium near Coventry. Several other crematoria
had refused to accept the body. Fred's simple casket, made of
pale wood, bore a plaque inscribed 'F. W. West'. The only
mourners were Steve, his wife Andrea, and sisters Mae and
Tara. They were matched in number by representatives of the
Sun newspaper, on hand to record the event for the next day's
edition.

The hurried ceremony lasted just a few minutes. There were
no hymns. The Reverend Robert Simpson read from the 23rd
Psalm, and added, 'We should have a quiet moment of reflection
for the life of Fred West and pray for his family. We must also
remember in our prayers everyone else who has suffered because
of these tragic events.'

Fred's casket then rolled behind the screen and was consumed
by the flames he had so feared. It is ironic that, on the very day
Fred was cremated, Hazel Savage was officially charged by
Gloucestershire police with discreditable conduct for trying to
sell her memoirs of the case. The news would no doubt have
given him satisfaction.

Rose let it be known that she had taken no part in the arrange-
ments for the funeral, and was not interested in the outcome.
But as she sat in her cell in the echoing vastness of Durham
Prison, with Myra Hindley a few doors away, it is hard to believe
that she did not reflect on what the future held for her without
Fred. She alone would now stand trial for their crimes; she alone

would suffer the retribution. Perhaps that is what Fred intended for her when he wrote this apparent suicide note[*] which was later found in his cell:

To Rose West, Steve and Mae,

    Well Rose it's your birthday on 29 November 1994 and you will be 41 and still beautiful and still lovely and I love you. We will always be in love.

    The most wonderful thing in my life was when I met you . . . our love is special to us. So, love, keep your promises to me. You know what they are. Where we are put together for ever and ever is up to you. We loved Heather, both of us. I would love Charmaine to be with Heather and Rena.

    You will always be Mrs West, all over the world. That is important to me and to you.

    I haven't got you a present. All I have is my life. I will give it to you, my darling. When you are ready, come to me. I will be waiting for you.

Underneath was a drawing of a gravestone. Fred had written this inscription:

In loving memory
FRED WEST   ROSE WEST
Rest in peace where
no shadow falls
In perfect peace he
waits for Rose, his wife

[*] Corrections have been made to spelling and grammar.

21

BLUEBEARD'S WIFE

THE WAIT FOR justice was a long one: Rose had been in custody for sixteen months before she stepped into the dock for what the tabloid newspapers were heralding as the 'trial of the century'.

Much had happened since Fred had died on New Year's Day. On a bright spring morning in April, Charmaine and her mother Rena were cremated at a small ceremony in the Northamptonshire town of Kettering, near the home of one of Rena's sisters. The remains of mother and child were placed in the same casket, and Rena's surviving daughter, Anna Marie, chose the song 'Memories' to be played at the service.

A few days later, over the Easter weekend, vandals desecrated the graves of both Walter and Daisy West in the churchyard of St Bartholomew's, Much Marcle. Doug West had recently paid for a new headstone for Walter and was distressed to find that both this, and Daisy's older memorial, had been pulled up during the night. There had been bad feeling in the village in recent weeks, partly because of sightseers coming to stare at the graves and partly because of a rumour that Fred's ashes were scattered there.

Rose made a preliminary appearance at Winchester Crown Court in May. In a tremulous voice she pleaded not guilty to ten counts of murder, two counts of rape and the indecent assault of two young girls in the 1970s. The fourteen charges took a full five minutes to read out. The judge was Sir Charles Mantell, the 58-year-old presiding justice on the western circuit, a genial-looking, avuncular man who often appears slightly red in the face. He set the date for the trial as 3 October; the venue would be this same room, Winchester's Number Three court. It had been chosen in preference to Gloucester, Bristol and London's Old Bailey because, among other reasons, it was felt that Rose could not receive a fair hearing in Gloucester – while Winchester was sufficiently far away to draw a fresh jury but close enough for the large number of witnesses to be brought to and fro.

Built in the 1970s, the court adjoins the ancient Great Hall of Winchester, where the infamous Judge Jeffreys had presided, Sir Walter Raleigh had been tried for treason and where the famous 'Rounde Table of King Arthur' hangs. The new building is a brutal concrete fortress specially designed to accommodate high security trials, including those of terrorists: the dock, for example, cannot be viewed from the public gallery.

Queen's Counsel Brian Leveson was the barrister who would prosecute the case. (He took over the job from Neil Butterfield, who had appeared for the Crown at the committal hearing but had subsequently been made a High Court judge.) Mr Leveson, a diminutive, balding man with formal manners, is a distinguished QC whose most notable case prior to the West trial had been the prosecution of the entertainer Ken Dodd for alleged tax evasion (Dodd was acquitted).

His opponent would be Richard Ferguson: a tall, eminent Ulsterman, former Unionist MP and Chairman of the Criminal Bar Association. The 60-year-old QC has a formidable reputation as a skilful cross-examiner and had famously, and successfully, represented the boxer Terry Marsh and the Birmingham Six.

Both QCs would be expected to claim approximately £250,000 from public funds for their work, including payments for their juniors and daily 'refresher fees' while the case was being heard.

As the legal teams prepared for trial, the West family continued to suffer its problems. In May, Rose's sister-in-law Barbara Letts, who had been so close to Rose over the years, pleaded guilty to assaulting a police officer who had gone to her Gloucester home to investigate a reported burglary. Barbara's family was in chaos. One of the children was behaving in a disturbed way, and her husband Graham, Rose's younger brother, had suffered a nervous breakdown. (One of Rose's other brothers, Gordon, was suffering from depression and in trouble with the police. Later on he too would be admitted to hospital after a breakdown.) Barbara was given a one-year conditional discharge.

In June, less than a year after his marriage, Fred and Rose's son Steve parted from his wife, Andrea. She took the couple's twin children and went to live in the Midlands.

TOWARDS the end of September Rose was transferred from Durham Prison to Winchester gaol, where she would be held for the duration of her trial. Her cell was a tiny cubicle, thirteen feet long by seven feet wide, sparsely furnished with a bed, chair, locker and combined washing and toilet fixture. It is within a suite of seven rooms intended to become a drug rehabilitation unit. Because Rose was a Category A prisoner, and could not associate with the gaol's 505 other inmates, all these rooms were dedicated to her care alone. They included a shower room and an association area, where she was allowed to watch television and play cards with the two female warders assigned to watch her round the clock.

Winchester is a genteel city with a splendid cathedral, famous public school and many fine buildings. The pedestrianised broadway leading from the statue of King Alfred by the Guildhall up the hill to the law courts is lined with fashionable shops. It is a prosperous, middle-class place – the ancient centre of England. Winchester Combined Court sits on top of the hill where a fort has stood since Roman times; the steps up to it follow the contours of the earthworks which have defended the city over the centuries.

The morning of Tuesday 3 October 1995 was mild, slightly damp with the threat of rain. Rose was awake by 7 A.M., and breakfasted on a boiled egg, cereal and toast. She then dressed in conservative clothes especially chosen for her trial, an outfit she would wear with little alteration every day for the next eight weeks: a long skirt, blouse and black jacket. She hung a small gold cross around her neck and put on gold-coloured earrings, circular with a filigree inlay. She applied a little rouge make-up to enliven her sallow cheeks, but despite the care she had taken to look her best, she still looked unhealthy, or 'buffeted by life' as her QC would later phrase it.

Rose was then led to the police van that would take her to court. She was triple-locked into a steel inner capsule with a bulletproof glass panel – designed to prevent escape and to foil any attack on the prisoner. Two prison officers sat on a bench beside the capsule, and a third officer joined the driver in front. The police motorcycle outriders then switched on their headlights and the group of vehicles swept down into Winchester, where camera crews and newspaper photographers jostled behind crowd barriers.

Number Three court at Winchester is an enormous, hangar-like space. Rose would later hear, to her obvious surprise, that 25 Cromwell Street could be fitted into the court with room left over. The ceiling features a large square of fluorescent lights. To the sides of this are windows covered with plastic, so they will not shatter in the event of a bomb going off. PVC panels, coloured a dirty cream and looking like the cushions of a 1960s sofa, cover two walls. The judge sits on a vast wooden dais, so gigantic and forbidding it would have been in keeping with the brutal architecture favoured by Mussolini. Behind the dais is an expanse of wood veneer and a drape of blue cloth.

Justice Mantell entered the court dressed in his scarlet robes and bowed solemnly before sitting. Between him and the dock sat the counsel, wearing black silk and white wigs. In an attempt to speed the trial along, the court stenographers – who sat beneath the judge – would type each word of the proceedings into a computer system known as CaseView, and Justice Mantell and the counsel all had LCD monitors in front of them. The police, including John Bennett, sat by the witness box, and the press and court artists were divided into two sections facing each other on opposite sides of the room. In annexes across the hall, dozens more journalists listened to the proceedings through speakers.

Rose stepped into the dock at 10:30 A.M., bowed awkwardly to the judge (although it is not customary for the defendant to do so), then sat and looked impassively ahead, with her lips slightly parted and her sleek brown hair flopping forward over her large spectacles.

A jury of eight men and four women, apparently ordinary local people who seemed both surprised and pleased to be told which case they had been selected for, were quickly chosen without objection. Then the court clerk read out the ten counts of murder. It had been decided previously that the rape and assault charges would not be heard at this time, but set aside for a possible later trial. To all ten murders the jury were told that Rosemary Pauline West had already entered a plea of not guilty.

The judge turned in his throne-like chair, smiled engagingly at the jury, and warned them not to be influenced by anything they might have read about the case, which he conceded had its 'sensational aspects'. He then dismissed them for the day so he could hear legal arguments. As the journalists scurried off to file long descriptions of Rose in the dock – although she had been as impassive as stone throughout – Brian Leveson and Richard Ferguson discussed legal technicalities about what evidence the jury should hear in the coming weeks.

Richard Ferguson for the defence said the evidence of Rose's sex life and the alleged treatment of Caroline Owens, Miss A and Kathryn Halliday had no place in the trial, and therefore should not be admitted – it was 'disputed evidence' and the whole Crown case was built on 'shaky ground'.

The prosecution, however, suggested the treatment of these women was 'similar fact evidence', meaning that it established a pattern of behaviour repeated in the killings. Justice Mantell decided the point by citing the legend of Bluebeard, who, as recounted in many folk tales, murdered a number of his wives and chopped off their heads. The judge said that if one of the wives about to be beheaded had escaped and told her story, then that would be admissible evidence of Bluebeard committing multiple murder. In the same way, he would allow the jury to hear about the ordeals of Caroline Owens and others. This was a considerable victory for the prosecution, because it meant that the jury would hear evidence of Rose's penchant for sadistic lesbian sex.

AFTER a day of rest, so Brian Leveson could observe the Jewish day of atonement, Yom Kippur, the case started in earnest on Friday 6 October. Brian Leveson's opening speech was a marathon piece of oratory, sixty-one pages long in document form. It would take all of that day and a portion of the following Monday to read.

Although some in court felt his delivery was not as effective as that of his predecessor Neil Butterfield, the content of the story he had to tell was moving and deeply shocking to those who, until now, had no detailed knowledge of what Fred and Rose had actually done to those young women and girls found buried in Gloucester. Standing with one hand resting on his portable shelf of law books, Brian Leveson described how in February 1994 the police had gone to Cromwell Street to find Heather West, and had stumbled upon secrets 'more terrible than words can express': the remains of dismembered and decapitated young girls 'dumped without dignity or respect' in holes beneath the garden, bathroom and cellar. An unprecedented police investigation had followed. He said that, for at least seven of the victims, 'their last moments on earth were as objects of the sexual depravity of this woman and her husband now dead'. In the dock Rose sat without apparent emotion, studied now by the members of the jury who looked keenly at her for the first time. She would later appear to cry, rubbing her eyes under her spectacles.

Brian Leveson said that Fred and Rose were 'in it together', and that although the evidence against her was circumstantial – because 'nobody says "I saw Frederick stab" or "I saw Rosemary strangle"' – the jury would find that evidence convincing. Mr Leveson continued: 'At the core of this case is the relationship between Frederick and Rosemary West; what they knew about each other, what they did together, what they did to others and how far each was prepared to go. Much of what follows can be explained in the context that both were obsessed with sex ... The Wests shared a knowledge of each other which bound them together.'

He went on to describe the macabre way in which the victims were found at Cromwell Street: young girls hidden in holes which formed a pattern in the cellar, a 'circle of death'. He said that, with the help of forensic scientists, these victims would 'speak from the grave as to what happened to them'.

The first witness for the prosecution would be Rose's mother. Now aged seventy-six, Daisy Letts cut a tiny figure in the witness box, all but obscured by the four microphones before her – a wizened, white-haired head dwarfed by the panoply of law. She answered questions in a small voice, addressing the counsel with unnecessary subservience as 'sir'. Rose watched her mother closely, and, at one stage between questions, Daisy darted a furtive look back at the daughter she had not seen in the flesh for many years. Their gaze met for a moment and then Daisy snapped away. This was the conclusive moment of their tragic relationship: mother giving evidence against daughter, recalling the moment half a lifetime before when Rose had said there was nothing Fred would not do, even murder.

When Daisy left the box after a little less than an hour, her handkerchief clutched in her hand, it seemed unlikely that she would ever face her youngest daughter again.

Next came Rose's elder sister Glenys, whom Rose had also not seen for years. Glenys glared at Rose as she entered the court, declining the offer of a seat. Her voice trembled as she told how Fred had explained to her his 'open marriage' with Rose, and asked if she had ever thought of trying it. With every movement of her body, every inflection of her voice, it was clear that Glenys felt acutely the shame into which Rose had finally dragged her family.

ONE of the early dramas of the trial was the evidence of Elizabeth Agius, the woman who had lived next door to the Wests in Midland Road, and who had baby-sat for them while they went cruising the streets for young girls. Mrs Agius had travelled from her home in Malta for the hearing, and was extremely unhappy about giving evidence. A ruddy-faced, middle-aged woman with tightly permed hair, she looked like life had worn her out. Under vigorous cross-examination by Richard Ferguson for the defence, she denied telling the police that she had ended up in bed with a naked Fred and Rose after drinking a drugged cup of tea, and that Fred had had intercourse with her. Ferguson said she was lying – a suggestion indignantly denied. She also denied sleeping with Fred while Rose had been in hospital giving birth to her daughter Mae.

It was then established that Mrs Agius had already been paid for interviews given to both the BBC and independent television, and had contacted the *Sun* newspaper even before speaking with the police. Asked why she had not told the press to go away when they knocked on her door, she tartly replied: 'They don't know what going away means, do they?' She then left the box and returned home to Malta. But the following day the court heard that Mrs Agius had indeed told a police officer that she had been in bed with Fred and Rose, but that she would deny this if asked in court because she feared her husband would leave her if he found out. This somewhat undermined her reliability.

A more effective prosecution witness was Caroline Owens, who had long prepared for her appearance. Still an attractive woman at thirty-nine, neatly dressed in dark jacket and white blouse and with her hair tied back, she retold the story of her ordeal at the hands of Fred and Rose that winter night in 1972, when she had been hitch-hiking home to Cinderford from Tewkesbury. Her evidence about being tied up, beaten and raped at 25 Cromwell Street was powerful, particularly as she recalled the moment when Fred had threatened to murder her and bury her 'under the paving stones of Gloucester', where nobody would ever find her. Under cross-examination she admitted having entered into a contract with the *Sun* newspaper worth £20,000. It was suggested that she had exaggerated her ordeal for commercial gain. But whatever damage this revelation did to her evidence was forgotten when the court heard the tragic story of how she had tried to take her own life after the rape. She then broke down in tears, sobbing that she only 'wanted to get justice for the girls who didn't make it. I feel like it was my fault.'

Up in the public gallery sympathy was expressed for Caroline Owens, with general agreement that if she was to get £20,000 for her story then she deserved every penny. 'I would have done the same,' said housewife Christine Reeves. 'I thought she was a very brave lady.'

Gallery seats had become much sought-after, and many of those who came to watch were, perhaps surprisingly, attractive young college girls: media or law students of exactly the age and type who had been murdered by the woman in the dock. They leaned over the gallery's glass barrier at each adjournment, stretching for a glimpse of the woman who was dominating the television news each evening, and were frustrated to find they could not see her because her chair was directly beneath where they were sitting.

THE evidence of Lynda Gough's mother, June Gough, was commanding in its poignancy. Now a grey-haired, retired council worker, she eloquently recounted the tragic story of how she had confronted Rose West on the doorstep of 25 Cromwell Street and seen her wearing her daughter's slippers. Mrs Gough's description of her rebellious but loved daughter was moving in its honest simplicity. She said that Lynda was 'cheerful, happy and friendly. She accepted some advice, but as she got older – I would say eighteen or nineteen – she started to rebel against our advice, like a lot of teenagers in those days as well as today. They think they are clever, and really they are only just beginning their lives.'

The court heard from former lodgers at Cromwell Street. Benjamin Stanniland, David Evans, and others who had rented rooms from the Wests in the 1970s were now grizzled middle-aged men with receding hair and lined faces. They spoke of the free and easy lifestyle of 'flat-land', and Benjamin Stanniland cheerfully agreed, under cross-examination, that some of them had been 'known to the police'. Many girls had been brought back to the house and girlfriends had been shared around – as had cannabis, and bearded David Evans nervously admitted to 'seven or eight' convictions for possession of drugs over the intervening years. Richard Ferguson was trying to establish that people had come and gone from the house all the time, that there had even been police raids for drugs, yet the police had seen nothing suspicious so why should Rose? Outside the court Stanniland and Evans posed jauntily for the ranks of assembled photographers before sauntering off into obscurity again.

Another former lodger, Liz Brewer, recalled how Rose had told her that when she retired she planned to spend all her time having sex. She remembered Rose's 'special room' and the constant lewd talk. 'Rose had her boyfriends and Fred his girlfriends. They were quite happy ... they seemed to have a bond between them,' she said. Just like Caroline Owens and Elizabeth Agius, this witness had entered into a contract to sell her story. She had also begun to write her 'memories' of life at Cromwell Street in book form. The message that Richard Ferguson was gently repeating to the jury was that many of the Crown's witnesses had something to gain from a conviction.

The court heard evidence of 'thumps, crashes, wails and shrieks' coming from Rose's 'special room' at Cromwell Street. They were wails of sexual excitement, but not necessarily of pleasure, and occurred late at night after male visitors went into the room.

Community nurse Jane Bayle, who had visited the house as a young girl, described how she had been unnerved by Rose, who had 'stared a lot and dressed as a child'. Another witness told how Fred had cheerfully introduced Rose as his wife and Shirley Robinson as his lover.

MISS A gave evidence on Monday 16 October, the start of the third week of the trial. A sad-looking young woman, in a black-and-white striped dress, her face and demeanour were marked by both her upbringing in a children's home and consequent adult life of poverty and domestic problems. When she first met Rose, she said, she had thought of her as a big sister, a shoulder to cry on, but then she had been savagely abused, tied up and raped.

Under cross-examination by Richard Ferguson, it emerged that when Miss A was only fourteen she had run away with Rose's brother, Graham Letts, who was aged nineteen at the time. They set up home above a café in Cheltenham. When a middle-aged neighbour discovered how young Miss A was, he blackmailed her into having sex. Miss A admitted that all this was true, but denied knowing that Rose was Graham's sister when she visited Cromwell Street – the unspoken inference being that she had a grudge against the family.

Then details of her mental health emerged: she had visited clinics on several occasions, wrongly convinced she was pregnant, and had attempted suicide. Mr Ferguson suggested she had seen a psychiatrist at the Coney Hill Mental Hospital, and had been experiencing bizarre hallucinations of a headless man. He said she tended to fantasise; she had also undergone a course of Electro-Convulsive Therapy and had heard voices in her head. Mr Ferguson asked if she had been diagnosed schizophrenic. Although Miss A denied this, she agreed that in her mind she had seen 'a man in black', and that this man was Fred West. The cross-examination had been a skilful one, based on her medical records, and the effect was to make the witness appear unreliable. Neither was the prosecution helped by the revelation that she, too, had agreed a deal with a newspaper, this time worth £30,000.

The next day, the twenty-fifth anniversary of Heather West's birth, the court heard about both the cruel and, surprisingly, caring side to the Wests. When Heather had disappeared in 1987 Rose had callously told neighbour Margaretta Dix that she was 'not bothered' if Heather was 'alive or dead'. But it seems Fred and Rose were also capable of compassion, for when Mrs Dix's husband died suddenly, it was the Wests who went to comfort her.

There was also unexpected testimony about Fred and Rose's relationship. A former girlfriend of Steve West told how Fred and Rose had argued, on occasion even leaving Rose with a black eye, and that Rose had once said, 'After everything we have been through together, he treats me like this.' Another witness remembered Rose saying she was lucky that Fred stayed with her.

A fascinating insight into Rose's life as a prostitute was provided when a middle-aged man named Arthur Dobbs came to give evidence. Grey-haired and dressed in a business suit, white shirt, floral tie and silver-rimmed spectacles, he looked like a GP. But Mr Dobbs' appearance was deceptive. After separating from his wife in 1985–86, he said he had visited a sex shop in Gloucester and bought a contact magazine. Through this he met 'Mandy', a woman he later discovered was Rose West. He had entered a bedroom at 25 Cromwell Street where he had been told by Rose to undress, as Fred watched. Fred then told him to 'get on with it' and left the room. Dobbs paid Rose £10. The relationship continued for eighteen months; after a while Dobbs carried out repairs on Fred's van in exchange for having sex with Rose for free. One day Rose told him that Fred had been having sex with the children. Dobbs claimed he had telephoned social services anonymously some time between 1986 and 1988 to tell them about what he had discovered. If this was true, it indicated another missed opportunity by the authorities.

Fred and Rose's former lover, Kathryn Halliday, became emotional when she exclaimed that the Wests had put children to sleep in the cellar, directly above where they had buried the remains of their victims. 'I find that totally horrendous,' she said angrily. 'They put them there. They let little children sleep on them. They knew about it.' Kathryn said she kept going back to the house, even after she had been abused by Rose, because she was like 'a moth to the flame ... He keeps going back until he singes his wings and can fly no more.' Kathryn admitted selling her story to newspapers and television for more than £8,000. Mr Ferguson suggested that her account of Rose's sadism was 'complete rubbish', but Kathryn was steadfast.

THE most dramatic evidence of the trial so far was the appearance of Rose's stepdaughter Anna Marie in the witness box (now preferring to be known as Anne Marie). A heavy-set woman with dark hair, she was unmistakably Fred's daughter, with his distinctive broad nose and blue eyes. She spoke in a trance-like voice, leaving long pauses between sentences and frequently breaking down. She referred to Rose as 'Rosemary' or 'my stepmother' in such a way that the phrase 'wicked stepmother' came to mind, and each time she described one of the sexual assaults she had suffered Anna Marie glared accusingly at the dock.

Asked by Brian Leveson whether she could remember her first sexual experience, she replied in a whisper: 'Yes ... I was eight.' There was absolute silence in the court as she went on to describe being raped by Fred and Rose, who told her that she should be 'grateful'. Anna Marie said she wished she were dead. She also recalled her stepmother beating her with her fists, a saucepan and a belt; Fred and Rose had spoken about beating her 'more on the torso than the face' so the marks did not show. Anna Marie broke down many times during her evidence, and the court was palpably shocked.

The following day, a beautiful bright autumn morning, the members of the jury were taken by coach to Gloucester to visit 25 Cromwell Street – something they had unanimously requested. The garden area of the house was covered over by a white marquee. Cromwell Street was blocked to cars, and elaborate arrangements were made so that the coach carrying the

jury could be driven into a covered area behind the house without the press or public setting eyes on them. Rose also had the
right to go, but declined, citing the excuse that it had been her
family home for many years and the experience would be
'unduly distressing'.

Dressed in overalls and wearing hard hats, the judge and jury
were led in through the back of the house and taken in silence
through each room (silence, that is, apart from the clatter of several helicopters hired by the press to take aerial photographs).
White tape marked out the locations of the human remains in
the garden. Inside the dank, stripped house the feeling of how
tiny the space was impressed itself upon everybody. There was no
furniture, but many quirky features were still present: the jury
saw a poster of a naked girl pinned up, and looked at the door to
'Rose's room' complete with its spy-hole device through which
Fred watched her having sex. In the cellar, together with the
graves of five women and the beams where Fred claimed to have
suspended the bodies of his victims from hooks, they saw cartoons and childish graffiti drawn by the younger West children.
After forty minutes, they were driven away from the city, back
across the Cotswolds and into Hampshire again – like emerging
from a dungeon into fresh air.

ON Thursday night Anna Marie again tried to commit suicide
(her last attempt had been at New Year, after her father's death).
She was taken to hospital, but was discharged later the following
morning. When she eventually arrived back in the witness box,
Anna Marie was cross-examined by Richard Ferguson, her evidence having been interrupted by the pre-planned visit to the
house.

The story of how she became pregnant by her father at fifteen
was revealed. She remembered being beaten and stabbed by
Rose, and how Fred had said her mother and stepdaughter were

working as prostitutes in Scotland and that Rena had 'all types of venereal diseases'. Anna Marie added that, despite the abuse she had suffered, 'I did love my father. I would have done anything for both Rosemary and my father.' Her agreement that she had accepted 'blood money' of £3,000 from a newspaper to tell her story detracted nothing from the power of her testimony.

On Monday a tape recorder was set up and four small speakers were arranged on the court clerk's desk. Recordings of several of Rose's police interviews were to be played.

The very first words the jury ever heard Rose speak (she had been utterly silent in court) formed a belligerent answer to a routine request from the police to state her name for the benefit of the tape. 'You don't know who I am?' mocked Rose. The next forty-five minutes continued in the same shrewish, often foul-mouthed way. Apart from her constant cursing, Rose's vocabulary was quirky – she frequently used malapropisms and curious words were repeated, like 'tricky', as in boys 'got up to tricky things'. The nature of what she said was also bizarre: she claimed to know Heather was a lesbian partly because the child 'knew exactly what kind of knickers the women teachers had on'.

The second interview tape ended dramatically, with Rose being told that Fred had confessed to Heather's murder. Her response was an almost unintelligible shriek – of horror or anger it was impossible to determine. In the dock, Rose clutched a tissue as if she were distressed.

She had recovered sufficiently by the next interview, taped just hours after the last, to offer her alibi: Fred had often made her spend the night with coloured men so she could not know what he was doing. She said Fred was the dominant partner in the relationship and 'what he says goes'. He made her sleep with other men even though she used to fight with him over it.

On another matter, Rose persisted with the story of giving £600 to Fred for Heather to go away with, but was told that

Fred had said it was only £100. When put under pressure like this, Rose's memory failed her. It seemed that there was a great deal which she simply did not remember, but the fate that awaited her appeared to be sinking in. Towards the end of the interview, she said: 'I ain't got a lot to live for now, have I?'

Despite her aggressive belligerence, in the next tape the jury learned something of Rose's extraordinary alternating personality – the concerned mum and then the callous harpy. She was asked about Heather's dentist (so the police could find dental records for identification of remains) and, like any mother, instantly remembered not only the name, but the full street address. Yet within the same interview she made harsh allegations about Heather, claiming that her daughter had hurt the other children, trapping their fingers in doors, giving them black eyes and making them drink obnoxious mixtures of 'vinegar and salt and stuff'. In fact, what she was describing was the abuse her children said *she* meted out to *them*.

In the tape Rose told the police that she was now certain she had spent the night with a coloured lover when Heather had vanished. Rose had to do what Fred told her: she claimed she had been hit when she was younger, and had once had her jaw twisted by Fred. Going with other men was something she was doing 'for our marriage ... He can be very persuasive, put it that way,' she said. But when asked for the name and address of this boyfriend, she could only remember that he was 'Jamaican ... big chap, I think', and in his fifties. His name escaped her; it was one of those 'awkward' names.

When Rose was informed on tape that the police had actually found Heather's bones, she was heard to wearily complain, 'Why have we got to go through this again?' She went on to repeat the lie that she had last seen Fred's first wife, Rena, when she came to take Charmaine away (the prosecution had already gone to some trouble to prove that Fred was in prison when Charmaine was murdered).

In his cross-examination, Richard Ferguson said that Rose had not eaten during these interviews and asked a police witness whether he thought she was in a fit condition to answer so many questions. But this meant little to those who had heard the shrill and very healthy-sounding voice on the tape, moaning about the daughter, Heather, who 'gave us loads of hassle'.

THE pathologist Professor Bernard Knight told the jury of how he had recovered the human remains at Cromwell Street. He described how many of the graves were 'quagmires' of mud and decomposed human organs, and listed the dismemberment and missing bones with scientific thoroughness, using the correct anatomical names. When asked to explain what a femur was, he reached down to a box by his side and produced a thighbone, brandishing it in the air for the jury to see.

The jury later looked though books of photographs taken of the bones and the instruments of torture. One showed Professor Knight holding the skull of Shirley Hubbard, the masking tape and tube still in place around the brutal death's-head. The mask was slack, he explained, because the flesh had rotted away. He told the court that to him Shirley Hubbard was simply 'Number Five' – the fifth victim he had excavated.

He afforded the court a macabre chuckle when asked how difficult it would have been to remove a shoulder blade: 'I could do it!' he exclaimed with some passion. The professor also gave the theoretical explanations as to why so many bones could be missing, but discounted them all bar one: the bodies must have been mutilated, and this would have involved a substantial amount of mess.

Dr David Whittaker, the oral biologist known to police as the 'Tooth Fairy', gave a demonstration of how he identified the remains using Facial Superimposition. The curtains in the court-room were closed and a photograph of Charmaine as an

eight-year-old child was projected on to a screen. The jury studied her grinning face: her lips were drawn back revealing little
teeth, some of which had not yet fully broken through the gums.
It had been taken in April 1971, just before she was murdered.
Dr Whittaker then overlaid the photograph of the child's skull as
it had been when found at Midland Road in 1994 – broken and
discoloured like a relic from an ancient tomb, now tinted blue to
contrast with the other photo. He pointed out the exact fit of the
empty eye-sockets and jaw-line, and where the court could see
teeth previously shielded by gums now matured and unprotected
in the most naked way. It was a highly dramatic demonstration,
but Rose looked on without emotion, for all the world as if she
were watching television back in Winchester prison.

The final witness for the Crown was Detective Superintendent John Bennett. He looked extremely nervous as he
stood in the witness box, holding his hands behind his back like
a soldier on parade and staring straight ahead so his gaze rested
somewhere above the heads of the jury. For months he had been
thinking about this moment, wondering what he would be asked
under cross-examination by the softly spoken but incisive
Richard Ferguson.

He was asked about Mary Bastholm, and replied that he had
compared her case with that of Lucy Partington but there had
never been enough evidence to charge Fred with involvement in
her disappearance.

John Bennett admitted that the police had launched a covert
operation to bug Rose's safe houses, but said this was entirely
legal (and had actually proved fruitless, as Rose said nothing
incriminating).

The police had long awaited the mention of Hazel Savage and
criticism of her plan to write her memoirs of the case. But even
this mine was defused by the time John Bennett was led towards
it by Richard Ferguson: he was merely obliged to confirm that
a female officer on the inquiry team had been suspended from

duties for 'discreditable conduct' – she was not even identified by name. After forty minutes in the box, John Bennett left with a spring in his step and it was not long before a relieved smile crept across his face.

Brian Leveson stood and told the judge, 'My Lord, that is the case for the Crown.'

A great many testimonies for the prosecution had been powerful, convincing, even shocking, and of course the jury faced the undeniable fact of where the victims had been found: that before Rose West moved to 25 Cromwell Street there were no sets of remains buried there, and when she left – after over two decades in the house – there were nine.

But it could not have been lost on Brian Leveson or his team that the evidence thus far had indeed, from a legal point of view, been no more than circumstantial – 'nobody says "I saw Frederick stab" or "I saw Rosemary strangle"' – and it seemed to some that Rose was still a long way from being found guilty.

22

ENDGAME

R ICHARD FERGUSON ROSE to his feet on the morning of
Monday 30 October, turned to his left, placed a clenched
hand on the wooden rail behind him and looked straight at the
jury sitting six feet away.

Some of the evidence they had already heard had been harrowing, he said, 'but I tell you now, as loudly and clearly as I can,
that Rosemary West is not guilty'. The fact that she may be a lesbian did not mean she was a murderer, neither did having sex
with her lodgers or being forced into prostitution. He suggested
the jury might consider it as 'plain as a pike staff' that Fred West
had committed all these murders on his own, and that Rose had
known nothing of what went on. He said the normal assump-
tions that a wife is always aware of what her husband is doing did
not apply in this case, because 'Number 25 Cromwell Street
was not your typical suburban household with 2.4 children . . .
It was a refuge of the flotsam and jetsam of modern life,' and
Rose was as much a victim of her husband's 'evil' ways as anybody else. As for the prosecution witnesses, he admitted he had
dealt with Kathryn Halliday with contempt, and suggested that
many may have embroidered their stories so they could sell them
to the media at a higher price. He concluded by telling the jury
that they would now hear from Rose West herself that she was

innocent. By the time he sat down he had succeeded in sowing
a seed of doubt in many minds.

It had always been thought that Rose herself would not give
evidence, because of the subsequent and potentially hazardous
cross-examination by Brian Leveson, but she had insisted against
advice that she should have a turn to speak.

As the second hand on the large clock on the wall clicked
together with the hour hand to twelve noon, Rose stood and
walked out of the dock, across the court, climbed up behind the
police seats and into the witness box. It was the first time the
court had seen her full length, and it appeared she was wearing
almost the uniform of a school girl – a long green skirt and flat
black shoes, together with a white blouse and her customary
black jacket.

She began poorly, by incorrectly giving her age as forty-two
instead of forty-one – a silly blunder, but indicative of what was
to follow. She then addressed a series of questions about her
childhood, sometimes answering with a half-smile and a chuckle
in her throat, a characteristic she shared with her mother. It was
her mother she seemed to want to talk about in these first few
moments of her evidence, claiming that when Daisy had left her
husband and taken the children to live with Rose's sister Glenys
and her former brother-in-law Jim Tyler, she had abandoned
Rose, and this consequently had had a devastating effect upon
the child. This is not a version of events that accords with the
memory of other members of her family, however.

She described her first meeting with Fred, and said her reaction to being chatted up by him was 'Shock! Horror!' – a
curious, and seemingly contrived, answer. 'He promised me the
world. He promised me everything,' she said. 'Because I was so
young I fell for his lies. He promised to care for me and love me
and I fell for it.' This was partly because she still felt vulnerable
after being 'abandoned' by her mother, she claimed.

Rose appeared to become emotional as she asserted her love

for the children she was accused of abusing and killing. Asked about her feelings for Heather, she answered perhaps a little too emphatically: 'I loved her very, very, very much.' But the rancour still showed when, minutes later, she told the court how Heather had 'been an awkward baby . . . I was inexperienced as a mother and she would sleep all day and be awake all night.' Charmaine, too, was a problem: 'misbehaving, not eating, running away and just generally disagreeing with everything I said or did'.

After lunch Rose's answers became longer, she seemed to pre-empt questions and give rehearsed answers. Worst of all, she made little jokes, about her always being pregnant, for example, about Fred drinking the vitamin supplement Sanatogen to keep his strength up, and she even made a derogatory comment about Lynda Gough's appearance. She did not seem to realise that, as she sat chuckling about Lynda Gough's 'grandfather' glasses, members of the jury were staring at her with apparent distaste.

When she was questioned about the time she had come home from hospital and allegedly discovered Fred and their former neighbour Mrs Agius together, the half-smile faded from Rose's face. She told of how she had barged into Elizabeth Agius' house 'very angry', shouting and banging on doors – 'I was getting louder and louder demanding either of them - I was angry.' There was no doubting her.

She also said that she and Fred had led separate lives, and that he often locked himself in the cellar with his DIY work.

Rose spoke about being bisexual, saying she enjoyed sex with other women because it was 'warmer . . . closer'. She said that Fred had manipulated her into trying to seduce Caroline Owens, and when she realised Caroline was not a willing partner Rose had stopped. Again she showed a flash of anger, when asked what she had said to Fred after the assault on Caroline. 'I asked him what the hell he thought he was doing,' she replied hotly. This did not seem to fit in with her earlier assertion that whatever Fred did, she had to accept.

At the end of the day Rose was shown photographs of the dead girls and was asked, in turn, whether she had known them or had had anything to do with their deaths. 'No sir,' replied Rose, but her nose turned bright red, she bit her lip and stumbled over her words. When Justice Mantell called for the court to be adjourned, Rose almost staggered back to the dock, completely exhausted.

RICHARD Ferguson seemed to have altered his style of questioning for the start of the second day of Rose's evidence. He became almost curt with her, trying to stop her long rambling replies and pressing her to address questions that 'have to be answered' when she broke down apparently in tears, as happened increasingly often. But again Rose showed herself to be unsympathetic witness: she made fun of Shirley Robinson, describing her as a 'silly . . . flittering' girl, and told an absurd story about Fred saying that Shirley's baby was his only because he was covering up for a respectable businessman who was the real father. Asked again about the £600 she had allegedly given Heather, Rose announced that she could remember now: this money had come from her post office account, a story never heard before. Asked about Miss A, Rose first said she had never met the girl, but later told the court that Miss A had been about to marry at the time of the assault – evidence not heard by the jury, who must have wondered how Rose could have known such a detail about a girl she had apparently never met.

Rose said her lesbian relationships had all been 'one hundred per cent consensual', a contrived phrase which she used repeatedly through the remainder of her evidence. Rose claimed that she derived no thrill from making people do things against their will. She spoke about herself and Kathryn Halliday playing records and talking about film stars – 'things that girls do' – as if they were innocent teenagers rather than two mature lesbians satisfying each other with dildos. She added that Halliday had agreed to everything. 'You don't come back if someone is hurting you,' she said, revealing more than she possibly intended.

Her evidence ended with her most dramatic, and bizarre, outburst of all. She informed the court that when she discovered Fred had confessed to killing Heather, she saw him in the guise of the devil. 'I hated him. I didn't see the man I had known all those years. He was just a walking figure of evil. I saw him – it might seem daft – but I saw him with horns and complete with a satanic grin. He never looked sorry for what he did or anything. He just used to grin, like it was some joke.' She added that she was not a murderer, and, sobbing loudly, that she could never have lived with a murderer.

Brian Leveson stood and began cross-examining Rose almost before she could stop crying. Starting quietly, he asked whether she had known nothing of the horrors committed between 1971 and 1994. 'That's right, sir,' she replied, quickly recovering. With increasing sarcasm Leveson asked if she had known nothing of the bodies, and of the blood on her husband's hands and clothes after he had cut them up. The questions, and denials, came thick and fast.

Within a few minutes Rose had lost her composure, and she became angry when asked about the day she had told her parents there was nothing Fred would not do, even murder. 'Right!' exclaimed Rose, with ill-disguised belligerence. 'I would like to answer that, sir . . . given the chance.' Brian Leveson glanced up at the judge with theatrical resignation and invited her to go ahead. Rose launched into a long, rambling explanation, the net result of which was her agreeing with what had been put to her in the first place.

The court was reminded of the love letter Rose had sent Fred, in which she had talked about how Charmaine liked to be 'treated rough':

BRIAN LEVESON: *You abused that girl, didn't you?*

ROSE WEST: *Not to the extent that you would like to think I have.*

BRIAN LEVESON: *You tied her arms?*

ROSE WEST: *No sir.*

BRIAN LEVESON: *Tied her to the bed?*

ROSE WEST: *No sir.*

BRIAN LEVESON: *You beat her?*

ROSE WEST: *No sir.*

BRIAN LEVESON: *You killed her and kept the body for Fred to bury . . . and from that moment on you were tied together forever.*

Cross-examination continued for the rest of that day and all of the next. It was an unmitigated and self-inflicted disaster for Rose's case.

Whenever she was asked a difficult question she replied 'I don't remember' or 'I don't recall.' Each time she was about to tell a new version of events she preceded it by crying, as if she were taking time to gather her thoughts. She became angry and blamed everybody apart from herself for what had happened. Most of all, she blamed Fred. Peevishly she complained: 'It's all very well for someone to say I said this or did that, because I'm the one now in the spotlight. Fred West is dead and I've got to take responsibility for what he's done.' It was noted that she said 'Fred West' now, as if she had never known him, not 'my husband' or even 'Fred'.

Asked if she would like to see the masks of torture found with her victims, Rose shuddered and said, 'I have seen enough of the horror, thank you.' Brian Leveson suggested that she had been lying and was trying to put all the blame on Fred; they had contrived a story the night before Fred was arrested, talking it over for hours.

Richard Ferguson's brief re-examination succeeded in proving that Rose was incapable of getting even the date of birth of one of her children correct. As this was discussed, one of the court officials choked on something and took some water to clear her throat – the noise of a woman gasping for breath seemed to divert Rose's attention. Like a bird eyeing a worm, she studied the woman closely.

A few minutes later Rose left the witness box: after three days of answering questions, and having impressed many in the courtroom that she was a wholly untrustworthy and unpleasant woman who had told lies – both petty and great – from the very first to the very last.

THE next defence witnesses were a succession of women who claimed to have been attacked or frightened by men who might have been Fred West. By calling these witnesses the defence sought to establish that Fred was capable of abducting women on his own, and possibly killing them. The first of these witnesses, Janette Clarke, said a man had followed her in Gloucester in 1966, and had tried to abduct her on two occasions. This had been reported to the police. In 1994, when she had seen Fred West's face on the television news after watching the *Antiques Roadshow*, she had been convinced it was her attacker.

The next witness, known only as Mrs C, told how she had been given a lift by a builder in 1966. The man attacked her and then masturbated in front of her. She thought there was a 'possibility' that it had been Fred.

Alison Clinton said she had been grabbed by a man in 1968, when she was aged thirteen, and that she thought he was Fred. There were other similar stories, but none of these women could be certain who their attacker was, and although most of them had informed the police at the time it was hard to identify any lack of diligence on their part because the descriptions of 'Fred' varied so wildly: one witness said he had 'fair hair', another that he had a beard, and a third that he had 'staring brown eyes'. The evidence these women put forward was slight, and, as Justice Mantell pointed out, it had never been disputed that Fred probably attacked a great many women.

ON Friday 3 November the court heard the voice of Fred West: four out of a total of 145 tape recordings of police interviews with Fred would be played to the court as evidence in Rose's defence. Again, this had been Rose's decision. She wanted the jury to hear her husband say loud and clear that he had committed the murders and that she knew nothing about it. (Rose had carefully read transcripts of Fred's interviews before making her decision.) She was warned that if some of the tapes were admitted in court the prosecution could call other evidence in rebuttal – evidence that might show Fred changing his story, and not always in Rose's favour. But she would not be dissuaded.

The first tape played had been recorded the day Fred was arrested for the murder of Heather. He was asked to say in his own words what had happened. Fred began, in this businesslike way: 'Right! what happened was . . .' and went on to tell a virtually unbroken, if largely imaginary, story of Heather's murder that lasted many minutes.

He quickly established that Rose had left the house to get some money for Heather, who wanted to leave home. His daughter was leaning against the spin-dryer in the tool room, and had told Fred that if he did not let her leave home, she would administer the hallucinogenic drug LSD to the younger children so they would 'jump off the church roof and be dead on the floor'. Fred claimed to have been enraged by this: he grabbed Heather's throat and held her until she turned blue. He tried to revive her, but failed. Her bowels opened involuntarily. He tried to force her corpse into a dustbin, but she did not fit. He then

fetched a heavy, serrated knife bought from the frozen food shop
Iceland, and set about dismembering her.

'I cut her legs off with that and I'm not telling you I have lived
that a million times doing that since then and then I cut her head
off and then I put her in the bin and put the lid on and rolled it
down to the bottom of the garden behind the Wendy house,' he
said. The casual voice on the tape was astonishing. The only
emotion came momentarily after Fred said he had cut his daughter's head off: he seemed almost to break down, but then
recovered.

Fred claimed he sent Rose out for the night to one of her
'coloured blokes', and used the time to dig Heather's grave.

The conversation then took a bizarrely banal turn as Fred
started looking at photographs of the garden to help the police
locate Heather's grave. The relationship between him and Hazel
Savage was so amiable that at one point she announced she was
just popping out to 'get [his] specs', because Fred could not see
clearly without them. When Fred had located the grave on the
photographs, with the aid of his glasses, Hazel Savage asked,
'And what's going to be in this hole in the ground?'

FRED WEST: *Heather.*
HAZEL SAVAGE: *In how many pieces?*
FRED WEST: *Three.*
HAZEL SAVAGE: *What?*
FRED WEST: *Two legs and a head and a body.*

After a pause, Fred announced that he had cut up the body in
the downstairs bath, above the grave of Lynda Gough. The court
had earlier heard a forensic expert say that, if there had ever
been bloodstains in the house, they would have worn away over
the years and it was not surprising that none were found.

He said he had loved Heather, but lost his temper when she said she was going to 'do the little ones'.

Rose was never far from Fred's thoughts, and he wanted to make it quite clear that she had played no part in this. 'The thing I'd like to stress . . . I mean, Rose knew nothing at all . . . [when] Rose finds out about this I'm finished.' At another stage in the interview this exchange took place:

HAZEL SAVAGE: *Right, who else knows what you've told us?*
FRED WEST: *Nobody . . . nobody at all. That is something I've had to live with for eight years. It's not easy, I'll tell you, because I loved Heather. That's why I was trying to persuade her not to go – I mean, what happened . . . in that brief moment when she was laughing about going to kill the rest of the children with acid, I couldn't believe it was Heather.*

The second tape had been recorded on 4 March 1994. Again, it was extraordinary how helpful and genial Fred was in interview, drawing diagrams for the police so they could find the victims in the cellar of the house he referred to as 'our place'. At one stage he even flirted with Hazel Savage, saying that when he first met her in 1966 she had to be 'about the beautifullest woman in Gloucestershire', and indeed it was a charming, rather than leering, observation – although Hazel's reply was curt: 'All right, let's stop the rubbish, Fred.'

He was anxious to explain why he had killed the girls. 'What 'appened, all these girls did exactly the same thing – it was made quite clear that I was married to Rose, and I don't want nothing to do with them, nothing serious, it was just thank you ma'am and finished, and every one of 'em did exactly the same thing of these: "I love you, I'm pregnant, I'm gonna tell Rose, I want you to come and live with me" and that was the problem.'

It was hard to image Lucy Partington, the cerebral medieval art student, begging Fred to marry her. But Fred even had an elaborate story to explain that girl's demise, an account the prosecution later said bordered on the obscene. He said he knew her as 'Juicy Lucy' because of the amount of vaginal juices she produced when they had sex, and that they had a secret affair — secret because of her 'other' boyfriend (Lucy did not have a boyfriend at the time). She had apparently wanted to make the relationship more serious, and had found Fred's home telephone number. Fred said he was furious. 'I mean I always made it clear to these girls that there was no affair, it was just purely sex, end of story.' They had an argument and he had grabbed her by the throat. Fred strangled her, drove her home and cut her up.

In yet another interview he gave an even more unlikely account of how his 'affair' with Lucy had ended: he said that she had become pregnant and had come after Fred, saying 'I have been bloody looking for you – I'm pregnant and want a thousand quid for an abortion.'

Fred agreed to try and help the police identify the victims — whom he referred to as 'the girls' — partly because he said he had come to like the police officers and thought he owed it to them, and partly because the families of the victims deserved a decent funeral. But his help was limited. 'As for these,' he said, looking at a plan of the cellar with numbers marked over graves, 'I 'ave no idea what their names are.' He later claimed to have picked them up at night, and had thus never seen their faces clearly. Again he was anxious to exonerate Rose: 'She knew nothing whatsoever about this.'

He claimed to have murdered Charmaine the same night he killed Rena (although this cannot be true because he was in prison when Charmaine died), saying he had strangled her while she was asleep in the back of his car – apparently panicking after killing her mother – and had buried the child behind the back of 25 Midland Road. Asked if he would go and help the police find Charmaine's grave, Fred breezily replied, 'Oh yeah, no problem.'

He was interviewed again the next day, and told detectives that two of the girls in the cellar at Cromwell Street were prostitutes he had picked up hitch-hiking. He knew them for what they were 'by their looseness'. One had started fondling his penis as he was driving, so they stopped, and, in Fred's words, 'made love' – but then she demanded £5 and said she would report him for rape unless he paid. 'We had a right set-to, and the next minute I smacked her up against the window and she just dropped and, um, anyway, I strangled her, or held my hands around her neck anyway, and um, that was it. She just slid down.'

He said he killed another girl for exactly the same reason. 'She said that'll be ten quid . . . I said, if you'd have said that in the first place I said I'd have told you to get lost and then she started shouting and said, you're the sort of person who goes with slags . . . and I just lost my head with her. Because as soon as she said that, I thought of Rose and Rose is no slag as far as I was concerned.'

All his victims 'were prostitutes going to know what they're doing', said Fred – a slightly different story to them all being in love with him and wanting to marry him. He said he had attacked a Dutch girl, knocked her cold, taken her back to the house and strangled her in the cellar. The belongings of all these girls were put into black rubbish sacks and left out for the dustmen. He said they had permed hair and make-up half an inch thick. Conveniently, when he came to bury the girls Rose would be away on holiday or out at the Jamaica Club.

In the final tape interview, DC Geoff Morgan was heard telling Fred that he had become upset in a previous interview when they asked about Rose's involvement. They then asked him about bondage. 'The bondage side of it was mine – Rose never had nothing to do with it,' he said. Asked about Caroline Owens, he indicated that she had indeed almost died. 'I think I would have went too far with it if Rose had been willing.' He added that he had been 'trying to get Rose involved with my sex life'. Fred also claimed that Caroline Owens had *wanted* to have intercourse with him the night they abducted her.

POLICE: *Are you saying she agreed to it?*

FRED WEST: *Well, she didn't do a lot about it, put it that way. I mean she could have screamed and the whole house would have heard her.*

POLICE: *Women don't always scream when they're being raped – they're terrified very often.*

FRED WEST: *Rubbish!*

His attitudes both to rape and to murder were revealed further in this exchange with Hazel Savage:

HAZEL SAVAGE: *You find things like that very difficult to cope with, don't you?*

FRED WEST: *What?*

HAZEL SAVAGE: *Allegations of rape.*

FRED WEST: *Well, yeah, 'cos I never raped nobody.*

HAZEL SAVAGE: *And yet you killed people.*

FRED WEST: *Yeah, see you've even got the killing wrong. You're trying to make out that I just went out and blatantly killed somebody.*

HAZEL SAVAGE: *No I'm not . . . they went through hell actually.*

FRED WEST: *No, nobody went through hell. Enjoyment turned to disaster.*

After the tapes had been played, Brian Leveson's junior, Andrew Chubb, questioned the interviewing police detectives for the prosecution to establish that these excerpts had only been part of what Fred said, and that he also told many insane lies. In an interview almost directly after admitting to killing Heather and burying her in the garden, for example, Fred told police that Heather was in fact not under the patio but 'in Bahrain working for a drugs cartel'. Fred had told the police 'lie after lie', for example that Shirley Robinson had sexually abused Anna Marie; that he had killed her because she was jealous of Rose having a 'black babby' and that she had called Rose 'that bitch, that slag, that cow'. Fred told police that after this insult to his beloved wife he had 'lost all sense' and strangled his lover.

He related a pornographic fantasy about the death of Lynda Gough, saying she had been tied up in the cellar, where they had been enjoying bondage sex together. 'She had a massive bust on her. She was all roped – kept laughing her head off and making weird noises.' Fred said she had been dangling over a hole in the cellar floor, supporting herself with her arms which were clasped around the beams. He had been smearing her with oil and 'love potions'. Then he went to answer the door, and when he came back she had slipped and hanged herself.

POLICE: *So she was strangled accidentally?*
FRED WEST: *I never killed anyone outright.*

The most damning evidence of all was that, on 29 April 1994, after consulting with his lawyers, Fred had instructed that a note be handed to the police by his solicitor. It read: 'I have still not told you the truth about this matter. The reason is that from the very first day of this inquiry my main concern has been to protect another person or persons.' There was little doubt who that person was.

★

BECAUSE the defence had convinced the judge to have Fred's tapes entered as evidence – on 'express instructions' from Rose herself – the prosecution was allowed to call new witnesses in rebuttal; in other words, to disprove material arising from the tapes. This was to prove dramatic.

The first witness was George Guest, a retired probation officer who had interviewed Fred at the time of the attack on Caroline Owens. The account he remembered Fred giving of the attack was quite different to the one heard in Fred's tapes. Mr Guest remembered Fred saying Rose had taken a very active, if not a leading part in the abduction and sexual assault. Furthermore Fred had explained that Rose alternated between heterosexual behaviour and being 'like a raging queer', depending on whether she was pregnant or not.

This was good evidence for the prosecution, but was superseded by what was to follow. The court first heard from a Detective Constable Steven Harris, who had interviewed Fred in May 1994 and recalled him saying that he was protecting somebody, but was not prepared to say who because he felt that his life, and the lives of his children, were in danger. Fred asserted that he was quite innocent: 'I had nothing to do with these girls' deaths at all. I have lied through the statements and at this moment I am not prepared to change that . . . I am not prepared to say who I am protecting in this case.'

With the next witness the finger of accusation began to point more towards Rose. Dr James McMaster had been the medical officer at Winson Green in Birmingham when Fred was held at the gaol on remand. Warders became concerned about Fred when they heard he was making arrangements for his own funeral, and on 1 August 1994 Fred sat down with Dr McMaster to talk about his feelings. At the beginning of the interview Fred was agitated and depressed, especially about his solicitor Howard Ogden, whom he felt was not representing him correctly.

The conversation turned to Fred's interviews. Fred said he was innocent of the charges and had been telling the police lies to protect another person. He then said that Rose was responsible for restraining his daughters while they were raped, that she was running a brothel in the house and had tried to murder him with a knife. He said that Rose enjoyed cruelty and abusing the children and that she had been burying people in the cellar without his knowledge; he did not know the bodies were there and had only been told to pour the concrete. 'He [Fred] claimed that he was protecting her [Rose], and was prepared to go to jail for life,' said Dr McMaster, who considered Fred to be rational when he made these allegations.

The prosecution then called Fred's 'appropriate adult': Janet Leach, a 39-year-old voluntary worker who had been assigned to become Fred's friend when he was taken into custody in 1994. She had sat in on eighty taped interviews and became a regular visitor and confidante of the prisoner, even receiving telephone calls from him at home.

In a broad Midlands accent, she told the court that when she had first met Fred, on 25 February, she did not even know what he was charged with. She sat through the interviews, listening to Fred's version of events, and then heard a quite different story in his cell when they were alone together (an extraordinary situation in itself, which was later picked up by the defence).

She claimed Fred had said he was protecting Rose, and that the girls found at Cromwell Street had been 'some of Rose's mistakes'. Mrs Leach explained: 'When he was arrested, he wanted to know whether Rose had been let out. That was important to him because they had made a pact that he would take the blame for everything.' When Rose was released on bail, Fred told Janet that the pact was working. Later Rose was arrested again and this distressed Fred. 'He was upset. He just said that the police were getting too close and that they would find out that Rose was involved.'

Fred told Janet Leach that there had been other people involved as well, including Rose's father; several coloured men; and somebody who (for legal reasons) can only be referred to as 'another person'. Janet Leach wept in the witness box as she said, 'I have got children growing up . . . and I needed to know that, if there was somebody else out there, that they had to be found.'

She said that Fred had told her fingers had been removed from the victims to foil identification, and indicated that he and Rose had chopped the victims up together (contradicting his earlier claim that he had only poured the concrete). Fred said he was not very good at sex, that Rose was very demanding and that he would do 'anything' for her. Fred had spoken about his own sexual tastes, saying he liked to 'break girls in'. He then changed his story yet again, claiming that the first he had known about the bodies in the cellar was when Rose telephoned to tell him the police were at the house in February 1994. 'He said he had a long discussion with Rose and Rose told him what had happened and where the bodies were.' Fred said he had suffered a black-out before he could return to the house.

He also stated that he had been in custody when Charmaine was killed, as the prosecution had claimed, and that it was Rose who had killed and mutilated Shirley Robinson, including removing her unborn child.

Under cross-examination Janet Leach said neither her nor any of the voluntary workers she knew who served as appropriate adults had ever encountered anything like this before. They were more used to dealing with juveniles. She had found the experience so disturbing that, at the recommendation of the police, she had been taken off the case and had then suffered a stroke.

When Fred died without confessing to what he had told her, she felt angry and confused about what she should do. She had never told anybody what Fred had said because she considered that they had been speaking in confidence. Richard Ferguson asked if it had occurred to her that Fred was using her, and she replied, with disarming simplicity, 'I suppose he was.'

She adamantly denied having been paid money by any newspaper, or having spoken to journalists, or that there was any substance in a rumour about her relationship with Fred going further than it should.

As the clock indicated it was time to break for lunch, Richard Ferguson informed the judge that he had not finished cross-examining the witness. Although much of what she remembered Fred saying clearly did not make sense (of course he had been involved in burying the bodies) many felt that Janet Leach's evidence had been like a breath of fresh air: at last somebody had told the truth – that Fred and Rose were in it together and that Fred had covered up for her. Janet Leach had been a very convincing witness.

The court was adjourned until 2:15 P.M., but minutes later Janet Leach turned deathly pale and suffered what later appeared to be another stroke, being unable to move or speak. An ambulance was called and she was taken to hospital. The court was adjourned for the rest of the day.

When the court reconvened the next morning Janet Leach was still in hospital, unable to give evidence for perhaps several days. But Richard Ferguson had dramatic news for the judge: it appeared that Janet Leach had lied to the court about her dealings with the press. Information had been received overnight that, far from not speaking with journalists, she had been paid £12,500 by the publishing subsidiary of a large newspaper group to write a book. In light of this, Richard Ferguson felt it was very important that he had a chance to continue cross-examining.

The hospital doctor was summoned to court, and it was agreed that the case could not proceed until the following week – and even then Mrs Leach would have to give evidence with a medical officer on standby, in case she became unwell. Considering that she was the last witness, the witness upon whom the whole case could turn, this long weekend could hardly have been loaded with more suspense.

ON Monday morning an ambulance brought Janet Leach back to court from the Royal Hampshire County Hospital, where she had spent the weekend. She entered the witness box in a wheel-chair, with a doctor standing behind her to monitor her condition, and looked both extremely unwell and very anxious.

Richard Ferguson skilfully cross-examined her, soon extract-ing her agreement that, contrary to what she had told the court the week before, she had struck a deal with a newspaper group – and a lucrative one at that. She had verbally agreed that the serialisation of her book would be sold to Mirror Group for £100,000. She had also told the police she would sign an affi-davit regarding her conversation with Fred in the 'worst case scenario' of a possible acquittal of Rose, to make sure that she was convicted. All this represented a body-blow to the prosecution.

It further emerged that Fred had written personal letters to Janet Leach, including one with the words 'keep it up, kid', but she denied any suggestion that she had become emotionally attached to Fred, as a police officer had said at the time, saying she had kept going to see him only because he was going to tell her more about the crimes.

In re-examination there was a revelation which dwarfed the lies she had already told: Janet Leach told Brian Leveson that Fred had claimed there were at least twenty more victims. Some were buried on farmland, and one was Mary Bastholm, whom he said he had picked up at a bus stop. She said Fred had told her other people were involved in these killings also: among them Rose, her father Bill Letts, at least two coloured men and the 'other person'. Fred said some of the girls had been killed outside Cromwell Street and brought back to the house by this 'other person', who had also apparently killed Anna McFall in collusion with Rena.

Much of this information – assuming Fred had ever imparted it at all – was clearly fiction, and there were many reasons for Fred to concoct such stories: he may have been trying to make himself more appealing to Janet Leach by shifting the blame on to somebody else; he probably wanted to keep her intrigued so she would return and see him; and Fred was also known to invent stories for visitors who he thought were selling information to newspapers in an attempt to catch them out (in the final months of his life he became jealous of the money made in this way).

But there may be a residual grain of truth to what Janet Leach claims Fred told her: a story that echoed what Fred told other visitors of a 'farmhouse' where victims, including Mary Bastholm, were buried. No doubt other men had been involved in the rape of girls alongside the Wests, but where the farm is and whether these men were actually participant in murder is another matter altogether. As Janet Leach said under cross-examination, Fred 'just talked all the time'. Truth and fantasy were one to him.

Despite this, it was the revelation of TWENTY MORE that made the headlines in the morning newspapers, not the fact that Janet Leach had lied in court.

BRIAN Leveson's closing speech for the prosecution included a detailed analysis of each part of the evidence. He spoke well, using slightly theatrical gestures – grimacing, and at one stage thumbing behind him at the dock when he said, 'He [Fred West] is not on trial, she is.'

He told the jury they had all travelled to a place that plumbed the depths of human depravity and there found a 'tough and resourceful' woman who was obsessed with sex – the perfect partner for Fred West – but, like the three brass monkeys, a woman who claimed to have seen no evil, heard no evil and spoken no evil, despite living in a house where women were raped, mutilated and buried.

He said Fred's death was the greatest gift he could have given Rose, because it meant he could not be cross-examined and (in all likelihood) proven in court to be both a liar and her accomplice. 'Picture him in cross-examination,' said Mr Leveson, and all eyes turned to the empty witness box, where the spectre of Fred West struggling gamely to deny Rose's involvement was all too easy to imagine.

He said there were common themes running though all the killings, and that those in the court who had seen the 'terrible pictures' of the exhibits, including Shirley Hubbard's mask with the pipe still in place, would live with these images for a long time.

The sky outside became overcast in mid-afternoon, heralding a storm that would soon drench the city. Suddenly the electric lights seemed to brighten the room and Mr Leveson concluded his speech in a sickly yellow glow: 'Frederick and Rosemary West were perfect companions and they were in it together. On that basis, you can be sure these allegations are proved.'

THE next day was the turn of Richard Ferguson for the defence. His approach was broader, even poetic. Rather than detailing the flaws in the prosecution case, he simply asserted that there was not a shred of direct evidence that Rose had killed anyone. He conceded that as a woman and a mother Rose may have fallen below the standards required, and that, if she had abused children, she would have to be tried for these crimes in this world or the hereafter. He agreed that the jury may not have liked her, or believed some of what she had said in evidence, but maintained that this did not mean she was a killer.

It was Fred who had committed these crimes, he said, and Fred had not killed himself to aid Rose's case, not being the stuff of which martyrs are made. Fred had been a depraved and morally bankrupt man who had opted out of the human race. He had killed before he met Rose, and continued to kill, without her knowledge or help, during their marriage.

Mr Ferguson finished with an inspired extended metaphor: Brian Leveson was a kind of mountain guide, leading the jury up a perilous path until they came to a gap, a void of no evidence. Mr Leveson had leapt across the gap to where the path continued on the other side and turned, beckoning the jury to follow, assuring them that it was quite safe. On the other side of this void, said Mr Ferguson, was a guilty verdict. But the void itself was a lacuna of hard evidence. 'Ladies and gentlemen,' he said, looking at the jurors. 'Don't jump. Don't jump.'

JUSTICE Mantell took no less than three days to sum up what he had already said was a remarkable case. He said the jury would have to consider carefully and individually each of the ten counts. They did not have to be certain that Rose had actually been responsible for snuffing out lives herself – she would be just as guilty if murder had resulted from a 'joint plan' with her husband to kill or inflict serious injury. The alternative, lesser verdict of manslaughter was open to them, he said, but they might think it was only a theoretical alternative, as there was a common thread through most of the killings. Unfortunately, they would have to spend time considering what was involved in killing and cutting up a human body. He then addressed the many other issues arising from the case with the same balanced, good sense, conceding that whatever he told the jury, and whatever had been seen or heard in court, only they could now decide on the verdicts that should be returned. Justice Mantell sent the jury out to consider their verdicts on Monday 20 November, forty-nine days after they had first been selected for the case.

★

THE jury deliberated for the remainder of that day and most of the next, carefully re-reading the transcripts of Rose's interviews before they began their discussion about verdicts.

The corridor outside Court Three became a waiting area for journalists and members of the legal teams, who paced back and forth expectantly. Jokes and predictions regarding the verdict were exchanged as the hours ticked by, and the air became thick with cigarette smoke. The court Tannoy system regularly intruded on this hum of conversation, and there would be a brief lull to hear which case was being called. Finally, just after 3 P.M. on Tuesday afternoon, the Tannoy voice requested that anybody having anything to do with the case of Rosemary West should return to court.

The jury had selected as their foreman a man in his early middle age, wearing a grey business suit. After being asked by the court clerk whether they had reached a unanimous verdict on any of the counts, he replied that they had. Rose, who was dressed in the same schoolgirl-like outfit she had worn practically every day for the last eight weeks, was called to her feet. Her mouth was slightly open and she appeared to be breathing deeply, nervously – for this was the moment upon which the rest of her life would turn.

The foreman was asked by the court clerk about the first count of murder, that of Rose's stepdaughter Charmaine.

'Do you find the defendant guilty or not guilty of murder?'

'Guilty,' replied the foreman, speaking so softly he was barely audible. There was a faint exclamation of relief, or anguish, from high up in the public gallery. Rose closed her eyes momentarily, as if trying to concentrate on what had just been said, and then opened them again.

The clerk read through the next eight counts, but the jury had not reached verdicts on any of these as yet. She came to count number ten, the murder of Heather West, and the foreman announced that they had a verdict in this case.

'Guilty,' he said again.

Justice Mantell sent the jury back to their room to continue their deliberations. Rose was taken down to her holding cell, where she collapsed in a spasm of tears and shock. But she did not have long to come to terms with what she had heard. At 4:30 P.M. the jury were called back. They had reached a third unanimous verdict, this time on the count of the murder of Shirley Robinson – again 'guilty'.

The foreman said he did not feel the jury could reach any more verdicts that evening, so court was adjourned for the day. Richard Ferguson went down into the cells where Rose was blubbing uncontrollably, her heavy shoulders heaving, her hands covering her eyes, the tears streaming down through her fingers.

The evidence for Rose murdering Charmaine, Heather and Shirley had been different to the evidence concerning the other seven women. The first three had been killed because Fred and Rose needed them out of the way, not because of a sexual motive. Now that the jury had accepted Rose to be a liar and murderess, they had to decide whether they agreed with Brian Leveson's 'similar fact evidence' – that the remaining seven had all died after being sexually abused in the way Caroline Owens, Miss A and Anna Marie had been.

At 12:15 P.M. the next day, Wednesday 22 November, the jury passed a note to Justice Mantell asking if the absence of any direct evidence was a hindrance to returning a guilty verdict in these seven counts. The judge said that it was not, so long as they accepted the Crown's case. They further asked if they could consider the evidence of Caroline Owens and the other women in relation to the charges of murder. Justice Mantell said the answer was yes.

The jury retired, but this time they were out for only thirty-five minutes. When they returned, Rose was told to stand. She then heard that the jury had unanimously decided on the seven counts, the seven girls whose remains had been found at

Cromwell Street together with masks, binds and other evidence of torture. The foreman said that Rose was guilty of murdering them all.

THE sentencing was as damning as it was brief. Justice Mantell first ordered: 'Stand up.' He then intoned these words: 'Rosemary Pauline West, on each of the ten counts of murder of which you have been unanimously convicted by the jury, the sentence is one of life imprisonment. If attention is paid to what I think, you will never be released. Take her down.'

Without a flicker of emotion having crossed her face, without any sign to the world she was saying goodbye to, Rose turned and was led away from view.

EPILOGUE

THIS BOOK IS entitled *Fred & Rose* because at its heart is a relationship between two people: their sadistic impulses; their
pact of silence; and, above all, arising out of that pact, their
obsessive love for one another.

Fiction based on genuine statistics has helped create a stereo-
typed profile of the multiple murderer, or 'serial killer': a young
man of lower-middle class, of above-average intelligence, who
murders on his own, often under the influence of alcohol, young
women, or young men, because he is sexually maladjusted. He is
usually caught when the number of his victims begins to escalate.
When he is depicted in film, the killer is often a salivating
lunatic, a man one would expect to be arrested each time he
ventured outside his door.

But Fred and Rose were nothing like that. They were most
obviously a married couple, man and wife acting together –
and, in their own strange way, a happy couple, 'ecstatically
happy' to quote Rose. They had a stable home where they had
lived for many years and where they intended to stay, a mortgage
which they worked hard to pay off and a large family. They
were the people next door, who waved a cheery hello to neighbours as they walked down the street.

This home was in the centre of an English city, just yards from a shopping centre and a police station, a street where hundreds of people passed by every week – hardly the domicile we would expect of a serial killer.

Also contrary to the accepted profile, the Wests were both of below-average intelligence, did not act under the influence of alcohol, and, in Fred's case at least, were well into middle age before their crimes were discovered (and apparently several years after they had last killed).

It should also be pointed out that the very fact of Rose's gender makes her crimes extremely rare, simply because such killers are almost exclusively male.

To discover clues about how Fred and Rose evolved into this murderous couple – so different to what one might expect of such people – it is worth briefly re-examining their childhoods and the early years before they met.

Ostensibly Fred's upbringing in Herefordshire was a rural idyll. His parents were poorly educated and had little money, but they were not drunks, or vagrants, or even Gypsies, as has wrongly been supposed. Nor were Fred's family in-bred, as has been somewhat unkindly assumed. They worked hard and appeared to be solid members of the community.

But something was very wrong at Moorcourt Cottage. Fred's father, Walter, was almost certainly a child-abuser, and I would suggest that Fred initially learned this behaviour from him. But more significant still was the fact of Walter's unapologetic and open attitude to his behaviour, considering what he did to young girls to be both normal and right. Little wonder then that Fred grew up with the same lack of morality, having sex with under-age girls, with or without their consent, from his teenage years. But that alone does not explain the genesis of a man who killed at least twelve women and children. Fred's development into a murderer is much more complex.

If Fred was abused by his own mother, that may have had

something to do with his attitudes to sex, but this is only hearsay.

Much has also been made of Fred's lack of intelligence, and the relatively unsophisticated 'backwoods' way in which he was brought up. But there is no logical reason why Much Marcle is more likely to create a murderer than any other part of the United Kingdom. Abuse and violence are present everywhere in these islands.

Apart from his father's influence, I believe – while accepting that their stories may have been exaggerated over the years – that Fred was initially and profoundly affected by the two accidents he experienced in his teens: the motorcycle crash and the incident at the youth club. There is ample evidence that head injuries can affect behaviour – causing epilepsy, among other dysfunctions – and throughout his life Fred exhibited numerous symptoms of brain damage: blacking out, unpredictable outbursts of anger, and an apparent inability to tell reality from fantasy. When Fred told the police of his 'friendship' with Lulu, was he pretending to be mad, or boasting in the naïve belief he would be credible, or did Fred think he really *had* known the singer? The last answer is surely the correct one. For much of his life, and for much of each day of his life, Fred was profoundly deluded, or as his own family described it, 'off in a world of his own'. That is not to excuse what he did, but maybe it helps explain.

How this unpredictable, fantasising dullard became a killer is a leap of evolution that is hard to understand. The truth can only be extrapolated from the evidence of his early life: we know Fred's relationships with women were all unsatisfactory and that he was an inadequate lover. In adult life he had sex in the same crude way as when he was a teenager – demanding immediate relief and expecting nothing in return apart from passivity (rape, in other words).

When the girls were not willing, Fred became violent. If girls failed to concur with the increasingly bizarre sexual behaviour he needed to arouse himself, he became violent. When a girl rejected him, he became violent. If he felt humiliated, as with his wife Rena and her lover John McLachlan, he became violent. I would suggest that this violence was also partly a result of the brain damage he suffered as a young man, as well as being a reaction to his own inadequacy.

What tipped violence into murder cannot be known for certain. Probably it first happened by accident: Fred may have lost his temper, had his hands around the throat of a girl who had angered him in one of these ways and then realised that she had died – turned blue, was urinating uncontrollably, just as years later he would graphically describe the death of his daughter Heather.

I do not believe that the first of Fred's victims was Anna McFall, even though she is the first that we know about for certain. Anna's remains were dismembered and were found together with bindings, in much the same way as Fred's later victims, and it seems unlikely that he would have carried out such extreme action the first time: it is behaviour too highly evolved. In Fred's own description of the slaying of Heather, he told of the panic that sets in after murder. By 1994, when he spoke about this, he was a man recalling a distant memory of fear and excitement at death, but these emotions must have been very real for him at the start of his murderous career. He could not have paused long enough to play at operations (a bizarre trait that had developed from his attempted DIY termination of Rena's baby years before).

Fred must have killed before, probably first in Glasgow, where his relationships with women were the most complex and unstable in his entire life. There were many other girls in England too. Where those victims are, and who they are, we shall probably never know; other than that they almost certainly include Mary Bastholm, who disappeared the year after Anna McFall.

★

THE problems of Rose's background are sadly obvious: her father was a violent schizophrenic who terrorised his wife and children, and quite possibly sexually abused Rose; her mother Daisy suffered from severe depression, lived through her marriage in a state of extended despair, and had undergone a course of electric-shock therapy while pregnant with her youngest daughter.

Rose herself was 'slow' from an early age, almost retarded, rocking herself relentlessly back and forth and exhibiting many other signs of disturbed behaviour, even as a small child. Statistics show that the children of the mentally ill stand an increased chance of similar illnesses, and it is interesting to note that, apart from Rose, her brothers Graham and Gordon have both led unstable lives involving petty crime and have suffered with depression. But Rose's siblings are quick to point out that they did not become murderers. It must also be remembered that Rose was unique among the Letts children in that her father did not hit her.

Members of her family have impressed upon me the fact that Rose was taught to know the 'difference between right and wrong' — a trite phrase perhaps (and certainly a lesson she forgot), but it is true that hers was an extremely disciplined home. Foul language and blatantly lewd behaviour were forbidden. The children were made to work and the house was run on almost military lines. Yet this prim home produced that rarest of criminals: a female multiple murderer, a woman who would kill her own daughter.

How this dull child became the creature in the dock at Winchester Crown Court is due in part to her over-stimulated sexuality. From a very early age, Rose was sexually precocious, probably because she had been initially abused by her father. She experimented with her brother and then went on to dalliances with numerous older men. She claims to have been raped at least twice as a child. Therefore when she met Fred she was an impressionable girl who already put little value on herself or her body, a girl familiar with abuse and cruelty.

THE peculiarities of Fred and Rose's characters combined to create something terrifying and unique. Steve West gives this insight into his parents: 'I think there was something wrong with Mum from when she was young. Dad wasn't quite right either, so there were two people who weren't quite right who got together, and it was a lethal cocktail. They encouraged each other in what they did. If they had both married someone else I don't think it would have happened to the extent it did – two wrong people brought together.'

Steve West's assessment makes sense: if Fred had not met Rose he would probably have committed impetuous violent assaults that would soon have landed him either in prison or in a mental hospital (with nobody to help him hide the evidence of these crimes). Without Fred, Rose may have become nothing more harmful than a prostitute. But Fred and Rose met, they fell in love and became a team, covering up for each other's excesses for almost twenty-five years – and it is this, more than any other single factor, that allowed their deviant ideas to escalate into murder and ensured that these crimes went undetected for so long.

When they first met, Fred was the dominant partner, a married man twelve years Rose's senior. He charmed this simple girl, enticing her to his caravan so she could play with his children. But the balance of their relationship began to change early on as Rose asserted her own, intrinsically stronger personality. In a letter to Fred written shortly after they met, Rose pledges that she will love him forever. Fred could not fail to be attracted to such devotion from a pretty, barely pubescent girl: the physical type he found most appealing. When Bill Letts forced his daughter into a children's home, hoping to end the relationship, he only succeeded in pushing his daughter towards the older man, her only ally in a hostile world.

The seeds of Rose's aggression had been sown during her childhood: she had become a bully to defend herself against pupils at school who mocked her. She then extended this aggression into a dominance over her younger brothers. When Rose was given care of Anna Marie, Charmaine and then her own baby, Heather, she found herself becoming aggressive again. She was 'a child looking after children', as her mother said, and soon found herself in squalid conditions that made this particularly stressful – her lover was in jail, she had little money and less experience as a mother. Two of the children in her care were not her own, and one, Charmaine, was old enough and spirited enough to defy her. Rose started to beat the children. She probably already knew that Fred was sexually abusing Charmaine (and Rose would not necessarily have recoiled from this: it was what her own father had probably done to her). It seems likely that Charmaine was killed by accident when Rose went too far in her chastisement, or when she simply flew into a rage. But even at this early stage there is the possibility of a sadistic element to her death, as indicated by her letter to Fred dated 4 May 1971: *'Darling, about Char. I think she likes to be handled rough . . .'*

As significant as Charmaine's death was the moment Rose told Fred about the crime, as she had to; it would have been impossible to conceal the body without his co-operation, and it would be Fred's job to dispose of the body, establishing a pattern for their subsequent crimes. If Rose did not already know about Anna McFall and the others (like Mary Bastholm), Fred must have told her at this stage. They swapped secrets, and with the exchange of guilt found themselves joined in a conspiracy of silence, a bond stronger than any wedding vow. Furthermore, they could now *justify* this murder to each other, the murder of a little child – and whatever one thinks of Rose it is hard to believe this did not have some effect on her then. She was only a teenager.

With the exchange of secrets, Fred and Rose were linked in two ways: by their interest in sex (Rose was amenable to any deviation Fred suggested), and by their agreement to view murder as an expediency. Anna McFall had threatened Fred's security by having a child, so she had to go (the subtext being that, as far as Fred and Rose were concerned, she got what she deserved); Charmaine was 'naughty', and her naughtiness was a bad influence on the others, so Rose was not to blame when she lost her temper with the child and killed her. These crimes did not make Fred and Rose bad people in their own estimation. They still considered themselves to be a 'family of love'.

Rose was never charged with the murder of Rena West, but she must have known about it even if she was not actively involved. Rena's death was another expediency – she was threatening the 'now until forever love' of Fred and Rose by asking after Charmaine. Fred decided that she had to be dealt with once and for all, and Rose probably had a say in this decision despite her later assertion that it was Fred's 'past life' and therefore of no concern to her. On the contrary, it was of the utmost concern to the girl who thought of herself as Fred's 'ever worshipping wife', because he was already married to Rena, her rival.

Rose was sexually attracted to women, so the Wests had a shared motive for picking up girls for sex. That this would be aggressive, bondage sex was as much Rose's taste as Fred's. She took a particular pleasure in sadism (exactly as her father had).

It was Rose's idea to abduct and rape Caroline Owens, and she who derived the most enjoyment from the assault. Fred raped Caroline only when Rose was not looking, weeping afterwards and begging her not to tell Rose.

The abduction and rape of Caroline Owens was a turning point in Fred and Rose's lives because of their decision to let her go. The Wests had deluded themselves into thinking she might come back for more, but instead she went to the police. It was lucky for the Wests that the magistrates took such a lenient attitude, but it served as a warning that such good fortune might not be repeated. In future they would kill their victims – if only to ensure they did not go to the police.

Most of the victims later found at Cromwell Street – being for the most part girls who would not take part in the Wests' bizarre sex games willingly – were so viciously abused that their deaths were inevitable, and maybe their extreme abuse followed on from the Wests' foreknowledge that they had no intention of letting them live. The use of the masks and tape was both to restrain the victims and to excite Fred and Rose, who abused with sadistic glee. Make no mistake: Fred and Rose were having fun. Raping, torturing and killing were an enjoyment, a leisure pursuit, and it is that attitude which puts them alongside the likes of Myra Hindley, Ian Brady and Charles Manson in the black museum of those who, as Richard Ferguson said at the trial, have opted out of the human race.

Whether it was Fred or Rose who finally snuffed the life out of these girls is irrelevant morally and in law: both were party to the tormenting and torturing which led to death, and therefore both are equally guilty of murder.

Fred never offered a wholly convincing explanation for why the bodies were cut up, only suggesting that he did it to save space and, in discussion with his appropriate adult, Janet Leach, that he had removed the fingers to foil identification. But the dismemberment of these young women went far beyond those practical reasons. Fred took pleasure in playing with corpses and cutting them up. It gave him complete power over women he could not hope to know or satisfy in any normal way. Rose may have been involved in the disposal of the victims, but probably only to a limited extent – maybe helping with the practical problems of getting rid of clothes, washing away bloodstains and helping Fred with the physical lifting and carrying.

It is also possible that the abuse of these young women

included the removal of parts of the body in life (the absence of fingers, fingernails, toes, and, in one case, hair, would suggest torture rather than simple dismemberment after death). It is a level of bestiality hard to comprehend, and it occurred to members of the investigation team that parts of the bodies had been eaten. People capable of such horrors are capable of cannibalism, too, and studies of other multiple murderers would suggest that this is not unlikely.

The murder of Shirley Robinson differs to that of most of the other girls found at Cromwell Street. She, like Kathryn Halliday in later years, was a willing partner to the Wests' unusual sexual activity. She was not killed to satisfy their pleasure, but because of her pregnancy and the threat it posed to the love of Fred and Rose. For above all, Fred and Rose still loved each other: a passionate love that had crossed over into insanity.

Apart from murder, Cromwell Street was also the scene of the physical and sexual abuse of children, including the Wests' own elder daughters Heather and Anna Marie. Talking and listening to the elder West siblings is rather like meeting the survivors of a corrupting religious cult. They lived in unbearable conditions and yet came to accept the most extreme behaviour of the mother and father for whom they still retain love – exactly like the relationship between cult members and their manipulative, abusive, and often deadly leaders. Their future lives will be fraught with difficulty.

Rose's barrister, Richard Ferguson, was correct when he pointed out to the jury that they were not considering a normal suburban family: 25 Cromwell Street was a bizarre place, filled with children, lodgers, Rose's male customers and Fred and Rose's victims and victims-to-be. So many people passed through the house, including policemen and social service workers, that it is apparently surprising that the murders and child abuse went undetected for so long.

Cromwell Street was, at times, almost an open house to every waif and stray looking for shelter. But whatever they witnessed, or whatever suspicions they had, these visitors were not the sort who would be inclined to go to the authorities. In many cases, they were in trouble with the police themselves, or runaways from institutions which they feared and loathed.

When Rose told the runaways who visited her from children's homes not to say where they had been, she knew well that they would not. Miss A did not tell anybody when she was brutally raped by the Wests. Instead she locked herself in her room, believing that everybody thought girls from children's homes were naturally 'bad'.

It is often asked why the neighbours did not know what was going on. The answer is that Cromwell Street is bedsit-land: a transient, down-at-heel corner of the inner city, where the Wests were among the most stable residents. At least they had a mortgage and brought up a family, both factors which made them a rarity in the street. There were hardly any regular neighbours, just people who came and went, with their own problems to occupy them, waving hello as they walked to the corner shop.

It is true that the Wests took in lodgers at one stage, and that these lodgers heard and saw many things, but nothing that was not easily explicable at the time. Maybe there was a lot of noise from the house, but Fred was a builder. They may well have suspected that prostitution was going on, but that would not be unusual for the area in which they lived. Young girls came and went, but it was that sort of free and easy place – there was no reason to suspect that women were being raped, tortured, murdered and buried in the cellar. At Rose's trial, the court heard from a string of witnesses who reported screams and odd conversations at Cromwell Street in the 1970s, but they were only giving this evidence because the publicity of the case had made them put two and two together (maybe some also thought there would be money to be earned from it). These stories would never have been heard otherwise.

Inevitably the authorities will be criticised, and there were occasions over the years when the suspicions of the social workers and teachers really should have been alerted. It seems extraordinary, for instance, that a child's disappearance from school is not investigated, as in the case of Charmaine.

THESE were the issues addressed at a major press conference held directly after the sentencing of Rose at Winchester. It emerged that the West family had come into contact with the authorities very many times over the years.

Their children had visited the Accident and Emergency departments of local hospitals, for example, on thirty-one occasions between 1972 and 1992. The medical records showed worrying complaints: a child who had apparently fallen on a knife, another who had hurt her chest 'falling off a gate', and a third with lacerations between the toes. Thrush and gonorrhoea had been present in the family and the children suffered from speech impediments and squints – classic symptoms of abused children.

Fred had also come into open conflict with teachers at their schools, opposing special care and even admitting punching one of his children.

One of the West children had been in contact with the NSPCC in 1989, but reports of this case had mysteriously been shredded. There had been an anonymous call to social services in 1988, saying children were being left on their own in Cromwell Street: the house was visited but nothing was found to be wrong – and the index card of this incident had also vanished.

Gloucestershire Health Trust announced it would review its procedures; the NSPCC agreed it needed to 'learn lessons from this tragic case'; and other authorities made similar statements, saying they would try and learn from any mistakes.

But we should remember two things before scapegoating

these institutions. Firstly, it is only in recent years that direct links have been established between schools, hospitals, social services and the police. If a child with Charmaine's history were admitted to a casualty unit now with suspicious puncture wounds, one would expect the social services to investigate *how* she came to be injured, and to remove her into care for her own protection if there was cause for concern. But in 1971 nothing was done, because there was no procedure, and Charmaine was murdered.

Secondly, and crucially as far as any criminal activity is concerned, the police had no reason to launch a murder inquiry in relation to the Wests until the 1990s simply because they had no firm information. It is, therefore, a testament to Fred and Rose's bravado that drug squad police could have regularly raided 25 Cromwell Street in the 1970s, and come up with little more than a few reefers, rather than a failure of the officers to be more observant.

There is another, more difficult fact to face here. It would be inappropriate to challenge too strongly those who have already suffered so much, but before anybody blames the police, the children's homes or the social services for these tragedies, the families of some of the victims must ask themselves why they did not contact the police straight away. In the case of Juanita Mott, for example, her known links with Cromwell Street may then have been investigated. Incredibly, six of the Wests' twelve known victims were not officially reported to the police as missing persons.

Rena, Charmaine and Heather are included in this list because, quite apart from Fred and Rose, they had relations who could well have contacted the police. The West and Letts families are large (as the family tree in Appendix II illustrates) and there were plenty of aunts and uncles, nephews and nieces, brothers and sisters who might have been expected to ask: 'Where is Heather?' or 'Why haven't we heard from Rena and

Charmaine?' But not one of Charmaine, Rena and Heather's relations contacted the police once in all the years these three were missing.

In the case of the girls who *were* properly reported as missing persons, there were thorough – and indeed extensive – police searches. That these searches did not take detectives to Cromwell Street was simply because there were no leads to point them in that direction.

When the suspicions of the police were finally aroused, it still took a long time before a warrant was granted and the garden of Cromwell Street dug up. That this was ever done at all is a credit to Hazel Savage MBE. If financial considerations played a part in the delay then that is a matter for the consciences of those who procrastinated.

Officially the last victim we know the Wests to have claimed was their daughter Heather, in 1987. But just as it seems improbable that Anna McFall was the first, Heather West was probably not the last (although the killing must have ended when the police investigation began in 1992). Nor were the ten women and children between Anna and Heather the extent of the killing.

There is an abundance of evidence that many other women have died: Fred himself boasted that he had killed many more – apparently telling Janet Leach there were twenty more – and made sinister allusions to other crimes and other grave sites; but most of all it is the *rate* at which he and Rose killed that arouses suspicion more than anything: three died in 1974 alone, and yet there were long periods of time when apparently nobody was killed. This is so unlikely it cannot be right. There must be more, but it is not known where they are because, unlike those at Cromwell Street, the police have not been fortunate enough to stumble upon their remains.

There are a host of other places the Wests could have buried these victims, and maybe even greater horrors are hidden elsewhere. The missing bones, for example; Mary Bastholm; and where did Fred go for so many hours the day he knew the police were about to excavate Cromwell Street? Maybe he blacked out as was later claimed, maybe he just sat and thought about his situation, as John Bennett has suggested. It is certainly odd that he did not take the opportunity to flee, knowing, as he must have done, that the game was up. Possibly Fred used the time to ensure that his other secrets were safe – maybe at another house, or an old farm building, or a café where Fred carried out some renovation work; maybe a lock-up, an allotment or a septic tank.

It has long been rumoured that Gloucestershire police will start looking for more victims in places such as this, but the practical problems in doing so are enormous: unless the police know the precise spot where a body is buried it is not feasible to dig up the countryside on a hunch, destroying property and creating another blaze of publicity in the process. Even when the police were told exactly where a victim's remains should be, as in the case of Anna McFall, the excavation can stretch to weeks of digging. Any further search would have all of these problems, coupled with the added disadvantage of Fred not being there to assist. It seems highly unlikely that Rose will ever choose to co-operate in the way Fred did, so further victims will probably only be discovered accidentally, by building or farm work in years to come.

After the verdict in the Rose West trial, Gloucestershire police announced they were reviewing 'potential avenues for further investigation'. This included their hope to trace nine young women who had links to Cromwell Street but had never been found. The police simply wanted to 'establish that they are safe and well'. Sketchy details were released.

Fred claimed that other people were involved in the murders, and the idea of a group of killers acting together is a sensational, perhaps fantastical one. As ever, it is important to remember that almost everything Fred said contained an element of make-believe.

All this begs the question: what is the total number of the Wests' victims? It is futile to try and fix a figure. All we know about for certain is Fred's casual approach to murder, and the rate of killing of the girls, together with what Fred said to people like Janet Leach and his son, Steve. From this admittedly sketchy evidence it seems likely that he had been killing fairly steadily (apart from when he was in gaol or under police scrutiny) – quite possibly more than once a year – for about thirty years.

There were times during this mayhem when Fred and Rose's marriage was tested to breaking point. Fred attacked Rose, and her him; other times she seems to have been preparing to leave him; and Fred clearly dallied with the notion of setting up home with Shirley Robinson instead of Rose. But these were temporary setbacks, and they always came back together again. In the final years before their arrest, Fred and Rose loved each other as much as, if not more than, ever before. The pact of blood had not destroyed them, like the couple in Zola's *Thérèse Raquin*, but preserved their love practically in its first flush, so they behaved almost like teenagers. 'I will love you always,' Rose wrote to Fred in 1992. She told Daisy Letts, 'I'm happy, Mum.'

Rose had been the most wonderful wife for Fred – a willing and enthusiastic partner to his excesses, a sexually voracious younger woman who would deny him nothing and support him in every crisis. She even seemed to enjoy the prostitution he was so keen for her to undertake. For Rose, Fred had been a good husband, a reliable provider who allowed her to have the large family she craved. He had also encouraged and condoned her passion for violent lesbian sex and been willing, in crude terms, to clear up afterwards. When they said they worshipped each other, they meant it. Fred and Rose were the perfect companions.

In 1992, when they faced prison because of allegations of

child abuse, Fred and Rose probably made another pact: if the secret of murder was revealed during the investigation it was agreed between them that Fred would assume all the blame, sacrificing himself for his beloved. Rose would be left with the security of the house, which she could keep or sell at a profit. After the Wests had been served with the warrant to dig up the garden, but before Heather was found on 26 February 1994, Fred and Rose must have rehearsed this agreement: Fred assured Rose he would take all the blame, and that her everlasting love was payment enough.

Over the next few days he told the police what they wanted to know, going out of his way to exonerate Rose. But the plan went awry. Fred talked about much more than Rose had bargained for: twelve killings, ten of which she could be implicated in. He talked for hour after hour, often making mistakes, letting little titbits slip that contradicted what Rose had said. She was furious with him. She ignored him when they were reunited at Gloucester Magistrates Court, and Fred's extreme hurt was plain to see. His spirit broke after this: his discussions with police became increasingly contradictory and then downright bizarre. In private he agonised over Rose's rejection while, in her gaol, Rose told visitors of her hatred for Fred. She now felt sick when she stood next to him: some change from her letters to him only twenty-four months previously: 'Remember I will love you always and everything will be alright.'

Fred became confused. He almost implicated her on several occasions, talking darkly about 'protecting' another person, or persons. In private discussions with visitors, advisers and even the prison doctor at Winson Green, Fred spoke in an unhindered way about his pact with Rose and how she had betrayed him. Fred last saw Rose at a magistrates court in December 1994. Again she rejected him. A few weeks later he killed himself, offering his life up as a sacrifice – the culmination of a mad and terrible love.

So we are left with Rose, behind bars now probably for the rest of her active life. Her decision to give evidence at Winchester Crown Court was a revelation to all who witnessed it. She showed herself to be tough and resilient, fighting for her freedom in any way she could: lying, concocting grief, blaming it all on Fred, together with her obvious resentment that she was there at all. Most telling was when she was put under pressure by the prosecution – then a little of her aggression showed through, and the court could clearly see she was capable of real violence.

This was the multiple killer of ten, maybe many more young women and children, and it appeared she felt no remorse for what she had done (her shows of emotion during the trial seemed almost entirely contrived). For two months she sat through harrowing evidence of what she had inflicted on others, but never once showed genuine compassion or seemed on the verge of telling the truth. Sometimes she even laughed. Her plan in giving evidence was to aid her defence, but it only served to demonstrate what a heartless, aggressive and potentially dangerous creature she is. Her adoption of a cross and a poppy as Remembrance Day approached during the trial were such obviously cynical gestures that she fell even lower in everyone's estimation.

For all these reasons, I do not expect Rose will ever tell the truth about her crimes, nor do I think she has any consideration for the families of those she killed.

THE interest in people like Fred and Rose is curious. I would suggest that we are fascinated because we can study them in detail while remaining completely safe. They are like specimens of rare poisonous spiders, impaled on pins and set in cases at the Natural History Museum: we peer through the glass in distaste, secure in the knowledge that we can come to no harm.

What we can learn from these macabre exhibits, what Fred

and Rose demonstrated so effectively, is that it is possible to kill repeatedly for many years without being caught (and the Wests might never have been caught, were it not for a few slices of luck) – if there is a partner who will both conspire in the crime and help camouflage it afterwards. A nondescript family home, it seems, is an almost perfect hiding place for the victims of such a violent campaign. If Fred and Rose were able to do this and evade detection for so many years, why should there not be other couples whose lust has twisted itself into similar sadism?

There might well be houses like 25 Cromwell Street in other parts of Britain, in the sort of shabby places we watch as the suburban train leaves a major city, the neglected streets we pass through on the way to the motorway. One of the many lessons of the story of Fred and Rose West is that horrors could be hidden in those houses, too; horrors of which we might never know.

25 CROMWELL STREET

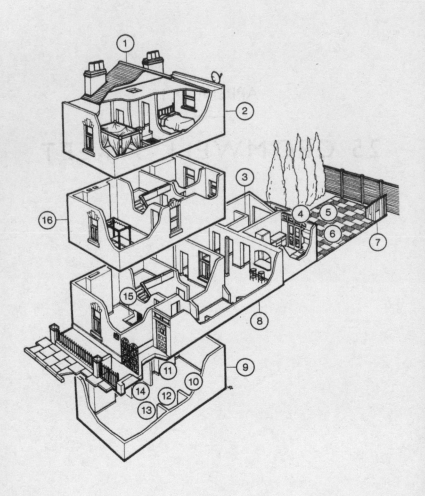

Three-dimensional plan of 25 Cromwell Street, showing what the house looked like when Fred and Rose West were arrested in 1994, and where the remains of nine of their victims were buried.

Key

1. The attic, where Fred and Rose stored boxes of pornographic photographs and correspondence.

2. Fred and Rose's bedroom.

3. The remains of Lynda Gough were buried here in 1973, in an old inspection pit under the bathroom floor. These remains were discovered on the evening of Monday 7 March 1994, the eighth set to be found.

4. The remains of Alison Chambers were buried here in 1979, in the garden, near the bathroom wall. Alison's remains were the second set to be found, at 5:20 P.M. on Monday 28 February.

5. The remains of Heather West, the first to be discovered at Cromwell Street, were buried here in 1987, near the fir trees halfway down the garden. They were found during the afternoon of Saturday 26 February.

6. The remains of Shirley Robinson, and her unborn child, were buried here in 1978, near the back door of the house. These remains were the third set to be uncovered, at about 9 P.M. on Monday 28 February.

7. The Wendy house.

8. The breakfast bar and children's living area.

9. The cellar.

10. The remains of Carol Ann Cooper were buried here in 1973, beneath the cellar floor on the right-hand side. Carol's remains were the ninth and last set found in 25 Cromwell Street, at 7:10 P.M. on Tuesday 8 March.

11. The remains of Juanita Mott were buried here in 1975, beneath the cellar floor in an alcove by the wall, where a staircase had once been. Her remains were the seventh set to be found, at around midday on Sunday 6 March.

12. The remains of Lucy Partington were buried here in 1974, in the 'nursery alcove' of the cellar. Lucy's remains were found early on Sunday 6 March, the sixth set to be discovered.

13. The remains of Thérèse Siegenthaler were buried here in 1974, beneath the cellar floor, and were later covered over with a false chimney breast. They were the fourth set to be found, just before lunch on Saturday 5 March.

14. The remains of Shirley Hubbard were buried here in 1974, in the 'Marilyn Monroe' area of the cellar. Shirley's remains were the fifth set to be discovered, just before 3 P.M. on Saturday 5 March.

15. Trap door to cellar.

16. The Black Magic bar.

APPENDIX II

—

THE WEST FAMILY TREE

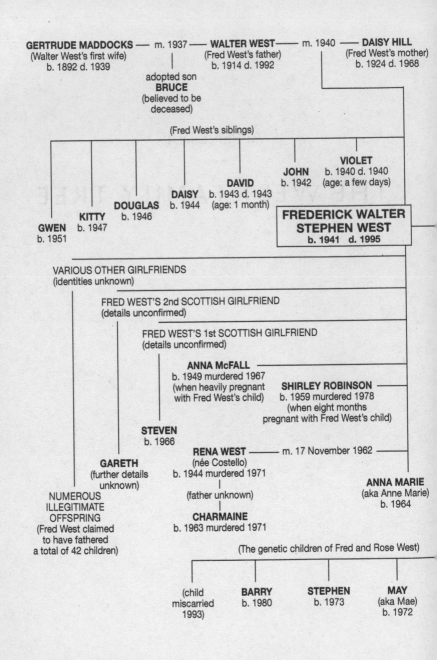

GERTRUDE MADDOCKS —— m. 1937 —— WALTER WEST —— m. 1940 —— DAISY HILL
(Walter West's first wife)   (Fred West's father)   (Fred West's mother)
b. 1892 d. 1939   b. 1914 d. 1992   b. 1924 d. 1968

adopted son
BRUCE
(believed to be
deceased)

(Fred West's siblings)

VIOLET
b. 1940 d. 1940
(age: a few days)

JOHN
b. 1942

DAVID
b. 1943 d. 1943
(age: 1 month)

DAISY
b. 1944

DOUGLAS
b. 1946

KITTY
b. 1947

GWEN
b. 1951

**FREDERICK WALTER
STEPHEN WEST**
b. 1941   d. 1995

VARIOUS OTHER GIRLFRIENDS
(identities unknown)

FRED WEST'S 2nd SCOTTISH GIRLFRIEND
(details unconfirmed)

FRED WEST'S 1st SCOTTISH GIRLFRIEND
(details unconfirmed)

ANNA McFALL ——
b. 1949 murdered 1967
(when heavily pregnant
with Fred West's child)

SHIRLEY ROBINSON ——
b. 1959 murdered 1978
(when eight months
pregnant with Fred West's child)

STEVEN
b. 1966

RENA WEST —— m. 17 November 1962 ——
(née Costello)
b. 1944 murdered 1971

GARETH
(further details
unknown)

ANNA MARIE
(aka Anne Marie)
b. 1964

NUMEROUS
ILLEGITIMATE
OFFSPRING
(Fred West claimed
to have fathered
a total of 42 children)

(father unknown)

CHARMAINE
b. 1963 murdered 1971

(The genetic children of Fred and Rose West)

(child
miscarried
1993)

BARRY
b. 1980

STEPHEN
b. 1973

MAY
(aka Mae)
b. 1972

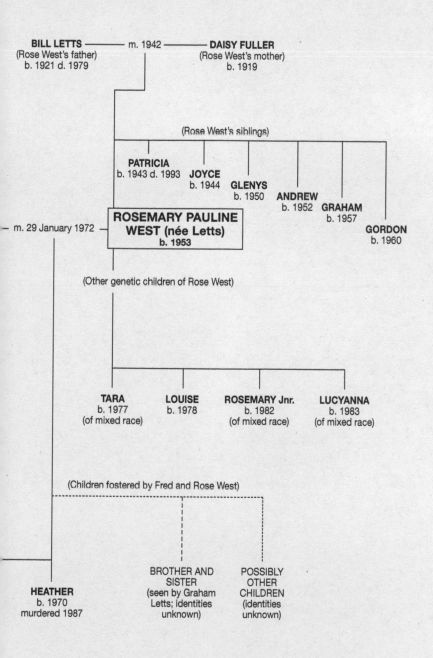

BILL LETTS ——— m. 1942 ——— **DAISY FULLER**
(Rose West's father)   (Rose West's mother)
b. 1921 d. 1979   b. 1919

(Rose West's siblings)

PATRICIA
b. 1943 d. 1993   **JOYCE**
                              b. 1944   **GLENYS**
                                                  b. 1950   **ANDREW**
                                                                     b. 1952   **GRAHAM**
                                                                                          b. 1957
                                                                                                    GORDON
                                                                                                    b. 1960

— m. 29 January 1972 —   **ROSEMARY PAULINE WEST (née Letts)**
                                              b. 1953

(Other genetic children of Rose West)

TARA
b. 1977
(of mixed race)   **LOUISE**
                              b. 1978   **ROSEMARY Jnr.**
                                                  b. 1982
                                                  (of mixed race)   **LUCYANNA**
                                                                              b. 1983
                                                                              (of mixed race)

(Children fostered by Fred and Rose West)

HEATHER
b. 1970
murdered 1987

BROTHER AND
SISTER
(seen by Graham
Letts; identities
unknown)

POSSIBLY
OTHER
CHILDREN
(identities
unknown)

PICTURE CREDITS

1, 2, 3: courtesy of Mr and Mrs Douglas West; 4: South West News Service; 5, 6: courtesy of Mr and Mrs Douglas West; 7, 8: South West News Service; 9, 10: courtesy of Mr and Mrs Douglas West; 11: courtesy of Mrs Daisy Letts; 12: courtesy of Mr and Mrs Jim Tyler; 13: courtesy of the National Missing Persons Helpline; 14: Howard Sounes; 15: South West News Service; 16, 17: Rex Features; 18: Howard Sounes.

19, 20, 21: South West News Service; 22: Popperfoto/Reuter; 23, 24: South West News Service; 25, 26, 27, 28: Popperfoto/Reuter; 29, 30, 31, 32: South West News Service; 33: Howard Sounes; 34: Rex Features; 35, 36: South West News Service; 37: courtesy of Mr and Mrs Douglas West; 38: South West News Service; 39: Rex Features; 40: courtesy of the *Daily Mirror*; 41: courtesy of the *Sunday Mirror*.

42: Rex Features; 43: Press Association/Topham (Barry Batchelor); 44: Popperfoto/Reuter (Paul Bates); 45: Popperfoto/Reuter (Russell Boyce); 46: Gavin Smith/FSP/Gamma; 47: Howard Sounes; 48: Frank Spooner/Gamma; 49: Press Association/Topham (Barry Batchelor); 50: Press Association/Topham (David

Jones); 51: South West News Service; 52: Press Association/
Topham (Barry Batchelor); 53: Popperfoto/Reuter; 54, 55, 56:
Howard Sounes; 57: Popperfoto/Reuter (Kevin Harvey); 58: Rex
Features; 59: South West News Service; 60: Popperfoto/Reuter
(Paul Bates).

THE STRANGER BESIDE ME

Revised and Updated Edition

Ann Rule

Ann Rule was a writer working on the biggest story of her life, tracking down a brutal mass-murderer. Little did she know that the young man who was her close friend was the savage slayer she was hunting.

Ted Bundy was everyone's picture of a natural 'winner' – handsome, charming, brilliant in law school, successful with women, on the verge of a dazzling career. On January 24, 1989 Ted Bundy was executed for the murders of three young women; he had also confessed to taking the lives of at least thirty-five more young women from coast to coast.

This is his story – the story of his magnetic power, his unholy compulsion, his demonic double life, and his string of helpless victims. It was written by a woman who thought she knew Ted Bundy, until she began to put all the evidence together, and the whole terrifying picture emerged from the dark depths.

'The most fascinating killer in modern American history . . . Ann Rule has an extraordinary angle that makes *The Stranger Beside Me* as dramatic and chilling as a bedroom window shattering at midnight' – *New York Times*

sphere

To buy any of our books and to find out
more about Sphere and Little, Brown Book Group,
our authors and titles, as well as events and
book clubs, visit our website

www.littlebrown.co.uk

and follow us on Twitter

@LittleBrownUK

To order any Sphere titles p & p free in the UK,
please contact our mail order supplier on:

+ 44 (0)1832 737525

Customers not based in the UK should contact
the same number for appropriate postage
and packing costs.